and tools. As such, it delivers a unique perspective on how his tradition is perceived and imparted by contemporary adherents today. The chapters on Magical Weapons and Folk Magic from Antiquity provides a further treasure-house of insights for readers of all magical traditions. Brian Cain's Initiation into Witchcraft should be added to the recommended reading list for all seeking insights into initiatory traditions of Witchcraft today."

—Sorita d'Este, author of *Circle for Hekate* and *Visions of the Cailleach*

"Brian Cain has written a brilliant new book on traditional Witchcraft that details our history and rituals in a concise manner. Too many people are being taken in by loosely-created magick circles and this book defines the difference of why it's important to go through the trouble to find a good traditional teaching coven. I highly recommend it to all who seek the initiatory pathways into the Craft."

—Lady Rhea, author of *The Enchanted Candle* and *The Enchanted Formulary*, Gardnerian High Priestess, High Priestess of the New York Coven of Witches, and co-founder of the Minoan Sisterhood

"*Initiation into Witchcraft* is a truly refreshing and honest offering throughout—a rarity among today's books on Witchcraft and magic. Brian Cain has provided a book that has been sorely needed in this modern era of the occult, written on a subject and presented in a style that I cannot remember seeing the likes of in a very long time. When in the presence of large amounts of pagans at festivals and events, I often lament to myself just how few of them have undergone the sacred rites of initiation when such gatherings were once filled with the voices of initiates. What Brian has done is provide a valuable book and inspiring guide for the seeker, and he has helped preserve tradition in doing so. Brian Cain demonstrates his high priesthood by offering something inclusive, encouraging, and educational, as well as hands-on spell and ritual work for the seeker on the path towards initiation. These rites and exercises work regardless of tradition—and this is not a common feat. As we straddle an era where many of our most sacred rites of humanity are being lost to technology, and the ever-present desire for the quick and easily accessible reign supreme over old-fashioned hard work, it's a true blessing to have a book that will surely reignite modern seekers towards the greatest spell before the gods—our initiation into witchcraft."

—Witchdoctor Utu, founder of Dragon Ritual Drummers and author of *Conjuring Harriet 'Mama Moses' Tubman and the Spirits of the Underground Railroad*

"While eclectic, do-it-yourself forms of Witchcraft and Wicca have enjoyed the spotlight for decades, an older, deeper tradition has continued to bubble and brew beneath the surface, seemingly invisible save to those few who would seek it out. Brian Cain is a welcomed voice in a growing movement that promises to alter long-held perceptions of Wicca, challenging the facile stereotypes and Insta-pop marketing trends that obscure the way to more profound practice. Here, you'll find direct, no-babying guidance should you be called to the initiatory path. Initiation into Witchcraft is a valuable book not only for seekers, but also coven students, new group leaders, and the curious."

—Thorn Mooney, Initiate, Gardnerian High Priestess, and author of *Traditional Wicca: A Seeker's Guide*

Initiation into Witchcraft is a must read for seekers who desire to expand upon their spiritual path in British Witchcraft. As a priest in two African Traditional Religions I say this, not as a witch, but as someone who understands why the path of initiation is important. Brian Cain expands upon this cornerstone of a magical tradition in such a way that it would be impossible for the reader to leave without understanding. The Ancestors of initiation (lineage) in and of itself holds a great power

Praise for *Initiation into Witchcraft*

"Initiation is one of the most difficult statures to reach in our Cabot-Kent Hermetic Temple tradition. It's like getting a degree from college, but it is only the beginning of the path to enlightenment. *Initiation into Witchcraft* is the only book I know of that truly addresses the importance of initiation, which hasn't been done before. Brian Cain's work will enlighten many people in their own traditions as to how initiation changes your entire world. They say that there is no hierarchy in Witchcraft. Well, there certainly is, because you've got the High Priestess and the High Priest, and they are initiated. That means they will carry on that tradition through thick and thin, until death do us part. Some go from one tradition to another, seemingly thinking that belonging to all these different paths is making them something better. I think it waters down the traditions. You must come into Witchcraft with a sincere dedication and devotion—and with an academic mindset as well. Witchcraft is still the fastest growing religion in America. It needs to be addressed in a serious and educated manner, and that's what this book offers. Its academic research has far surpassed nearly any Witchcraft book being published today. Witchcraft becomes a fervor in your heart and your mind. You are drawn to it, and this book is for such people who are truly serious about becoming a Witch. Because of that alone, *Initiation into Witchcraft* is a book that has been needed for ages."

—Laurie Cabot, Founder and High Priestess of the Cabot-Kent Hermetic Temple and author of *Laurie Cabot's Book of Shadows*, *Power of the Witch*, and *The Witch in Every Woman*

"Witchcraft is the fastest growing spirituality in America. The seeds of this remarkable growth were transplanted here by British Traditional Witches like Ray Buckland and others, and cultivated within hidden covens. Profound and life-transforming rites of initiation and the sincere training of priestesses and priests were offered to those fortunate few granted entrance to this concealed spiritual community.

"In the midst of accelerating popularization driven by public information ranging from the wise to the witless, the history and practice of modern Witchcraft are worth remembering, honoring and preserving. Brian Cain has done all of these and more, demonstrating in this thoughtful, thorough and generous book the divinely magical reasons for initiation and for disciplined training. He offers the gifts of a genuine priest of the initiatory path, sincerely guiding those with the courage to make the assay, simultaneously revealing and concealing the Great Mystery that, ultimately, can only be known through personal experience. It is a unique and worthy contribution to the literature of the Craft of the Wise."

—Phyllis Curott, founder of the Tradition of Ara, activist attorney, host of The Witch Within online course for Hay House, and author of Book of Shadows, Witch Crafting, Wicca Made Easy, and more

"Brian Cain's *Initiation into Witchcraft* isn't just an excellent introduction to initiatory British Witchcraft, it also re-establishes the Witch-Cult as a religious and spiritual practice. More than just a "how to" book, Cain has crafted an excellent resource for both beginners, and long time practitioners. Highly recommended for anyone looking to join a traditional coven or simply seeking to take their practice to a deeper and higher place."

—Jason Mankey, High Priest, Initiate, and author of *Transformative Witchcraft: The Greater Mysteries*, *The Witch's Athame*, and *The Witch's Book of Shadows*

"This perceptively crafted tome reflects the knowledge and experiential perceptions of a 21st-century Alexandrian Witchcraft Initiate on the history and development of British Traditional Witchcraft, its practices

that not only serves to edify and strengthen the magic of the initiate, but also to protect the tradition that continues to blaze the trail to magical growth and understanding. This book was birthed out of the heart of a priest and a witch and it is abundantly evident once the reader opens the pages.

—Hoodoo Sen Moise, author of *Working Conjure: A Guide to Hoodoo Folk Magic*, rootworker, Houngan of Haitian Vodou, and Tata of Palo Mayombe

"Amidst the whirlwind of eclectic approaches to modern witchcraft, Brian Cain's book is refreshing for its reaffirmation of witchcraft as an initiatory mystery tradition, and of the warmth and wisdom of the coven's hearth, while attesting also to its age-old operative magical current. This is the Craft of the true and sincere dedicant, before whom unfolds the path of occult knowledge and power that burns bright at the heart of the witch's art."

— Gemma Gary, British Craft initiate, folk-magician, Dyawles of the coven Ros an Bucca and author of *Traditional Witchcraft: A Cornish Book of Ways*, *The Black Toad*, *Wisht Waters*, *The Devil's Dozen* and *Silent as the Trees*

Brian Cain outlines the rich history of initiatory traditions in witchcraft as a journey through time to be traveled by all who wish to know more. For the sincere seeker, he also issues a challenge to prepare both mentally and spiritually for the effort. To assist them in accomplishing these goals, a wealth of practical information is provided, all gained from notable sources as well as from the author's own years of training initiates. More seasoned practitioners will also enjoy reading through the detailed descriptions of both ancient and modern traditions, and reviewing the myriad of resources and sample rituals. This book is a handy reference for seekers, initiates, and priesthood, encapsulating both the practice and the practical, and it has been added to my personal list of recommended reading.

—*Christine Stephens, High Priestess of the New Orleans Coven, Witch, teacher, and lecturer*

"*Initiation into Witchcraft* is rich with insider history, integral philosophy, and a wealth of rare spells and well-crafted rituals that can be utilized by anyone with the dedication to learn the true Craft. Brian Cain's diligent research and obvious devotion will resonate with seekers and seasoned practitioners alike. This book belongs on every coven's required reading list and every occultist's bookshelf."

—*Sandra Mariah Wright, Alexandrian High Priestess and co-author of Reading the Leaves: An Intuitive Guide to the Ancient Art and Modern Magic of Tea Leaf Divination*

"There only a few witchcraft books that can be called reference books, special books that have the ability to illustrate the practice of the Witchcraft in one form or another. Brian Cain's *Initiation into Witchcraft* not only instructs but inspires those who want to be part of Traditional Wicca. Historically accurate, delightfully written, this book is already a classic."

—*Karagan Griffith, author of Pelo Cálice e pela Lâmina (By the Chalice and the Blade), a title in Portuguese.*

"Stepping into the pages of Brian Cain's *Initiation into Witchcraft* is a lot like falling into the deep end of the pool. His crisp, "take no prisoners" style of writing is unexpectedly refreshing. The author does not, as the saying goes, suffer fools gladly, yet what he has to say about initiation into what may be the oldest of priesthoods is of immense significance.

"But *Initiation into Witchcraft* is so much more than an intimate reflection of the author's personal journey. The book is packed cover to cover with more information on the history of witchcraft and magic than one will likely find on several shelves of your local bookshop. It's virtually one stop shopping for both novice and experienced practitioners alike.

"But wait, there's more. The author's generous inclusion of a grimoire (complete with requisite tablets of correspondences), as well as a series of extraordinary and provocative photographs of a working coven, place *Initiation into Witchcraft* into a class by itself. Highly recommended."

—Jimahl Di Fiosa, Alexandrian High Priest and author of *A Coin for the Ferryman: the Death and Life of Alex Sanders*, *All the Kings Children*, and *A Voice in the Forest*

"Brian Cain has managed to find the balance between his obvious love for the Craft and his responsibility to his tradition, and has created a highly informative and invaluable introduction for any seeker of initiatory Craft. His concise account of the history of British Traditional Witchcraft in America is extremely interesting, and his use of the archetypes in his exploration of the Witches' Gods is an eloquent description of the way in which Craft incorporates the Gods of many pantheons into its practices and beliefs. His presentation of the magical working system of "Alexandria", well-adapted seasonal rites, and charming collection of modern and traditional spells and workings are a lovely addition to the extensive background information he has provided. I predict that this book will be found on many a true seeker's book shelf: a modern Traditional Witchcraft classic."

—Val Hughes, High Priestess of the Oswestry Coven, Witch, teacher, and lecturer

"Dare to learn how the power of initiation can transform your life. *Initiation into Witchcraft* is an innovative book that inspires and informs those who are curious about witchcraft. This book is a comprehensive, informative guide to prepare the student for their own magical initiation.

Experienced members of the Craft will find Brian Cain's voice engaging, and the subject matter tantalizing. He brings to light a fresh perspective that is a must-read."

—Leanne Marrama, High Priestess of Celtic Traditionalist Gwyddonaid and co-author of *Reading the Leaves: An Intuitive Guide to the Ancient Art and Modern Magic of Tea Leaf Divination*

"When Brian first told me of his intention to write this book, I was nervous. Not because I had any doubt of his integrity or knowledge on the subject, but because I found it hard to imagine how he could possibly achieve so monumental a task as to summarise initiatory Craft in a way that fully communicated its power, allure and beauty. I am very happy to say that, in my opinion, he has nailed it.

"This book is a perfect blend of essential information, advice, and reverence for the Craft that we—as initiates—hold so dear. Brian has successfully captured the spirit of magic, mystery and personal responsibility that sets the priesthood apart from, although never above, the uninitiated. Those of you who are seekers have no idea how lucky you are to have access to this book, and I certainly wish it had been around when I began my own magical journey. To the seeker, take note! To the initiated reader, enjoy! And to Brian, thank you and Blessed Be – your faithful sister and daughter in Craft."

—Rozi James, High Priestess and Witch in the Oswestry Coven, author, teacher, and lecturer

INITIATION INTO WITCHCRAFT

Brian Cain

Foreword by Maxine Sanders

Warlock Press™

Initiation into Witchcraft

Brian Cain

© 2019 Warlock Press

All rights reserved. No part of this publication may be reproduced, stored in a retrieval system or transmitted in any form or by any means, electronic, mechanical, photocopying, recording or otherwise without the prior permission of the publisher or in accordance with the provisions of the Copyright, Designs and Patents Act 1988 or under the terms of any license permitting limited copying issued by the Copyright Licensing Agency.

Published by:
Warlock Press
1219 Decatur Street
New Orleans, 70116 LA, USA

Typesetting and Cover Design: Christian Day

Cover Photo: Scott Lanes

ISBN-10: 1-7332466-0-6

ISBN-13: 978-1-7332466-0-6

This page intentionally left blank.

I dedicate this book to my mother who brought me to my first Esbat, to the priestesses who aided and guided me in my journey, Shawnee Gardner, Sandra Mariah Wright, and most of all, Val Hughes, who taught me how to teach! To my first Coven and the New Orleans coven for all your magic and continued inspiration. To my husband without whom this book would not have been written, thank you for being a slave driver and for believing in the work. Last, but not least, thank you to Maxine and Alex Sanders whose teachings lead me to my tribe.

Contents

Foreword   *XVI*

Introduction   **XVIII**

CHAPTER 1
Stepping onto the Path 1
   The Roots of Modern Witchcraft 3
   Getting Proper Witchcraft Training 7
   How to Know if You're Ready 8
   Things to Work on Before Initiation 10

CHAPTER 2
Covens **15**
   Joining a Coven 18
   What to Look for in a Coven 21
   What Might be Expected of You 26
   Coven Leaders 28
   Coven Meetings 29
   Types of Covens 31
   Coven Rules 34

CHAPTER 3
The Cultural Origins of Witchcraft **38**
   The Celts 39
   The Romans 41
   The Saxons 42
   The Egyptians 42
   The Melting Cauldron of Britain 44

CHAPTER 4
The Power of Lineage **46**
   The Gardnerians 49
   The Alexandrians 57

CHAPTER 5
The Flame of Initiation **72**

    Initiation in the British Isles 78
    The Cult of Dionysus 84
    The Cult of Isis 87
    The Cult of Diana 90
    A Path to Modern Magic 97
    The Secret Orders 100
    Initiation within Witchcraft 101

A Collection of Coven Photos   **107**

Chapter 6
The Goddess of the Witches 116
    The Moon Goddess .119
    The Triple-fold Goddess 120
    The Goddess of Magic 123
    The Goddess in Polytheism 124
    The Goddess in the Stone Age 126
    The Goddess in Early Civilization 127
    The Goddess of the Tribes 127
    Iconic Witch Goddesses 129

Chapter 7
The God of the Witches 147
    The Horned God 148
    The Sun God 154
    Iconic Witch Gods .156

Chapter 8
Magical Weapons 178
    History of Occult Tools 179
    Witchcraft Tools 182

Chapter 9
The Grimoire Occultatum 203
    Psychic Powers 204
    The Arts Magical 209
    The Five Elements .210
    The Witch's Pyramid 212

The Threefold Law 213
The Witches' Rede 214
The Seven Hermetic Principles 217
A Dedication to the Gods 218
Occult Exercises .221
The Rites of Alexandria 226
The Witches' Mass 232
Sabbat Rites 233
Folk Magic from Antiquity 245
Magical Systems .268
Recipes 276
Poems, Invocations, and Chants 278
Tables of Correspondences 287
Magic Words 291

APPENDIX A
Suggested Reading List. 293
General European Witchcraft 293
Western Occult Classics 294
Gardnerian & Alexandrian Initiates 296

APPENDIX B
Resources 298
Witchcraft, Magic, & Occult Shops 298
Magical Events 300
Facebook Groups .301

Bibliography   302

Index   312

About the Author   320

Foreword

Since the early days of 1964 when fear of ridicule and the need for secrecy was the way to avoid the persecution that was only a bigot away, the evolution of the Craft has raced itself into 2019 often falling into disarray before rising with even more traditions and ways of magic.

Today we have such choice of practice from fairy to high ceremonial and a veritable plethora of traditions in between. Not only traditions but Occult conferences, festivals, workshops creating a stage where knowledgeable practitioners teach and sometimes the not so enlightened beguile the innocent.

There are so many books; it is usually challenging to choose or recommend; indeed, I rarely do as every book is only another person's opinion making it difficult for the seeker to know what is fact, illusion or just plain rubbish.

Every so often, a good book comes along, usually when the need for it is acute. It is one of those times, and *Initiation into Witchcraft* is one of those rare books.

Do not be fooled by its cover, Alexandrians are known for their flamboyance, and magic.

Meeting Brian and his husband Christian was memorable. They were intelligent, humorous, and outrageous with just a touch of mystery about them to make one curious. Not long after our first meeting Brian was sitting in my living room, and he had received Initiation into the Alexandrian Tradition. There was an energy within him that needed honing; this was no run of the mill Initiate.

My work as a priestess entails accepting the responsibility for the well-being of Initiates who need direction.

Brian was burning with the vocation of the priest and the desire for training in the Inner mysteries of the Alexandrian Circle. He willingly became the pupil of a remarkable priestess well practised in the art of witchcraft and magic.

Brian and Christian are Razzmatazz showmen, successful in business and generally outrageous in their public appearances, which makes Brian's book *Initiation into Witchcraft* all the more impressive as within its leaves, it is occult.

It is the book I too would have cherished all those years ago as I approached the Circle of the Craft. It has the feeling of care and protection that surrounds the vulnerable soul as it journeys towards the centre of the Circle and beyond. It is also an extremely interesting read for those like me who consider themselves rather old in tooth; it just goes to show, we are never too old to be taught by the young. *Initiation into Witchcraft* contains surprises both simple and deep and in parts worthy of the title 'grimoire'.

This book is balanced, informative, and to the point, which is just what the seeker needs; indeed, it gives the pitfalls that have become more sophisticated and the 'how's' that are so necessary in today's confusing occult world.

Initiation into Witchcraft gives a brief history of British Traditional Witchcraft and does come up with surprising information which somewhat contradicts the controlled accounts of yesteryear.

Within its pages are gentle workings for the would-be Initiate that attune and prepare the soul and body for that which can only be truly experienced by those with the vocation that leads to the priesthood of the Witch and the well of knowledge that never runs dry.

— Maxine Sanders

Maxine Sanders is the Co-Founder of the Alexandrian Tradition of Witchcraft and author of Fire Child: The Life & Magic of Maxine Sanders.

Introduction

This is a book about the religion of Witchcraft. It honors the old Gods, the ancient mysteries, and the secrets of magic. This book will immerse you into the magical arts of Witchcraft and will dispel many of the false myths that persist about Witches. It is an enchanted window into what Witches practice and what we believe. While this book does contain rites, recipes, exercises, and lore, it is not a how-to for those seeking to be instant Witches or for those looking for immediate spiritual gratification. Rather, it is an exploration of the timeless traditions, essential ethics, and the awe-inspiring power of our Craft as well as providing basic practices that will help you to embrace the deeper ways of the Witch. It is a signpost for those seeking the path that begins the journey of initiation into Witchcraft. It is also a primer of occult techniques and rituals to prepare you for that journey. Witchcraft is personal empowerment magnified through a relationship with the old gods. Through it, you can direct the course of your life and find a path to your most powerful self!

Witches are healers, sorcerers, and shapeshifters, as many of the tales of Witches portray, but, like those tales also tell, we are a priesthood as well. No, we aren't worshiping the evils of Christian fantasies. Our Gods are far older, perhaps the oldest gods in the world, but gods we do have. Witchcraft is an ancient religion and, like many of the mystery cults of old, it requires the solemn rites of initiation in order to enter into those mysteries. Some of today's instant practitioners may scoff at the concept of initiation but Witches know that the ancients did not see things this way. The great emperors and kings of Greece and Rome and Egypt were seen as god-kings on earth and were worshiped by their people, and yet many such venerated leaders would not dare to use their status as incarnate deity to ignore the call of initiation. They took the arduous path into the Mysteries at such holy places as the great Temple of Eleusis in Greece—knowing that to not do so would deprive them of the hidden wisdom they needed to effectively guide their people. Unlike today's mages of the mall, the god-kings of old wouldn't dream of looking down their nose at these ancient practices. Witchcraft is a survival of these mysteries. It is a force of significant power—and initiation is the key that unlocks that power. Initiation transcends culture. It transcends religion. It takes a community to manifest to priesthood and it takes initiation to become a priest … and a Witch.

Witchcraft transforms you and changes you. It challenges you. It compels you to penetrate the darkest parts of the self and the deepest realms of the soul. You must delve into that abyss and shadow to find your light and power. I became a Witch because I had an unending need to unleash the power within—and that power does indeed come from within. Through initiation into the Craft, I was able to unlock my true potential and propel forward the evolution of my soul. Witchcraft allows you to become something greater than a mere mortal, but it takes great courage and daring. It is dangerous, but it is also richly rewarding for those who take the path to godhood … to Godhead. To those who climb Mount Olympus or the great pyramids and to all those who would steal fire from heaven, the power of Witchcraft is just that: you are stealing fire from heaven. Witchcraft is the ecstatic wonder of the Goddess in springtime, the awestruck terror and desire of the Horned God, the blazing power of the midday sun and the pull of the tides of the moon. I became a Witch because I sensed the forbidden power that lies hidden within the Craft. I perceived its force before I ever even knew what it was. Like a search for the Holy Grail, I sought that power out. It was only through initiation into Witchcraft that I was able to discover my own true magic.

For years, I have received inquiries from new seekers to the Craft, getting a firsthand look at how Witchcraft is perceived in the information age and how much actual information people really don't have. There is so much alleged knowledge out there that it's almost impossible to filter the truth from the lie and seekers are given no real sense of direction. Whether these seekers ever become Initiates into the true Craft, the fact that they are interested in Witchcraft and yet know so little of its enigmatic history and rich power means that there's still lots of educational work for Witches to do. I wrote this book as a guide for people interested in real Witchcraft. I also hope that it can become a useful tool for covens that they may recommend it to potential students so that these seekers may discover whether the Craft is right for them.

This book offers guidance and techniques of pure magical power and wisdom and provides a roadmap to true Initiatory Witchcraft. It is an accurate compass to use on your path. It's a book I wish I'd had when I first started out and it has taken me thirty years to learn some of the things that I will be teaching you in these pages. Let these ways empower you as they have me, for Witchcraft is a limitless well of power upon which to draw at times of need and is a source of joy and reverence in your everyday life.

CHAPTER 1

Stepping onto the Path

From my earliest childhood, I was fascinated with mythological stories of witches and wizards and so the idea that magic could be real came naturally to me. I was first drawn into the world of the occult at the age of 13, when I would visit the home of a friend whose mother had a number of books on magic. I didn't know at the time that she was practicing Witchcraft, but my friend and I would secretly read her books and practice the spells therein. It all seemed somehow forbidden, taboo, and that made me want to do it all the more. I was enthralled with the idea of practicing magic. Eventually, I came across Raymond Buckland's *Complete Book of Witchcraft* when I was 15 and that was the moment that I fell in love with the idea of Witchcraft as a religion. Buckland's big blue book was a massive awakening for me in that I'd never contemplated people worshiping a goddess before, much less a horned god. To my 15-year-old mind, it was an epiphany that God might actually be a woman and that a god could have horns, not because he is the source of all evil, but rather because he is the embodiment of nature, sexuality, and lust for life. By the age of 17, I began training under my first priestess who prepared me for the rites of initiation.

At 19, I received my first initiation into Witchcraft, which started me on a journey that ultimately lead me to the magical city of New Orleans, where, eventually, I would become a high priest of the Alexandrian Tradition of Witchcraft and form the first Alexandrian coven in the Crescent City. It was also in New Orleans where I met my husband, Salem Warlock Christian Day, who had moved to New Orleans out of love for the deep magic there.

You may have noticed that I avoid the word "Wicca" in this book. The word Witch comes from the Old English roots "wicca" and "wicce," and were pronounced with the palatal consonant /tʃ/ (like the "ch" sound in "chip") and would have sounded like Witch-ah [wɪttʃɑ] and Witch-eh [wɪttʃe], respectively, not the more commonly mispronounced "wick-ah." Also important is the fact that the roots "wicca" and "wicce" are not actually two words. Unlike Modern English, Old English was a gendered language and so "wicca" and "wicce" were gendered variations of the same word. If you remove those variations, you simply get the word "Witch!" Hence, continuing to use the word "Wicca" with a *k* sound doesn't make any sense. While it has been said that Wicca with a *k* is an old word for Witch, the truth is that *Witch* is the old word for Witch! Our ways are called Witchcraft and Witchcraft is the very source of the pastiche of practices that are now called Wicca with a *k*—a word that has gone on to be applied to many derivative Pagan religions, pseudo-spiritual therapy encounter groups, and donut social gatherings. However, Witchcraft is the authentic core of our priesthood, and our traditions continue to thrive in spite of the many bastardizations that come from the misuse of the word Wicca. Therefore, I am punishing that word by not using it.

To truly begin your own journey towards initiation into Witchcraft, we must first define what Witchcraft is and where it comes from. We will explore the lives and legacies of the major players of the modern Witchcraft revival. And, I'll help you to understand the deep roots of the ancient magical priesthood you are endeavoring to explore.

The Roots of Modern Witchcraft

From mankind's earliest roots, there have been magical religions that served both spiritual and practical purposes in the lives of traditional peoples. From Paleolithic cave paintings such as the famed Sorcerer of the Cave of the Trois-Frères in Ariège, France (13,000 B.CE) that symbolize the success of the hunt and the spiritual embodiment of the horned one, to countless goddess figurines that celebrate the fertility and life-giving power of women, mankind has long had a relationship with both the divine feminine and masculine. They saw themselves in the divine and the divine within themselves and so the procreative process of fertility was fundamental to their understanding of both religion and magic. And, being so close to the harsh challenges of nature, traditional peoples used the power of magic daily to influence their lives for the better. Witchcraft has always been at the heart of these mysteries, embodying both magical religion and fertility cult, dedicated to the power of creation and how it can influence both spirit and matter.

Later, as Christianity took power in the Western world, the old fertility cults, such as the cults of Isis, Bacchus, Dionysus, Diana, and the Druid priests of the Celts were forced into the shadows, hunted over centuries of persecution, and became known to the masses as Witches—diabolical outcasts seeking only to harm the people. There are hints and glimmers of the word Witch being connected to the Iron Age tribe of Dobunni and medieval Hwicce (pronounced "Witch-eh") of Central England.[1] They are said to have worshiped a goddess associated with a cauldron, so there are clues as to where the word Witch may have come from and how it came to factor into the consolidation of fertility cults as agents of the Christian Devil.

Everything began to change with the enormous surge of interest in occult and Eastern spirituality in the second half of the 19th century. Luminaries such as Madame Helena Blavatsky and, later, Arthur Edward Waite and the infamous Aleister Crowley, stoked the public interest with

---

[1] Stephen J. Yeates, *The Tribe of Witches: The Religion of the Dobunni and Hwicce* (Oxford: Oxbow Books, 2008), 4-5.

all things mysterious and unknown. It wouldn't be long before the fascination with ancient Kabbalistic grimoires, secret tomes of the Catholic Church, and Eastern Vedic texts turned to an interest in the old ways of Witchcraft. In 1899, Charles Godfrey Leland published his notorious work, *Aradia: Gospel of the Witches*, in which he claimed to have been given the texts of an Italian Witch named Maddalena.

While academia may have been less than embracing of Leland's claims, a far more renowned scholar soon came along to propose an idea even more profound than Leland's localized theories. In 1921, notable Egyptologist Margaret Murray published her momentous work, *The Witch Cult in Western Europe*, a dramatic assertion that the Witch trials records and folklore of Witches revealed the existence of an ancient Witch Cult. Murray published her second work on the subject, *God of the Witches*, in 1931 and, between them, these two works convinced many in both academia and in the general populace that Witches might actually have been a true fertility cult of magical practitioners. I sometimes wonder if Murray herself was not drawn to the power of the myths she studied, having devoted her life to the study of Ancient Egypt and its gods. While Murray has fallen in and out and in again where academic credibility is concerned, her work inspires us to seek the truth of the Witch from the shadows of the past.

Perhaps the most significant developments in the modern Witchcraft revival occurred in 1951, when, urged by the then-popular religious movement of spiritualism, England's Witchcraft act of 1735 was replaced with the Fraudulent Mediums Act. This paved the way for authentic spiritualist mediums to continue to ply their trade while, not-so-incidentally, opening the doorway for Witches to finally emerge from their broom closets—and a Witch named Gerald Gardner was about to do precisely that. In 1951, the Museum of Witchcraft and Magic was established in Castletown on the Isle of Man and featured Gerald Gardner as its resident Witch, a man considered by many to be the father of modern Witchcraft. Gardner was a civil servant, an amateur anthropologist and archaeologist, and a Master Mason. He also held a charter in Aleister

Crowley's Ordo Templi Orientis before eventually taking up the mantle as the world's first media Witch.

Gerald Gardner described his initiation into a cult of Witches in England's New Forest in 1939. While this has been called into question, much research has verified that this coven did indeed exist. Whether it was a survival of Murray's ancient Witch cult or practices inspired by Murray herself, it is clear that Gardner did, in fact, find practicing Witches in the New Forest. Gardner later founded his own Bricket Wood Coven and worked to combine what he found in his research into other traditions. Gardner drew upon the works of Leland, Murray, Crowley, Freemasonry, and more because he saw vestiges of the Witch Cult in each of these practices. Gathering these materials together with what he had discovered in the New Forest, Gardner created what is known as the *Book of Shadows*—the liturgy and rituals passed down from Initiate to Initiate. In 1949, Gardner had published a fictional work titled *High Magic's Aid*, within which some of the practices of Witchcraft were hinted at. His most iconic work, *Witchcraft Today*, was published in 1954 with a foreword by Margaret Murray and he later went on to release *The Meaning of Witchcraft* in 1959. Gardner did this work in hopes of saving what he felt was a cult in decline, and it did generate considerable interest. He was featured in numerous publications and television shows and was even invited to Buckingham Palace.

Gardner initiated a number of powerful, influential, and iconic Witches, who themselves would go on to influence the liturgy and practices of the Craft, represent Witches in the media, and write some of the great written works on the subject of Witchcraft. Priestesses like Doreen Valiente, Lois Bourne, Patricia Crowther, Eleanor Bone, and Monique Wilson became the leading lights of Witchcraft for years and eventually came to be known collectively as Gardnerian Witches. The Craft was later brought to the United States by Raymond Buckland, a prolific author whose work continues to help popularize Witchcraft throughout the world. I wonder if old Gerald could have imagined how the Witchcraft cult he discovered in the New Forest would spread across the globe into the modern belief system it has become today.

Even though Witchcraft had thrust itself back into the world, a royal couple was about to truly bring the Craft to the center stage of public consciousness. In 1963, Alex Sanders was initiated into Witchcraft and was later declared "King of the Witches" by a gathering of his peers and to the consternation of some of the known priestesses at the time. In 1965, Maxine Sanders was initiated into the Craft and, together, she and Alex would appear in countless media outlets as the first couple of modern Witchcraft. Together, they founded the London Coven in 1968 which would later become the foundation for the Alexandrian Tradition.

Alex and Maxine were controversial right out of the gate. For starters, Alex claimed to have been initiated by his grandmother at the age of seven in a ritual that he asserted involved a sexual act between the two. It was a brutally provocative statement to make at the time, even for the sexual revolution of the 1960s. I explore this scandalous claim more in-depth in Chapter 4 but, suffice it to say—and bearing in mind that I wasn't there—I would guess that this story was quite colored and that Alex was more likely initiated by the Gardnerians. While it is possible that he may have had magic in his childhood, his introduction into the Craft probably came much later.

In May, 1973, the Sanders parted ways, divorcing several years later. Alex relocated to Bexhill-on-Sea while Maxine remained in London, pulling together the remnants of the London Coven and eventually developing it into the Temple of the Mother, perhaps the most well-honed incarnation of Alexandrian Witchcraft. Maxine Sanders continues to work on behalf of the tradition today. She is responsible for a large part of the highly-developed training and occult practices used within the Craft today.

In 1988, Alex Sanders—the King of the Witches—passed beyond the veil, leaving a legacy of magic and spiritual practice that continues to thrive today as a living, breathing tradition. Alexandrian Witchcraft—founded and developed by both Alex and Maxine Sanders—remains at the pinnacle of not only the Witchcraft revival, but occultism and the Western mystery traditions as well.

British Traditional Witchcraft is more relevant now than ever. Sadly, the pendulum has swung too far in matters of religion, with people melding politics and spirituality to the point where the old magic no longer matters. This is especially true in America where it has come to the point where so-called practitioners of the Craft dispense with tradition entirely. Such people want do-it-yourself Witchcraft. They want whatever feels right—no matter how little their practices resemble actual Witchcraft. In the age of absolute self-identity, these pretenders to the Craft define it as whatever they want it to be—while they continue to culturally appropriate the actual beliefs and practices of British Witchcraft. In the 1990s, such free-for-all Witchcraft became the norm with the authors of the time churning out as many Witchcraft "traditions" and non-traditions as they could dream up. This terrible trend has continued, but what is not spoken of is just how much of those practices continue to be appropriated and, quite frankly, mangled by those who should know to have respect for the traditions of other cultures.

Despite these attempts to cloud the Craft in vague and lifeless terms, people have begun to crave actual substance again. You find this even within Christianity and Catholicism. Seekers are going back to the core of belief, practice, and principle in search of both depth and divinity. They want the timeless traditions of old and they're realizing that the spirit roaming wild often returns from the wilderness without sustenance. To be a Witch is to honor those ways of old and to draw power from the time-worn path.

Getting Proper Witchcraft Training

While many aspiring Witches insist on going it alone, Witchcraft is a priesthood. We are members of a mystery tradition, a fertility cult, and a magical religion. Proper Witches meet in covens and train their postulants to become dedicated and effective Witches themselves. The coven is the heart of Witchcraft—a place where we come together for worship, training, magic, and celebration of the seasonal rites. A Witches' coven keeps their particular tradition's worldview and beliefs, its code of ethics, its collection of teachings and wisdom, and the entire culture that goes along with it.

As it is said, "You may not be a Witch alone." You can't teach yourself something that you simply do not know; you can't initiate yourself into a priesthood that requires other people, and you cannot perceive tradition from the mere bits and pieces of knowledge scattered haphazardly into the mangled tomes of today's Witchcraft book market. Unfortunately, circumstance sometimes thrusts such loneliness upon us, and so we try to keep the old ways alive as best we can without the benefit of our brethren. But the heart of Witchcraft will always pull us back to its core—which is the coven—and so, seeking a coven is fundamental to becoming a Witch and we will explore how to find the proper one in the next chapter.

How to Know if You're Ready

How do you know if you're ready to become an Initiate of Witchcraft or to join a coven? When is it the right time? The first thing I ask a seeker is, "How many books on Witchcraft have you read? How much do you know about Alexandrian Witchcraft? How much do you know about Gardnerian Witchcraft, if that's what you're seeking initiation into?" Today, many, many books have been published over the last seventy years by Alexandrian and Gardnerian authors. My best advice would be to read as many as you can, including this one. If you haven't attempted to absorb as much information on the subject as you can before seeking the Craft then, no, I don't think you're ready. You need to do your research. And no, that doesn't just include Google, Wikipedia, or Facebook groups, but actually reading the rich and varied books by serious Initiates of the Craft and wrapping your brain around their traditions.

The books on Witchcraft are not going to tell you everything about a tradition, as many secrets remain unpublished, but they will give you the flavor. They will provide you with enough to know if the Craft is something that you're drawn to. Are you enjoying these books? Do you want to devour the material? Are you excited to practice the rites therein? Is it something that you feel incredibly drawn to? Are you prepared to approach the Craft with the seriousness of a truly valid priesthood?

If you do not approach the Craft with the same dedication and fervor that a Catholic would have upon entering the seminary, then no, you're not ready. If you're not completely serious about the Craft as a priesthood—one that you want to join, train in, and make a vocation and spiritual foundation of your life, then walk away. This is a fertility cult. It is a mystery priesthood. It will become and transform your whole life. If you're not ready for that kind of transformation, if you're not ready to be a true priest or priestess, then you are not ready for the true initiation into Witchcraft. It is perfectly ok if you're not ready. Take all the time that you need. Read every book you can find on the subject. Educate yourself. Immerse yourself in the history, timeline, culture, and legacy of the Craft.

You simply cannot prepare yourself for initiation just by reading a few beginner Witchcraft books or because you've made some witchy friends on social media. It's not enough to be excited about the idea of being a Witch. Witchcraft is not a hobby or casual pursuit. You must actually study and make a real connection with Witchcraft on the inner planes before you're ready to take the leap. I can guarantee you that no one decides to become a rabbi without first immersing themselves into the ideology and culture of Judaism. You must do the same in the Craft if you're really going to open the doors of initiation. Ultimately, you'll know when you know. It's quite like falling in love. You do not have to ask the question, "Am I in love?" You know when you're in love, so when you feel you're in love with the Craft enough to penetrate the Mysteries of initiation and become a priest or priestess of Witchcraft, then you're truly ready. I promise you that the magic will find a way.

Things to Work on Before Initiation

If you do begin working with a coven, the preparation required for initiation will vary to some extent depending on that particular coven's training style. One practice that has become common in America is the outer court system, which originated in American Gardnerian Craft but has been adopted by some Alexandrians as well. The outer court is used to prepare and evaluate seekers before initiation is given. Traditionally, there was no such thing as an outer court. The more common custom is that seekers were initiated, and then the training would begin. My coven does not have an outer court, but we understand why some would utilize the practice as a means of assessing potential Initiates.

I have already stressed the importance of reading and researching on the subject of the Craft, but I would also advise you begin your own inner work before initiation—the personal mental and spiritual development that can ready you for the task ahead. Most Initiates can tell you that their transformation began long before the initiatory rite and continued long after.

There's an old story about a disciple seeking out a teacher for initiation and, after a long journey, the seeker throws himself at the feet of the master saying, "Master, master, I have come for initiation!" The master says, "Oh, again? Again, you've come for initiation? Oh, you mean the rituals and whatnot? We will begin that in the morning. Your initiation began the moment you left on your journey to see me."

This is not to say that the rituals of Witchcraft and its initiation are unimportant. They are vitally important to the Craft. However, the process of initiation—or the journey towards it, begins within. The rites of initiation are the crowning jewel of this great work.

Understanding the philosophies, beliefs, ethics, and culture of Witchcraft are important but books do not paint the full accuracy of these concepts. You will get a lot of the flavor if you read books by actual Initiates, but you simply cannot glean the heart of the Craft through books alone.

Learn from Nature

One of the easiest ways to begin making inner contact with the Craft is to go out into nature. Immerse yourself in the elements of earth, water, air, and fire. Embrace the strength of the element of earth as you lay upon the earthen ground of a forest meadow. Explore the element of air as you gaze upon the clouds and look for patterns in their shapes and movement or simply close your eyes and feel the wind upon your face. Discover the element of fire as you peer within the candle flame or into the crackling blaze of an open campfire. Divine the secrets of the element of water as you contemplate a pebble in a stream or submerge yourself into the ocean's waters at a secluded beach. How does this exploration make you feel? What do you sense when you focus on these elements? Write those impressions down in a magical journal so that you can continue to relate them to your study of the elements on the magical planes. It has been said that you can learn more about the spirit of Witchcraft by gazing at the full moon than you can from any number of books. The Witches' gods and guides are all connected to nature so it is essential that you tap into these forces in the living and breathing world around you and that you work your magic in the natural world as much as you can.

Commune with the Witch Gods

You can also begin your path by making contact with the gods of Witchcraft—the Moon Goddess and the Horned God. Once you're initiated into your chosen tradition, the gods in those covens will have specific sacred names that will be given to you. These names may or may not be secret in the lower degrees of the Craft but, in the higher degrees, I can assure you that they are secret as such secrets are part of the power of these mystery traditions. Whatever names they are given, these gods are far older than the names themselves. They are the oldest gods in the world. They are the first primordial forces—the Goddess of fertility so often associated with the moon and the Horned God that embodies the hunt and who would also represent mankind's first exploration of death.

To make contact with these gods, and to see if they resonate and call to you, is one of the first signposts on the road to true initiation.

I would suspect that you're already feeling the pull of the Witch Gods if you're currently seeking initiation, but I urge you to make a connection to them regardless. Set up a devotional altar to them. Consider choosing a mythological god or goddess that represents the Moon Goddess and Horned God concepts for you. Perhaps it's Isis and Osiris. Maybe it's Diana and Pan. The gods you choose at first may not be the ones that you continue with and will most likely change with proper training, but it is important to begin embracing the energies they represent.

The contact you make with the Witch Gods will continue to become more and more potent as time goes on. You are making a connection to powerful primordial energies that are essential to the work of the Witch. Statues are not required for your altar but can help you to visualize the link to your chosen deities. You can put whatever prospective representatives of the Witch Gods you like on your altar, so long as they help you to strengthen the connection, which we explore further below. This book is not going to tell you how to be a do-it-yourself Witch. Many, many books already do that, and you can incorporate some of those practices, or even practices you've developed on your own, into your work with this book so long as you understand that the purpose of this work is not ultimately meant to be conducted alone. Neither this book nor any other can replace the proper training that you will receive upon initiation. This book is intended to prepare you for it. I do, however, share exercises and rituals through this book that will help get you started on the path.

Ritual Baths

A most powerful practice on the path to initiation is the ritual bath. Water has been seen as both a physical and spiritual cleansing from time out of mind and is one of the simplest and most powerful ways to prepare yourself for working with the gods. The only ingredient you really need for a ritual bath is salt. Most Witches prefer sea salt, but any kind of salt may be used in a pinch. You can add other ingredients to enhance the experience and to create more potent magic. Oils, herbs, creams and even spirits (the liquid kind) may be used. Here in New Orleans and in many areas of the South, we find that a few drops of Florida water are usually more than enough for a protection and cleansing bath. Upon filling the bath, infuse your intent into the waters by blessing them, saying (and truly feeling) the following words: "May this water purify my body and make me clean and ready to stand before the gods."

The Devotional Altar

Ancient Witches and other spiritual peoples often had devotional altars set for their house spirits or local deities. This practice is still very much a part of the modern world of Witchcraft. In our own home, we have many altars, including an altar for the dead, as well as altars for love, the Moon Goddess, the spirit of place of New Orleans, the higher self, and even some of the naughty creatures one encounters in magic. Our main altar is that within our Alexandrian temple, as it is the central place where worship of the Witch Gods takes place, circles are cast, and magic achieved. Your altars can be as grand or as simple as your taste and lifestyle allow. Like all things in the Craft, our main Witches' altar is something we are trained in how to set up explicitly for the work involved, but your other altars may be as wild as your imagination and space will accommodate. They can even be hidden amongst the items of your everyday life, for not all practitioners can be open about their Craft. If you must be discreet, natural objects might be ideal for representing the Witch Gods, such as a seashell to symbolize Aphrodite or a panpipe to signify the goat-footed God.

Making Offerings

A relationship with the Witch Gods is a two-way conduit. If you want the blessings of the Old Ones you must be ready, willing, and eager to bless them as well. This can be done at your devotional altar or at a place in nature that feels sacred to you: perhaps a hidden brook, a secret meadow, or a grove of trees. If you're lucky enough to live near an ancient sacred site, this a powerful way to connect with the Witch Gods of old. Visit your altar or sacred place often—especially on a full moon—and leave offerings to the Gods of Witchcraft and the other natural spirits that dwell there.

Before you make your offerings, make sure you have taken a ritual bath as this will make you clean in both mind and body and is a sign of respect to the Gods that has been considered an essential practice among all mystery cults. The offerings can be made up of flowers, coins, cakes, oats, grains, breads, honey, cream, or spirits—mead, wine, and ale are all appropriate. My first coven and I used to make candied violets and pour mead in acorn caps for the fairies. Another very magic offering is honey or spirits in eggshells. When you make your full moon offering, invoke the Witch Gods thus:

"Oh, Queen of Witches, I come before the spirits of this place. I come before the Shadowy Lord and all the prevailing Gods of Witchcraft. Accept these offerings and may my service to thee be pleasing before thine altars!"

After you make your offering, it is a perfect time to reflect and meditate on the moon, the stars and the forces of nature around you. If you are indoors at your devotional altar, gaze upon the statues and symbols thereupon. If you have a great need for the Witch Gods to address, a petition may be made that can be written or spoken at this time.

CHAPTER 2

Covens

A coven is the name of a magical working group for practitioners of Witchcraft. The word coven, like the word Witch, has obscure origins. Some believe it is derived from the Latin *conventus*, meaning a gathering or assembly. It shares a common root with words like convent, covenant, and conventicle. Historically the Church believed in the existence of covens, and the word appears throughout trial records. It is interesting to note—although pure speculation—we do find a few pieces of evidence of words relating to coven within Britain in both place names and pre-Christian peoples.

The Celtic scythed chariot used by Queen Boudicca was called a *covinnus*[1]; there's also the mysterious goddess Coventina. I've often found it curious that no writer on the subject has ever speculated an association between Coventina and the word coven. Coventina is a three-formed goddess that was discovered near Hadrian's Wall. [2]

---

[1] Michael Harrison, *The Roots of Witchcraft* (Secaucus, NJ: Citadel Press, 1973), 168.
[2] "Coventina's Well," PastScape, accessed June 4, 2019, https://www.pastscape.org.uk/hob.aspx?hob_id=1013364

In folklore and trial records covens numbered anywhere from three to thousands, although more common were assemblies of thirteen Witches. Regardless of origins, this number is the standard for most covens today, although some covens do choose to work in smaller groups of eight for the purpose of having a tight-knit magical group, and these groups will generally very rarely introduce a new Initiate; this often only happens when a former member has died or left.[3]

Several recorded trials mention groups of thirteen witches, with the trials of Dame Alice Kyteler, the Somerset Witches, and Isobel Goudie being some of the more famous examples. In the trial of Dame Alice Kyteler, twelve witches are named with the devil.[4] The Somerset Witches were said to have had two covens, each consisting of thirteen members. One of the most influential trials was of a Scottish woman, Isabel Goudie, who in her confession stated that each coven in her district had thirteen persons.[5] Both Emma Wilby and Ronald Hutton speculate that this trial may have very well introduced the word "coven" as the official label for a group of Witches.[6]

Groups of thirteen can be found in many mythologies and magical systems. Jesus and his twelve disciples, Robin Hood and his Merry Men, and in some legends Arthur and his Knights of the Round Table equal thirteen in number.[7] The Olympian Gods, although twelve in number are really thirteen in total. Hestia mysteriously stepping down for Dionysus. It could be speculated that Hestia's removal represents the thirteen-month lunar calendar becoming a twelve-month solar system. Another case of this is the zodiac, which some astrologers believe was once thirteen in number and you will find many articles and books on the subject.

---

[3] Doreen Valiente, *An ABC of Witchcraft Past & Present* (New York, NY: St Martin's Press, 1973), 91-92.

[4] Ibid, 252.

[5] Margaret A. Murray, *The God of the Witches* (Oxford: Oxford University Press, 1952), 69.

[6] Ronald Hutton, *The Witch, A History of Fear, from Ancient Times to the Present*, 2017 E-book ed. (New Haven and London: Yale University Press, 2017), Loc: 4785, Kindle.

[7] Doreen Valiente, *An ABC of Witchcraft Past & Present* (New York, NY: St Martin's Press, 1973), 96.

The number thirteen is deeply rooted in folklore and superstition, earning the nickname the "Devil's dozen." It has been seen as bad luck so much so that hotels avoided having a thirteenth floor; it also has its own holiday, Friday the thirteenth. It is possible that covens of thirteen were simply church propaganda, the devil and his twelve witches being a mockery against Christ and his twelve disciples. However, I believe the number thirteen has its occult origins from the moon as I have previously mentioned. Before the Julian calendar, we had thirteen moons or months, so the year was measured by moon cycles. When it became solar we turned into twelve months. The solar system, being somewhat flawed, cannot escape the old year, and every so often a year still has thirteen moons; we refer to this additional moon as a blue moon. Witchcraft is a lunar cult and being priests and priestesses of a moon goddess, we serve in orders of her number on most occasions. Each coven member represents a station in the ancient seasonal year.

In modern Witchcraft, covens are alive and well with active groups throughout the world. The first recorded modern coven is the New Forest Coven of England. Modern myths link this coven to alleged hereditary covens found throughout Britain. Others believe the coven was created by an occultist who believed profoundly in reincarnation and channeling. They were inspired by the works of Leland, Margaret Murray, and Reginald Scott, as well as the witch trials. Of course, it is possible the truth is somewhere in between. I believe that members of this coven had family magic, folk knowledge, occult training, initiation, and a belief in past lives, some of which were memories of having been witches previously. It is also important to realize they did make genuine contact with the old gods of Witchcraft. It is almost unquestionable that Gardner did make contact in the New Forest, and it was from this group that he received the seeds he used to start his first independent group, the Bricket Wood Coven.[8]

---

[8] Frederic Lamond, "Gerald Gardner," in *Fifty Years of Wicca* (Sutton Mallet: Green Magic, 2004).

Since that time the Craft has had many influential covens, now considered historic. Notable covens like the ones in London, Sheffield, Manchester, Perth, and New York have become groups of legend among Witches today. Originally most covens were named by place, a practice carried on by many today. Our own coven, the New Orleans Coven, was named for this reason.

Joining a Coven

In the old days, to find a teacher or a coven, people would often have to write authors, travel long distances, and rely on word of mouth. Seekers would write letters to Gerald Gardner, Patricia Crowther, Alex and Maxine Sanders, or other notable Witches because they saw them on TV, read about them in the newspaper, heard them on the radio, or read one of their books. It has been said that Witchcraft is a cult of personality and that's probably why those authors and other notable Witches were more successful. In their day and age, they were the poster children of Witchcraft and the only faces available at the time. These tried and true methods still work. Reaching out to the lights of the British Craft can help guarantee that you're getting exceptional training. However, contacting authors today can also be a double-edged sword since, these days, anyone can write a book on Witchcraft and the checks and balances of yesterday no longer exist.

Before you even seek out a coven, you should establish what it is you actually want. What are your expectations? Do you want initiation into a lineage, and why? Do you want to be Alexandrian, Gardnerian? Do you wish to join a particular tradition? Do you want to make friends? How important is discipline? Are you expecting to join a coven that has rigorous occult training and develops you on an intense level? Is this a vocation or exploration? Are you hoping to join a priesthood? This is extremely important if you want to join a traditional Alexandrian or Gardnerian coven—to understand that it is a priesthood. I will not accept members who are not going to have a serious vocation towards the Craft, and I doubt very much I stand alone in this viewpoint.

Once you know what you're looking for, the quest perilous begins. In today's world, the options go far beyond authors, media Witches, and good old-fashioned word of mouth. You can also find your gateways into the Witchcraft traditions via such methods as occult stores—which can be found in countless cities and towns throughout the world, magical festivals, moots and soirées, and, of course, the Internet. The Internet unleashed the floodgates of communication for those seeking the old ways of Witchcraft. With sites like WitchVox.com, Facebook—including my own British Traditional Witchcraft group, YouTube, and even Twitter, seekers are finding potential teachers like never before. Vouching—the process of verifying whether the lineage of a practitioner of the Craft is valid—is a much quicker process than in the old days of handwritten letters sent through the post or cryptic midnight phone calls. However, this, too, has been a double-edged sword. Unfortunately, when bombarded with so much information, the would-be seeker might find it difficult to distinguish between fact and fiction. Moreover, in the age of the one-minute news cycle, any ambitious YouTuber can become an instant-celebrity Witch, but this notoriety does not necessarily confer expertise.

In Britain, it is easier to find legitimate Alexandrian and Gardnerian Covens and teachers; it is where I found mine. This is where these traditions were founded and because it is a smaller country Witches have in the past had better communication. Because of this, most false claims are quickly exposed, though the British tend to prefer doing so behind closed doors. Unfortunately, in America and other countries, this is not the case. America is a vast country, and unfortunately, most states do not have Gardnerian or Alexandrian covens operating. This is one of the reasons why America has so many self-declared eclectic traditions.

If you genuinely want initiation, you might have to travel for it. You might have to move for it. But as I said earlier, if this is actually a vocation for you, you will find a way to pursue initiation. You will move, you will travel, or do whatever it is you need to do to achieve the goal of the priesthood. It is up to you, and you can't just expect people to hand it to you. There won't be an online Internet course, and you can't just get on the computer and hope to become a priest or priestess.

If you wanted to become a Catholic priest or nun or a Buddhist monk, you would have to go where the training was available. When we go to college, it is often our first experience leaving the nest and entering into adulthood. This may be the level of dedication required if this is your calling; this is just a reality. I think it actually separates the wheat from the chaff, in many cases! The good news is that our training does not cost anything.

People have been traveling for initiation for thousands of years. The Craft first entered the United States in this way through Raymond Buckland after corresponding with Gerald Gardner. He and his wife, Rosemary, went to the UK for training and initiation. It was a bit more difficult in those days. He only had twelve days of training with the High Priestess, Monique Wilson, and came back to the United States with a *Book of Shadows*. Returning to America, he set off the first Gardnerian coven in our country. Buckland was willing to do what he needed to become a Witchcraft priest.

In my own coven, I have a few processes that have worked well. If I'm contacted by someone through correspondence, email, social media, or what have you, this would be the first medium I have for communication. If it progresses, then I will have phone calls with the individual; I think this is very important. Finally, if things proceed, I will meet the individual in person in a public setting.

If you are going to meet with a coven for the first time, I advise you to make sure it is in a public setting. There is no reason why it should be a private meeting. If a teacher wishes you to meet them in the middle of the woods or have you come to their house, I would be wary. If the group charges money for any of their teachings, this is another red flag. We do not charge money for teaching our craft. There should be no required payment for the training. If they insist on this on any level, they are not Gardnerian or Alexandrian. It is quite reasonable to ask for contributions such as wine, flowers, and food for the feast. That's normal and many covens do have a coven bank, but it's not required, and it should not be required. These are offerings that you make. It is necessary that you contribute, as it should not be solely on the coven leaders to foot the bill for everything. However, the teaching and the Craft do not cost money.

In my own coven, I have had long-distance students who have come to New Orleans for initiation, and they've repeatedly come to New Orleans for training. I even had someone move to New Orleans for a while to try to assist in his training. Unfortunately, it does take years to reach high priesthood, so you are better off if you are living in the area if that's your goal.

I have developed some long-distance training methods, but this is not my preference, and I think it best avoided. I would rarely agree to attempt it. I just do not believe that some of the training can be done long distance. You can discuss things. You can even, now, have private video sessions where you can go over ritual. But it is not the same as being in the ritual itself. The Craft is not as intellectual as it is ecstatic. The Mysteries must be experienced. Discussing or reading about them is all fine and good, but you cannot truly penetrate them with these methods. This is why you cannot really learn the Craft by reading books. It is not an academic process. The only true way you can learn the religious side of Witchcraft is by being in a coven and experiencing the Mysteries within that coven.

Whichever way you find the coven that best suits your journey, it is more important than ever to make sure that your potential teachers have both the knowledge and the credibility to impart the practices and beliefs of Witchcraft. If you look hard enough, you will likely find a coven suitable for you. This will not be easy, and it's not supposed to be, but it can and is done every day.

What to Look for in a Coven

If you're hoping to receive initiation into the priesthood of Witchcraft, then it is essential to know what it means to be a priest, and you will want the proper training that will confer such priesthood upon you.

Each coven and tradition will often have its particular styles of practice and emphasis on specific areas of teaching, so it is essential to research the tradition you wish to join (see Chapter 4: The Power of Lineage to learn more about the traditions of the Craft).

Once you find the coven that represents the tradition that you wish to be initiated into, and the dialogue begins with its leaders, it is vitally important that you ask lots of questions. It is also crucial to ascertain that they have clear expectations of their students and that they have a strong focus on training. If training is not the primary focus, it is a potential red flag that this group does not have the proper training to actually pass on to you. If the teachers you've met do not talk about training in your initial conversations, and if they don't appear to make training the number one priority in their work, then they're probably not going to actually train you. It makes me sad when I meet a dedicated Initiate who has worked tirelessly for years and yet has received little or, worse, false training. You are seeking to represent a true priesthood and, as such, you should want to receive proper, solid instruction in your prospective tradition, and so you need to thoroughly investigate the teachers involved and ask lots of questions to ensure that they are who they claim to be.

Another thing you should ask for when you interview the teachers of a prospective coven is a vouch for their lineage. Who initiated them? What covens have they participated in? How long have they been teaching? If they provide suspicious answers or if they're purposely mysterious about their origins, then there's probably a good reason why. If they sound shady, they probably are shady. With the enormous popularity of the Internet, including social media groups and other online social forums, it's really not that hard to investigate people. If your potential teachers cannot get another known Initiate to speak in favor of them, do not waste your time. Vouching, by which both covens and seekers ascertain the validity of Initiates, is an entirely acceptable system within the Craft. Both Gardnerians and Alexandrians employ this practice. It wasn't something that was done at the beginning of the Witchcraft revival because the Craft was a relatively small movement in England at the time and it was easier to verify who was who. With the popularity explosion of Witchcraft, especially in America, it has become imperative to be able to trace the authenticity of people claiming to belong to these traditions because not everyone does know one another. Public Witches are more easily approached, which means it's easier to figure out who is authentic and who isn't. If they are hiding things about themselves, they are very likely lying to you.

The world is filled with all manner of religious frauds and this includes many who claim Witchcraft traditions they have no right to claim. Some of these include those who sincerely believe that they were initiated into Gardnerian or Alexandrian Craft but were not. Such sincere practitioners were lied to—fooled by those who were more interested in ego than in the work of the priesthood. Other teachers are simply willful frauds, tossing around unverifiable backgrounds about nameless teachers of their own who were most likely invented as part of their backstory. The unsuspected seeker can be lured in by such deceptions when they should be seeking teachers who were properly prepared. There's simply nothing wrong with vouching and there's nothing wrong with asking for a vouch. If one cannot be provided, then buyer beware.

Another thing you should probably ascertain is the purpose of the group. If you're going to join a coven, you need to be capable of embracing a psychic hive mind, as the energies raised weave and intersect between each member. You need to be of the same purpose, so if the coven you're seeking to join is a healing coven and you have no interest in healing, then it doesn't do you any good to join that group. If you want initiation into a particular tradition and have not practiced it before, then a training coven is the best choice because you will get a solid background in that path.

You should also explore the social dynamic of the group you're seeking to join. Are they all friends? Is this the kind of coven where everyone considers one another to be family? Are they all very close-knit and do they socialize with each other in their mundane lives? Or, is this a coven that takes a stauncher occult approach where there's no socialization outside of temple life, and where the focus is on the work? It's up to you which you think will be more beneficial to you. But, if you're looking for a serious training coven or working coven, they're probably not getting together for tea and crumpets. They're probably not holding Tupperware parties or game nights. They're probably not bar-hopping together on any kind of regular basis. And they certainly aren't merely getting together as a therapy encounter group or emotional crutch. They're too busy focused on the work and they're probably going to have a dedicated nature and focus. My coven practices the "no-socializing rule" established by the Temple of the Mother. We do not allow socializing for most new Initiates because we believe that this dilutes from a sincere focus on the work of the priesthood. Naturally, some circumstances bend these rules; they're not the Ten Commandments. But we employ the no-socializing rule so that Initiates can focus on learning the Craft. In my coven, students come to learn Alexandrian Witchcraft. We have promised to teach them Alexandrian Witchcraft. That's the purpose of our coven. It's not to make friends. It's not to interfere with one another's personal lives. Our students already have families. That's what works for our group and it's made for a very efficient and powerful coven. It also keeps people from attempting to join just so they can hang out with us, especially since we have so many public members so this could be a real issue for us if we did not follow this rule. If someone wants to be initiated and we tell them beforehand that there's no socializing, and that we're not going to be their friends, it'll turn the social seekers off if their actual intention is simply to hang out with the cool Witches or whatever they're thinking.

If the true intent of the seeker is to learn the Craft, then they won't be bothered by rules of socialization. They're going to get precisely what they're asking for—which is priesthood—and that is the purpose of a coven. However, some might prefer to run a coven where everyone feels like they're close family and in one another's personal lives. This is not my way nor is it my preference, but if that's what you think you want then you need to make it clear and ask the question, "What are your stances on socialization? Can I hang out? Can I become friends with other coven members?"

Ask as many questions as you can and try to get to know your prospective teachers. Do you like these people? Are they people you want to spend time with, even if it's not in friendship? Do they seem intelligent and well-informed to you? Do they answer your questions or are they unnecessarily mysterious? Are they too hesitant to answer your questions? Do they seem happy, healthy, and successful? These are all things to be considered. Ask many, many questions and see how many questions they're asking. How eager are they? Are they willing to just hand initiation to you just to get a new member, or are they trying to ascertain if you're of good quality?

A good coven is concerned with quality, not quantity. Does the coven you're seeking just want lots of members? Do they think having a large coven gives them power? I've heard some Witches say that having a larger coven makes their coven more powerful but more numbers does not necessarily equal more talent if participants are lackluster and uncommitted. Is the group just looking for members? Remember, magic is more than just a numbers game.

You also need to know how often your prospective group meets. If they're only meeting once or twice a month, when is the training taking place? In our coven, we meet weekly. There's always training taking place. Some covens only meet once a month because they're primarily worship-based covens, so they do not have a strong focus on training. I don't think you can really get proper Craft training once a month.

Another thing to consider is whether you meet the time commitments of the group. Can you meet on all of their scheduled dates, and how far are they away from you? I get contacted by people all the time who could not possibly make it to coven meetings because they live one or two states away. However, we do have one member of our coven who does live in another state and regularly makes long-distance journeys, staying for as long as possible to get the training that he needs.

Some covens have what's is called an outer court that you are asked to join before initiation, and they work with you in this system for at least a year and a day. It's a really great way to establish whether someone is suitable and really watch them. My coven does not have an outer court, nor did the original Gardnerian and Alexandrian covens. I prefer a more organic process when it comes to receiving new Initiates. However, the results are intended to be the same.

The last thing I would be concerned about is if you get any vibes that the coven leaders might be sexually interested in you. Inappropriate jokes right out of the gate or too many personal questions about your love life may be a warning sign. The Craft is not a dating service. Although Witches do fall in love with each other and many well-established couples—both heterosexual and gay—do exist within the Craft, it's not the point of a coven. One of the reasons why we follow the no-socializing rule is because we want to really try and avoid those entanglements when possible. It is also important to note the Craft never requires you to have sex with anyone. No initiation requires sex, and doing so is unquestionably a form of rape.

What you might be looking for in a coven is both circumstantial and personal. While geography might be an issue for some, for example, it may not be for others. In the Craft, we do not give the location of the covenstead to outsiders, but most can give you a general idea of where they are. Is the group you're seeking compatible with your needs, and are you compatible with theirs? These are fundamental questions and, if the answer is no, that is ok. If the answer is yes for both seeker and student, then congratulations! Magic has found a way.

What Might be Expected of You

While each coven has its own unique style and I cannot speak for every one of them, I think that there are some essential assets that a majority of covens might look for in a potential student and so it is vital for you to consider these qualities in yourself when ascertaining your readiness for initiation into Witchcraft. Because the training of Witchcraft involves a journey into the inner planes of self and through the magical doorways of reality, it is crucial that the student is in a place where he or she is ready to receive such wisdom and power.

The coven interview process varies, with some even having actual applications. Regardless of their methods, be prepared to answer a lot of questions. They are also going to be measuring your personality. Do they want to spend an immeasurable amount of time with you? Will you be a good fit for the group? More than anything, I think that most covens will want to know that the seeker is sincere, dedicated, and humble, and possesses a strong moral compass. They will also likely want potential Initiates to be intelligent and capable of performing their duties to the coven, and that both their attendance and participation will be consistent and reliable.

Speaking as a coven leader, I also want someone in my coven whose life is already together, and so stability is paramount as well. I don't want somebody whose life is in chaos, whether it be emotionally, spiritually, or in the mundane world. If you're currently without a job or an income, you should be focusing on getting employed, not on getting initiated. Moreover, if your home life is unstable, your temple life will almost certainly suffer as well, so getting your own house in order is crucial to pursuing the priesthood of Witchcraft. Within the Craft, a healthy dose of skepticism is a wonderful thing—almost expected, but both skepticism and cynicism within the circle itself can be quite detrimental. In the Arts Magical, one must be able to let go and allow the magic to flow. If you put one person in your circle who's constantly wondering if the spell will work or, worse, expecting that magic to fail, then it's going to affect the power raised within the coven and impair its overall consciousness. Experienced coven leaders will be able to psychically ascertain these harmful attitudes and deal with them accordingly. I also wouldn't initiate anyone into my coven that I knew from the beginning was going to derail the group in any way. You might find an exceptional coven with a dedicated group of people, but they just might not be the right fit for you. For example, that steadfast coven you found might hold its meetings deep in the woods at midnight while you might be allergic to mosquitoes.

Coven Leaders

Covens do have a hierarchy, a word terrifying to those of the New Age mindset or immersed in social justice politics. However, this is necessary within an intense magical environment. If you dabble in any magical system without proper training, it can become destructive. Your ego alone will not protect you from the forces you seek to command. Good ritual and beautiful equipment do not give the impostor power or wisdom; in magic, you do play with fire. I have had the experience of working with untrained magicians, and although the rites they were performing were not part of the Craft, the consequences were as equally destructive as those who misuse Witchcraft without the training to understand it. Using spirits, angels, and demons to make your dreams come true may appear easy, but without true knowledge, discipline, patience, and the priestly disposition you might just be ringing the dinner bell—and the main course will be you.

In the Craft, it often takes many years of development and training to become a leader and teacher. The traditional coven is led by a Third-Degree high priest and high priestess, who jointly govern the group in a working partnership. This varies a bit depending on lineage and understanding. Sometimes due to circumstance, a coven may have a singular leader. This happens when no one is suitable for the higher degrees. It is quite clear that Gerald Gardner started his first group, the Bricket Wood Coven, in such a way as he did not hive off with a priestess from the New Forest Coven. Alex Sanders similarly started working as an independent leader, and today many covens have done so, mine included. The New Orleans Coven was founded originally by myself and two priestesses, one of which has gone on to become the high priestess.

My own Craft training has taught me that we can utilize our first degrees for any capacity within the magical circle. First degree Witches are Witches and can perform any of the tasks necessary. It is irresponsible and harmful to prematurely elevate someone simply so that you are able to perform specific functions necessary to lead a coven. It is best to give them the time and proper development so that they can rise on their own occasion. There are lineages within both Alexandrian and Gardnerian Craft that insist that the working partners must hive off together and, in some cases, they must be sexual working partners. I refute this as nonsense and will state clearly: these lines are not following the original *Book of Shadows* and they do not know their history. These practices were put into place by those of a dubious nature. The Craft never requires sexual intercourse, consensual or not.

Some Gardnerians will allow the formation of what they call maiden covens. These covens are run by second degrees under the guidance of their mother coven and third-degree priesthood. The idea or necessity for such a coven is often based on geography so that the group can get started, but it is not felt they are actually ready to be independent. This is not an Alexandrian practice. Alex did give the second degree upon a couple occasions separately from the third. However, it is not standard for our tradition as I state elsewhere in this book. We generally would not do such a thing.

Covens also have various offices, with the coven maiden being one of the most well-known. She's a sort of runner-up and primary assistant to the high priestess. Equally, the high priest has his own lieutenant, often called the summoner. Other offices are employed to fulfill the various needs of the coven. The position of coven elder—not to be confused with craft elder—is given to second- and third-degree Initiates who do not hive off and are not official leaders of the coven. These elders will assist in leading rituals and training new Initiates; they are often choosing to remain to further their instruction in the higher workings under an experienced high priest and high priestess before they finally hive off.

Coven Meetings

Covens traditionally have a boundary of three miles between them; this is called a covendom. It means that the coven has a territory that other covens should respect. When a new coven branches out it is supposed to do so outside of this boundary. Today this rule is difficult to follow with covens sometimes popping up on every street corner. This rule can still be practically applied in other ways; if one group is holding a meet-up at a pub and you are aware, your group should pick another pub. The Witches' meeting place is called the Covenstead, or simply the Temple in Alexandrian craft. The location of both the covenstead and covendom are kept secret from outsiders, as is the membership list, without express permission.

Covens generally meet on the full moons for esbats. The full moons are a celebration of the Moon Goddess, a time to work magic. Witches also gather on the eight Sabbats. These are the eight seasonal festivals, which are as follows: Halloween, the Winter Solstice, Candlemas, the Spring Equinox, May Eve, the Summer Solstice, Lammas, and the Fall Equinox. Some covens celebrate the Sabbats on the full moon closest to the Sabbat. Some also meet explicitly for training, though there is no hard rule about this.

As I have mentioned previously, covens often have exterior work, whether it is an outer court or some sort of community outreach such as soirées, meet-ups, and public festivals. This is a way for the coven to highlight itself to its local community, so sincere seekers know that they are available for training that there is a place that they can go for initiation. Alex and Maxine, in the London coven, met every Saturday, so they would celebrate the full moons and the Sabbats on the closest Saturday. When there was not a full moon or a Sabbat, other training would go on, though it is said that daily training often took place in their original groups, the London coven and Maxine's Temple of the Mother.

I adopted this way of practicing here in New Orleans. We meet weekly: once a week, at the same time, every week. I implemented this method because it makes it easier for people to actually get together and plan their lives. If a coven is planning its meetings to try to be on the exact Sabbat or on the exact full moon, they must constantly juggle their schedules to get together, and I have found in the past that this creates lower attendance. My coven members or anyone who joins this temple knows that there's a day set aside that has not changed since we instituted this method. It is no different than joining a church. You know when the services are, and you have to make that time available if you wish to be a member. People who join this coven realize that they need to keep that day and that time free, and if they cannot, they might as well not join the group.

Types of Covens

It is essential to understand that not all covens function for the same purpose. Although rare, some have a specialty they are known for, although they may not select a distinct label, they might have strong leanings towards a particular way of practicing.

It must be noted that there is a difference between a traditional coven and an ad-hoc coven. Traditional covens, Gardnerian or Alexandrian, practice the religious system of Witchcraft as it has been passed down to them, and they function as priesthoods. But the world is now filled with ad-hoc covens. These are covens that are formed by eclectic Witches, often do-it-yourself, self-trained Witches who may have a particular style. These are not traditional, even if they call what they do a tradition. You'll find that there are many, many traditions out there. The truth of the matter is, most of them aren't traditions. They are a coven, and somebody's created a system, and they call it a tradition, but until it's been passed down or propagated to multiple covens, it really isn't a tradition. It is a system that they've created, and they simply labeled it.

Every coven does have its own methods. Even among Alexandrians and Gardnerians, there are unique developed rituals or workings that the coven has created. This is perfectly acceptable, and there is nothing wrong with being an ad-hoc coven. That might be the only thing available to you in your area. You may not be able to belong to a lineaged coven at a given time, and many Initiates originally began working in other systems before they were initiated. Generally, they put their toes into the pool of Witchcraft long before they sought initiation. Things have changed a great deal from the early days when the only way you could learn about Witchcraft was by joining a traditional coven. Now people are learning from books and other methods. However, traditional covens are out there, established, and ready to receive those who choose the path of priesthood.

Aside from worship and training, the Witch's coven is also something that becomes a force unto itself. When a group works long enough, it begins to build a thoughtform of its own. The established coven thereby becomes a magic battery that each individual member is tapped into, their constant working adding to the energy and the spirit of the coven, and they are able to draw from it as a resource when needed. You will also hear Witches refer to the "hive mind." Coven members do quickly establish strong psychic ties with each other, intensifying their magical workings. When you are working with someone in a coven, you will start to share each other's thoughts. You will start to pick up on things. Many, many times, I find myself opening the door as a coven member is arriving; I just knew they were there. It's just commonplace. We don't even think about it. Covens do have their own egregore—or shared magical current—and consistently invoking the same gods and performing the same rituals magnifies these forces for the individuals involved.

Worship Covens

Most covens are fertility or worship covens. These groups do not really have a specialty and are content with the practice of Witchcraft as a religious system. All covens provide Witchcraft training, but these covens are more of a jack-of-all-trades and offer a cursory education in the principles and practices of the Craft.

Training Covens

Training covens are stricter and have an immense dedication to the preservation of information and technique. These covens are not for the faint of heart but provide a great foundation. Those who hive off may choose a different method but are generally well developed. Training covens may not be called precisely that; a "training coven" is more of an Alexandrian term. In Gardnerian Craft, you might have certain high priests and high priestesses who are very focused on nothing changing within the system or nothing changing within the lineage that they were given. They want to preserve and pass on that knowledge in a strict, rigorous, and regimented way. These would be training covens by another name.

Fertility Covens

As I have stated previously, Witchcraft is a fertility cult, and indeed, this was the primary purpose of the old covens. All Witches still work for fertility in the seasonal rites, in their commitment to the protection of nature, and the healing of our Mother Earth. Today, we work for the fertility of the mind, spirit, and the potency of our magic. Specialized fertility covens are extremely rare and tend to exist only in rural farming areas as they did in days gone past. Their concern is still associated mainly with agriculture and animal husbandry. City-based covens are typically far removed from natural cycles and thus they might experience fertility in more conceptual terms such as the fruits of their magical and tangible labors. Even today, farmers seek Witches to bless their crops. I have personally been asked to bless both apple orchards and wheat fields!

Healing Covens

Healing covens are an example of a more specialized area of magical focus; such covens are often sought out for their results in working with the sick and not for general Witchcraft. After ensuring that a patient has received proper medical diagnoses and care, these Witches will often engage in remote healing techniques and offer herbal advice for a more holistic approach to the healing process. Although not all Witches specialize in the healing arts, all Witches are trained in them to some extent.

Specialized Covens

Healing is just one of the many topics a coven might explore. Just as the interests of magical individuals vary, so too do those of covens. An experimental coven is a coven that explores various forms of magic. A power coven is dedicated to the development of magical power. Other covens may choose a magical specialty of their own. These covens want results and do not wish to develop new Initiates. This can undoubtedly be a factor in the style of coven you choose to join. Fertility, worship, and training covens tend to use the traditional 3- to 13-member model. The more specialized covens tend to be rarer and more secretive, often meeting in smaller groups of eight or fewer and rarely accepting new members.

Coven Rules

One of the questions you should ask is about the rules and structure of the coven itself. How do you operate? How long have you been running the group? Have you a fully-trained priesthood? What is the primary purpose of the group? How do you train? What do you do for a living? Perhaps most importantly, can you provide proof of lineage?

As far as rules, the answer or lack thereof is of great importance. In my opinion, if they have no response to this question, be wary. In the Craft, there are both laws and general guidelines that every initiatory coven should follow. It will be noted that not all covens adhere to all of them, but as they are in the *Book of Shadows*, they are the only operating foundations that some lines have in common. It is and should be assumed that they are being followed in a general way. Communication is usually forbidden between groups without the Coven leaders' permission. The online world has made this a bit problematic for some.

Each coven should be autonomous, and it is up to the leaders to run their group, hopefully within the proper framework of the tradition. The coven leaders get to decide how they're going to run their coven. It's not up to anyone else, and if you're not comfortable with those leaders' rules, it's not the coven for you. You've got to find a more suitable one. If you're initiated, be prepared to have such guidelines. It is normal; the Craft is not a democracy.

Within our own coven, we practice a stricter law called the no-socializing rule mentioned above. I think it is a misunderstood rule. The foundational purpose of our coven is deep occult training and research, the serious development of priesthood, and the practice of the Arts Magical. We want to avoid members who are merely seeking a social circle or an emotional crutch. We do not desire mere worshipers but dedicated practitioners. We want people who are coming because they want to develop their own powers on the inner planes. This does not mean that we do not have love, joy, or fellowship; many of us have become very close, but this came after the priority of the group was firmly established. The no-socializing rule has helped protect our temple from the mundane and achieve our magical and spiritual goals.

Some covens do socialize, and that is up to them and up to their leaders, but this will often bring the mundane into their circles. Conveners, just like all friends, have strife, and the more mundane interaction they have, the more mundane conflict will be pulled into your coven. Unfortunately, common everyday concerns do dissipate spiritual power.

I once led a coven for over twenty-five years. It was not an Alexandrian coven, and we did socialize. Although the members stayed for many years, and we loved worshiping together—indeed, many of us are friends to this day—our mundane interactions dispersed the power, eventually. In the early years of that coven, there were a lot of younger people, and it was filled with potent power; our work was magnificent, and I can look back at some of the magical experiments and the fantastic feats that were performed, and I delight in it to this day. But eventually, that coven became useless because it became complacent. People became too comfortable, didn't want new members, and didn't want to try anything new. It just really wasn't going anywhere. I think the socialization was the main reason it had become a family and not an occult magical working group.

When I founded the New Orleans coven, years ago, it was the first Alexandrian coven to be established here, in Louisiana. We started out not really sure how we were going to proceed with our practices. Fortunately, we had the great pleasure to meet with Maxine Sanders in her home in London, and she sent me to work with a temple in Wales. Upon arrival, I met the High Priestess who would become my true mentor in the Craft: Val. Her temple was so disciplined and so magical that it had great ritual power. I'd never seen a Witchcraft circle like that in my life, so I immediately knew I wanted to know more. I immediately knew I did not know enough about the Alexandrian tradition, and I wanted to learn everything I could. I asked Val to take me under her wing, and eventually into her lineage, and that's when this coven really, truly started to become what it is today.

The practices that Val taught me are derived from the Temple of the Mother. I probably shouldn't say this, but I do feel that we are probably more of a product of Maxine than Alex, although he is the patriarch of our tradition and absolutely has contributed significantly to everything that we now do. One of the rules that we decided to adopt from the Temple of the Mother was the no-socializing rule. I had learned from my mistakes when I looked back at the coven in my early days, and how it had lost the power and how it had become complacent. I also looked at what I was being given, the training that I was given at Val's hands, and realized how special and rare it was and how I wanted to preserve it and pass it on to others to the best of my ability. I'm still doing this today. I'm still learning. Our coven is still learning, and Val will always be my teacher. I've had many teachers. Every Witch who's ever contributed to my Craft has been my teacher, and I always say that my best teachers are my students.

You're going to have to decide what it is that you want out of the coven you're joining. If you were to come to my coven, you would be told we practice the no-socializing rule. New Initiates who live here are not going to be able to socialize with anyone else in the coven. The elders can. Yes, the high priest and the high priestess can certainly spend time with Initiates. They're the teachers. It's not an easy rule. There is a vast spiderweb of complications when it comes to the no-socializing rule. For instance, my husband is a First-Degree Initiate. It does rather change things. We're never cruel. If two people have an established relationship or a friendship, we don't get in the way. They're just given separate boundaries. They're to keep their mundane relationship out of the temple and they're not to discuss the temple life in their mundane relationship. A difficult thing to enforce, but you can't deny love. You cannot deny friendship. These are not the goals of the no-socializing rule. Eventually, as the years pass, those of the Priesthood do often become your most faithful friends, and the no-socializing rule goes away for them.

Other covens prefer socialization. They prefer the bond that it brings. There may be those who found other ways of working around the obstacles that socialization and the mundane may create. I would always be curious to see how this was done, but for me, at present, this is the best system and training that I have received. I have Initiates who are well-disciplined, well-trained, and powerful. And they've each gone on into the world to leave their own mark.

One thing I will definitely say about my coven, as arrogant as it might sound, is that I am not the superstar; Christian's not the superstar; Christine's not the superstar; we are, collectively, all superstars. Every member of this coven is a genuine occultist, gifted, and able to bring the power through. It manifests in their lives. This is what I wanted out of a coven: a coven that would build each other up and become powerful, potent, and fertile.

CHAPTER 3

The Cultural Origins of Witchcraft

I did not set about to write a history book, nor am I especially interested in becoming the supreme authority that every Witch looks to in order to validate or prove the antiquity of Witchcraft. There are many books already written on the subject that I believe do demonstrate the deep and ancient history of the Craft—and I include a number of them in the recommended reading list at the end of this book. The purpose of this chapter is to establish that what we call modern Witchcraft originated in Britain and was popularized by the founders who first made the world aware of this mystery cult in the 1950s. It has gone on to become the vastly popular religion that some have come to call Wicca—though we Initiates still call it Witchcraft.

The Witchcraft of Britain is a modern fertility cult and priesthood that celebrates the ancient classical mystery traditions. It has developed into two primary branches—the first and oldest sects of modern Witchcraft—the Gardnerian and Alexandrian traditions. Much has been written about whether or not Gerald Gardner was truly initiated into the New Forest coven he described in his iconic 1954 book, *Witchcraft Today*, and much has also been written about the various tales of how Alex Sanders came into the Craft. Proving the authenticity of these founders or the antiquity of their work is not my priority. Each of us must decide for ourselves how we feel about those who paved the path and whether or not we think that initiation, and the work beyond it, really works for us because we will never actually know the truth. After decades of practice, I know that Witchcraft works and is a powerful doorway between the worlds of men and the realms of the Gods.

Human beings desire to know facts. We hate few things more than an unanswered question. Many authors, Initiates, and even scholars have spent decades developing and honing their personal opinion on the origins of Witchcraft. At the end of the day, even the most historically informed opinions have often amounted to little more than a best guess or even outright mythology regarding both Gardner and Sanders. Unless you were present for their initiations, you simply do not know. My personal work on the inner planes has led me to believe that both of these priests were, in fact, initiated into Witchcraft. I also feel that the God and Goddess of Witchcraft made real contact with the world at that time, a world very much in need of them.

What is the spiritual power behind the Witchcraft of Britain? What is its egregore—that mutual concept that has been created over millennia through the collective power of thought? Three major peoples have influenced those we know today as British and it is no coincidence that this same influence has directly impacted the Craft.

The Celts

Perhaps the earliest cultural influences on modern Witchcraft were the Celts, a group of tribes that at one time spanned most of continental Europe and Britain. The vestiges of that culture still exist today in Ireland, Scotland, Wales, and Cornwall, the Isle of Man, and there are even some sections of it in Brittany in the west of France. The Celts had their own priesthood—the Druids. We know very little about them except that they were somewhat organized and communicated and worked together in some way through the tribes of the Celts, that they were well-educated, that they had secret rites and initiations, and that they worked with the old gods of Britain. The Druids considered Britain—and especially Anglesey—to be the spiritual heart of their ancient faith.

Legends have often ascribed mysterious origins for the Druids. Some say that they hailed from the lost city of Atlantis upon its destruction beneath the waves. Others describe their arrival from the four island cities of the Tuatha Dé Danann spoken of in early Irish myth. We know that Celts were employed in Egypt as mercenaries,[1] under the Ptolemies, and Caesar wrote that the Druids used Greek characters.[2] The Egyptian connection could be entirely plausible given recent genetic research that discovered that up to 70 percent of the modern British people share DNA with the historical pharaoh Tutankhamon.[3]

We know that these priests went by many other names and titles. Druid is an English word and not Gaelic or Brythonic. Some people have suggested the word's roots in "*duir*," meaning oak, and "*wid*," a root word for "Witch," so Druid might accurately be defined as an oak Witch. It is undoubtedly connected to terms such as the Old Irish "*drui*," or "sorcerer," the Welsh "*drws*," or "door," and the Greek "*drýs*," or "oak-tree."

Like most ancient peoples, the Celts embraced the gods of other cultures. The current concerns regarding cultural appropriation would have been an alien concept to ancient peoples as it was common practice for cultures to overlap not only in religion but in other areas of life as well. When they looked at the moon and said, "Diana," and someone else said, "Selene," or "Isis," everyone understood that they were talking about the Moon Goddess.

---

[1] "Celts," *Ancient History Encyclopedia*, accessed June 17, 2019, https://www.ancient.eu/celt/.

[2] Julius Caesar, "De Bello Gallico" and Other Commentaries of Caius Julius Caesar, ed. Ernest Rhys, trans. W. A. Macdevitt (New York: J. M. Dent, 1915), 119.

[3] Alice Baghdjian, "Half of European men share King Tut's DNA," *Reuters*, August 1, 2011, accessed June 13, 2019, https://uk.reuters.com/article/oukoe-uk-britain-tutankhamun-dna/half-of-european-men-share-king-tuts-dna-idUKTRE7704OR20110801.

In the past several decades, Celtic music and culture have become increasingly popular in Western society and, perhaps due to this, there were those in the Craft who have attempted to brand the origins of Witchcraft as purely Celtic, but Witchcraft is not an ethnic faith and has several cultural influences. Still, the Druids were the last great priesthood of pagan Britain and their influence can be felt today within the beauty of the rituals of the Craft. I believe that modern Witchcraft carries the true spiritual inheritance of these ancestors.

The Romans

The Roman contribution to modern Witchcraft is often overlooked, perhaps because they began in Britain as foreign invaders. Still, they ruled over much of Britain for over four hundred years which eventually made them locals. We often forget that, at one time, our British ancestors were Romans. When the Romans settled, they brought with them their gods and mystery cults. These gods were often worshiped alongside their Celtic predecessors and were also often merged with them, as was the case with Sulis Minerva who guarded over the sacred springs of Bath, England.

The Romans had a wealth of knowledge that they spread throughout their entire empire, including the Mysteries of nearly every culture in Europe, Egypt and the Middle East—the Eleusinian Mysteries; the Cult of Dionysus, which would become the Cult of Bacchus; and the cult of Isis, perhaps the most significant and influential initiatory goddess cult known to modern history. If the Mysteries were not already among the peoples of Britain, then this may have been the most powerful impact that the Romans would have. In either case, the Romans certainly brought much of their vast tapestry of religious cults and mystery traditions to Britain. The magical and cultural contributions of the Empire would have a lasting effect on the peoples of the island. When Rome withdrew, it was not a time of rejoicing but was the beginning of the decent into barbarism in the void of Celtic authority.

The Saxons

As the Romans withdrew from Britain and their influence waned, a new group of invaders arrived upon the British shores—the Saxons—a Germanic tribal people. The Saxons had been vying for a foothold in Britain for centuries and had tried invading only to be beaten back by the Romans, so when the Romans departed, the road was clear. We know that the Britons had been invaded by the Germanic Vikings and other peoples over the centuries but the Saxons truly established a lasting Germanic influence in Britain. The Saxons do not appear to have any sort of priesthood to speak of, but if they did, it has been lost to history. Their magical peoples functioned more like local shamans and magicians, cunning folk, and wise people which would definitely have influenced the practices of what would come to be called Witchcraft.

The most substantial impact of the Saxon settlers was their language, for it was through them that much of what we call English was derived. Germanic roots such as *"weik"* ("to curve or bend"), *"wigol"* (prophetic), and *"wiglian"* (to practice divination) gave way to the uniquely British Anglo-Saxon word, "Wicca," and the later word it became: Witch. The presence of the Saxons completed a triad of Celtic, Greco-Roman, and Germanic influence in British life and culture that became the core influences of modern Witchcraft.

The Egyptians

One might question why I would include a section about the Egyptians when talking about the cultural identity of Witchcraft in the British Isles. Clearly, they did not directly impact Britain through migration or invasion. Egypt did, however, have a lasting impact on Britain and the modern Witchcraft revival. Aside from the DNA findings, mentioned above, that King Tut had Celtic ancestry, as well as old myths and pseudo-histories—such as the Egyptian princess Scotia—associated with both Scottish and Irish legends, the British and the Egyptians are very distinct and separate. This does not mean there was not influence. Egypt left its stamp on the entire world forever.

In Roman Britain, cults to Isis and Serapis would be established in both York and London. Statues of the Greco-Roman-Egyptian gods have also been discovered in other Roman temples, such as the famous Temple of Mithra in London. We do not know how many followers this cult amassed in Britain, or how long the gods were remembered, but we do know that for hundreds of years, gods born in the Nile of Egypt had become British.

Many have speculated that the gods of Rome are merely soldier cults. I defy this. The Roman soldiers that inhabited Britain for more than 400 years intermarried with the British people and had generations of children and families. Romans often adopted the local gods and merged them with their own, a common practice in most pre-Christian peoples. Yes, Isis and Serapis were foreign gods originally, but the same is true of all the British gods, including the Celtic and Germanic.

Then there is the Egyptian craze of the Victorian age. We must remember that Egypt lost its independence during the Napoleonic invasions, eventually leading to its absorption into the British Empire. The antiquities of the Nile flowed into Europe and were embraced in a frenzy by the Victorian mind. It was not uncommon to discover the relics of the pharaohs as everyday home decor in Britain. Like the Greeks and the Romans, Britain was being seduced by Egyptian culture and magic. With the occult revival, the old gods of Egypt would encounter new devotees in the island kingdom.

Pioneers like Helen Blavatsky, Karl Lepsius, MacGregor Mathers, Dion Fortune, Aleister Crowley, and Gerald Gardner would lead and belong to groups that used Egyptian deities or symbology, such as the Freemasons, Golden Dawn and the Ordo Templi Orientis. It is a small wonder that much of the magic of Egypt found its way into the western mind. Fortunately for the occult world and modern Craft, the Egyptians documented many of their magical practices. This remains a vast resource for practitioners today. Modern witchcraft is, in part, pure occultism. It is without a doubt influenced by the mystery cults of old, much of which came into our practice through preservation of esoteric works.

The Melting Cauldron of Britain

The Celtic, Greco-Roman, and Germanic influences of Britain led to a great melting pot. When Christianity took root with the arrival of the Roman Catholic Church, the vestiges of magic and mystery cults that still remained in Britain were conflated and lumped together as Witchcraft and designated as an evil best to be avoided. Whether or not you believe that there is a continuation of an ancient priesthood that existed all the way up to the time of Gerald Gardner and beyond, or that either Gardner or someone before him reconstructed Witchcraft from the tatters of history, the elements of modern Witchcraft contain a thread of power that encompasses the very heart of spiritual Britain. This can clearly be seen in our liturgy:

> *"Listen to the words of the Great Mother, who of old was also called among men Artemis, Astarte, Dione, Melusine, Aphrodite, Ceridwen, Diana, Arianrhod, Bride, and by many other names."*

We work with the Greco-Roman gods. We work with the ancient Celtic gods, the pre-Celtic gods, and even the Egyptian gods. And we're definitely influenced by the Anglo-Saxon culture that gave us our language, as we are the Angles—the English. The British people have become a unique culture unto themselves and modern Witchcraft reflects this. We are not a specifically cultural religion as we are not uniquely Celtic, Saxon, or Greco-Roman. Rather, we have elements of all of these cultures. Each coven may be drawn to its own cultural egregore. Each tradition of the Craft may have its own resonations but, in every case, we remain a mystery cult. The modern Witchcraft movement is a religion, and the only culture that we actually originate from is the British culture, a vast and powerful cauldron representing the synthesis of its influences. The ancient Roman city of London is one of the great international cities of the world and the home of many peoples, religions, and magical practices. Perhaps this is why our modern Craft has always thrived there.

The religion of Witchcraft should not divide people but rather bring them together whether we are of British descent or simply magically drawn back to the ancient isle of Anglesey. Britain is a place that has been filled with ancient peoples that we know little about, with magical practitioners whose ways we do not remember, and with great priesthoods nearly forgotten. Britain is the home and birthplace of modern Witchcraft, but the stone circles still stand, and magical priesthoods and ancient gods have returned to stand with them.

CHAPTER 4

The Power of Lineage

In Witchcraft, high regard is given to the lineage of the Witch—the initiatory line of priestess to priest, priest to priestess, going all the way back to the founder of that Witchcraft tradition. It is a record of your modern magical ancestors, your teachers, and those whose shoulders you stand upon. Through the rites of initiation, the Witch power is passed through a magical current bestowed upon you by every ancestor in the chain directly back to the source. If you're Gardnerian, you can trace your lineage back to Gerald Gardner. If you're Alexandrian, you will be able to trace back to Alex and Maxine Sanders.

Another reason that lineage is so vitally important is that it is the only way that the seeker can truly ascertain that people are indeed who they say they are. If you do not have valid, unquestionable lineage tracing back to Alex and Maxine or to Gerald Gardner, you cannot claim to be Alexandrian or Gardnerian, respectively. The vouching system is used among Initiates to ascertain that the lineage claimed is true.

If you ask a Witch what his or her lineage is and you're not an Initiate, he or she may not be keen on telling you because some of those individuals in their line may be secret Initiates. Vouching is a system whereby

Initiates work together to verify the lineage being claimed. Usually, a publicly known Initiate can be used by the seeker for this purpose. There are also several Facebook groups created where you can verify lineage, like my own group, British Traditional Witchcraft.

It is said that lineage has become increasingly more important in recent years, particularly in America. In the Britain of the 1950s and '60s, the community of Witches was much smaller and more closely connected. The Initiates knew one another. It was not that hard to investigate would-be claimants. Today, the Craft has grown to vast proportions and is spread out all over the world. In the United States in particular, we often have to deal with frauds wishing to gain converts to their personal ego trip by claiming lineages and traditions they do not actually possess. Numerous covens are claiming on websites and social media to be Gardnerian or Alexandrian, and they are simply not. Worse still, many claim these lineages intentionally. There are shop owners who claim false lineage and even prominent authors as well, so today's Initiates rely on the vouching system to ascertain whether someone has the proper Craft background.

Lineage is a living history, so we must go back to the source—or at least as far back as we can go in the case of modern Witchcraft. This brings us back to the New Forest Coven of 1930s England. The New Forest has always been a magical place and has been associated with Witches and Witchcraft since the medieval era. Authors like Gerald Gardner and Sybil Leek have fueled the myths of secret magical meetings held in the depths of the New Forest. It is without question that both magic and occultism were occurring there in the 1930s. We know that there was an active folklore society, as well as societies like the Woodcraft Chivalry that seemed quite favorable to Paganism and used such deities as Dionysus, Pan, and Artemis in their liturgy. They reveled in nature—perhaps inspired by the Victorian era interest in mythology and the occult. The New Forest also had an active Rosicrucian society, exploring the mental mysteries of the hermetic sciences, but, was there really a coven of Witches in the New Forest?

It's likely that we'll never know and, even if we did, we'd then have to ascertain that coven's own origins in the timeline of history. Were they simply a re-constructionist group based on the works of famed anthropologist Margaret Murray? Were they occultists who simply claimed the word Witch as a sign of power? Or, were they in fact practitioners of an ancient cult of Witchcraft? Much research and speculation has been made in recent years, and some rather exciting theories have developed about what was really happening in the New Forest and what its famed coven was actually up to.

Gerald Gardner formed the world's first Gardnerian coven, called the Bricket Wood Coven, in 1949. In this coven, he would initiate Barbara Vickers, Doreen Valiente, Jack Bracelin, Lois Bourne, and many other priests and priestesses—some of whom would go on to form covens of their own. Gardner would independently initiate other priests and priestesses to form covens throughout Britain, people such as Patricia and Arnold Crowther in York, Eleanor "Ray" Bone in London, and Monique Wilson in Perth, Scotland.

Then there is the mysterious and often speculated-upon Alex Sanders. Alex emerged on the scene in Manchester, England, working the rites of Witchcraft—the very same rites passed down through Gerald Gardner—but how did he come to the Craft? Who initiated him? Perhaps these remain unanswerable questions.

Many lines have developed as the popularity of modern Witchcraft has grown, and some members of the priesthood have substantially altered the original practices to such a degree that it may now be worth asking, "What kind of Gardnerian (or Alexandrian) are you?" We must also ask how close to the original praxis these practitioners actually are. This clarity of lineage matters more than ever as some lines have even changed or added to the original *Book of Shadows*—the sacred text from which Witches draw their secret rites, spells, and lore. The original *Book of Shadows* was rather small. Over the decades, it has been changed and altered so that now, various Gardnerian and Alexandrian lines may have different versions of the book that all descend from the same source—the original *Book of Shadows*. Versions of The *Book of Shadows* can be found that run anywhere from 55 pages to around 900, and which version you have depends on which line you have copied yours from.

Many Initiates today—myself included—have more than one *Book of Shadows* in their possession. I have four versions of the Alexandrian tradition's first book alone and two versions of its second book, and yes, it's all basically the same material, give or take thirty to fifty pages. Likewise, I also have the California Gardnerian *Book of Shadows* and a Whitecroft one as well that have both been passed on to me by several different Initiates in my line. Still, other than the occasional spell or incantation, I do not require most of these various editions as I only work from the Alexandrian Books of Shadows that I have received—and those were copied directly from Maxine Sanders' own. I don't mix my drinks, but a spell is a spell.

Lineage does matter, but in truth, there is not a lineage in the modern religion of Witchcraft that is entirely unquestionable in some way. Each line works from its own version of the *Book of Shadows*, and each line may have variations in their practice, but let us look to the fruits of these lines and the fact that the power has been willed through all of them. It is for this reason that these lineages continue thriving to this day, ushering forth new priests who continue to bring magic into the world once more. While there are now many lineages in today's Craft, we address some of the more well-known lines below.

The information I have presented on the following lines of the Craft has been based on in both written sources and in personal conversations I have had with Witchcraft elders and historically-minded Initiates over the years. I have verified all of this information to the best of my abilities, but it may be updated and expanded in further editions.

The Gardnerians

The first Gardnerians—who were initiated by Gerald Gardner himself—got their materials directly from the source. Likewise, those directly trained and initiated by Alex and Maxine Sanders received direct instruction in their original teachings. These first modern covens tended to function in much the same way. Now, with so many generations, so much passing of time, such vast geographical spans, and just plain poor training, several lineages have made great changes to the original practices—whether it was altering them or merely adding to them. However, some of the original priests and priestesses of modern Witchcraft are still with us, and so we often seek them out to find out how things were done.

The Sheffield Line

Notable author, High Priestess, and Witch Patricia Crowther would go forth from her initiation by Gerald Gardner to lead the Sheffield line. Patricia was very fond of Gerald and admired him deeply. In fact, it is said to this day that she continues to see Gardner and his work as infallible. Because of this, the Sheffield line did not alter the practices within their *Book of Shadows*. However, they did add a great deal of beautiful poetry and expanded upon the seasonal rites. Within the Sheffield line, the spirit of place plays a significant role, and the ancient *nemeton* (or sacred grove) is incorporated into their practices—whereas members often prefer rituals held outdoors in nature. When working inside, the Sheffield covenstead is filled with plants, flowers, and other natural adornments.

While Gerald Gardner gave Patricia the title of "Queen of the Sabbat," the Sheffield line—along with nearly all of the Witchcraft lines in Britain—are distinguished from many of the Gardnerian lines in America in that lineage is traced through priest to priestess, priestess to priest—male to female, female to male. In certain American Gardnerian traditions, a new system of "Witch Queens" has emerged by which only the female lineage is acknowledged. There are no Witch Queens in Patricia's line, and lines are traced in the old way—which includes male Initiates as well.

The Bone Lines

Another Witch matriarch elevated by Gerald Gardner was Eleanor "Ray" Bone. One of the two lines that descend from her is the eponymous Bone line. Eleanor was a nurse by trade and a natural healer, and this focus on healing had a major influence on her practice and has continued to be further developed within the branches of that line.

The other line to spring from Eleanor Bone is the prolific Whitecroft line, which was established by High Priestess Madge Worthington and her high priest Arthur, both of whom were Initiates of Bone. The Whitecroft line is named after the street where their first covenstead could be found—Whitecroft Way. It is a flourishing line and perhaps one of the larger Gardnerian strains existing today. It is a common joke among the Craft that the Whitecroft line breeds like rabbits. This humorous descriptor originates from the line's symbol, which includes both a hare and the moon. A unique and sometimes controversial element said to be practiced by some branches of the Whitecroft line is that they alter the names of their gods from the standard names of lore to names based on the geographical location of the particular coven within that branch of the line.

The Olwen Lines

One of Gerald Gardner's last Initiates was Monique Wilson, whose Craft name was Lady Olwen. While I have been told that Wilson does have lineage still remaining in Europe, I've heard little about it beyond rumor. However, Lady Olwen has gone on to have a considerable downline in the United States as a result of her most famous student—popular Witchcraft author Raymond Buckland.

After a period of correspondence between British-born American Buckland and Gerald Gardner, Gardner directed Buckland to Lady Olwen in Perth, Scotland, where Buckland was then trained over a course of twelve days. Upon completion of this condensed training period, Lady Olwen initiated Buckland with Gardner himself present as witness to the rites.

Upon initiation, Buckland returned to the United States and formed the very first Gardnerian coven in America out of Long Island, New York. Yes, it is certainly problematic to think that one can obtain the kind of effective training one needs to start a coven in only twelve days, but this kind of thing was actually quite common in the early days of British Witchcraft in America. Still, Raymond Buckland was a sincere and dedicated priest who did the best that he could, and so the magic found a way. The lines of Olwen's tree continue to flourish here in the United States and those branches remain strong.

Perhaps the largest group to claim descent from Lady Olwen is known as the Long Island line, named for the area where Buckland's first American coven put down its roots. This sturdy branch of the Olwen line had its humble beginnings in 1964 with the first coven to be firmly established in the United States, with Gardnerians and Alexandrians already having been established throughout the United Kingdom for some time. Raymond Buckland and his wife, Rosemary, strictly adhered to the rites of the *Book of Shadows* and to the teachings they received from Lady Olwen, but those that Buckland passed those teachings onto would gradually make considerable changes to them.

In one of his last interviews before his death in 2017, Buckland describes how two of his successors who would go on to truly define the Long Island line—Theos and Phoenix—made tremendous changes to the materials he had given them and that, to his chagrin, many of these changes had been erroneously attributed to Buckland himself. Buckland goes on to say that "Theos and Phoenix probably did more harm to Witchcraft than did the whole of the Christian persecutors back in the Middle Ages!"[1] This would be quite an insult from any teacher in the Craft, much less one as respected and iconic as Raymond Buckland.

Theos and Phoenix added hundreds of pages to the *Book of Shadows* and—in one of their most significant departures from the source—created a form of lineage by which men are excluded from the line of descent and lineage is traced solely through a succession of Witch Queens. These queens would, in turn, maintain a system of control over their

---

[1] Terence P Ward, "An Interview with Raymond Buckland, American Wicca Pioneer," The Wild Hunt, June 1, 2016, accessed September 15, 2018, https://wildhunt.org/2016/06/an-interview-with-raymond-buckland-american-wicca-pioneer.html.

subsequent downlines. In addition to this change, men would also be prohibited from casting the circle in which initiations were to take place. Another of the components added to Long Island line practice was that of reculement—a form of excommunication in which the initiator or Witch Queen within the line has the authority to cast one out of the Craft. The Long Island line has used the practice of reculement to compel other American Gardnerians into adopting their party line—something that would earn them the nickname, "the Hard Gards." Perhaps the most significant change made by the Long Island line is that of the secret names of the Gods. They are entirely changed, and the myth of their line is that Gardner and Olwen "changed the locks." I would find it odd that all of the other UK Gardnerians would be left out of such a change, which leads me to wonder that this may have been a change enacted by Theos and Phoenix to further an agenda of control that seems to have pervaded their leadership style.

The Long Island line was successful in absorbing many Initiates of other branches of the Olwen lines, with a few exceptions. Those exceptions would lead to a great schism—an all-out Witch war that would rival any that had ever happened in the UK.

I am not picking on the Long Island line. This is just the truth as I understand it from discussions with members of its priesthood and from what is a matter of public record, and I think it's essential for this book to document what each line represents. The Long Island line is populated with many truly devout priests, some whom who have begun looking to Witches in the UK and some who have even reverted aspects of their practices towards original Craft tradition. This is the advantage of the modern age. Knowledge can be obtained and shared far more quickly and efficiently than in days gone past.

Whatever one might feel about them, the Long Island line is the most prominent lineage in American Gardnerian Witchcraft and has made the Craft accessible to so many who might otherwise not have discovered it. It has a vast network and a history that has evolved in this country. Although some of its teachings may be uniquely different from other Gardnerian branches, it has developed some admirable qualities, including dedication to both the priesthood and to its practices. If I were to assign to it a key attribute, it would be that it is the most matriarchal and matrilineal line. If you are looking for a genuinely goddess-oriented sect that places its priestesses on the highest pedestal, it is well worth looking into.

The Kentucky line is another lineage of descent from Lady Olwen. It evolved from the Coven of the Silver Trine founded by Theo and Thane, a couple initiated by Raymond Buckland in the 1960s. From what I have been able to glean of it, the Kentucky line appears to be closer in praxis to the Gardnerians of the UK and, in more recent years, has been influenced by the primarily UK-based Whitecroft line. The Kentucky line was once more prominent than the Long Island line which has lead to some confusion about which is the oldest, though they seem to have evolved concurrently.

The Kentucky line may be of great interest to you as a seeker because it was formed independently of the Long Island line by early Initiates of Raymond Buckland and may, in fact, be closer to the original teachings that Buckland received from Lady Olwen than any other American line. One of the differences found in the Kentucky line is in the casting of the circle for initiation. The Kentucky line allows for men to do this while most other Olwen lines do not.

The California line of Gardnerians may be one of the more tumultuous stories of modern Initiatory Witchcraft, but it is also a tale of survivors who persevered through much adversity to maintain their deep spiritual bond to the Craft and to one another. The California line was a truly proper offshoot of the Long Island line—declared the "California line" by some of its elders due to the line's own additions to the *Book of Shadows* and, as one might imagine, its geography as well. The California line sought to carve out its own independence amongst the lineages of American Craft. In perhaps the starkest example of the differences between the west and east coasts, one of the California line's prominent Witch Queens, Judy Harrow, chose to make specific changes within her coven that were completely unsanctioned and disapproved of by her East Coast contemporaries. Harrow removed the scourge from its traditional place on the Witch's altar and proposed that the prohibition of same-sex initiation be reviewed for possible change. This and other alterations within her coven coming to light eventually led to Harrow forming her own sub-sect of the Gardnerian tradition named for her Proteus coven—the Protean tradition. Although Judy never formally left the Gardnerian tradition, this difference of opinion created a massive schism within Gardnerian Craft across America and even affected those within the California line who did not join the Protean tradition. If you were in any way connected to Judy Harrow then, you were considered to be invalid in the minds of certain American Witches—especially the "Hard Gards" of the Long Island line.

What gave this battle such powerful gravitas was that Harrow's infamous "Protean declaration" took place in 1991. The timing of this cannot be overstated as it is also the year that America Online took off as a compelling digital communication platform and, with the Long Island line said to have been the most vigorous earlier adopter of online communication within the Craft, so too did the battle against the "Harrowtics" become a particularly widespread one. This, in turn, set the stage for the countless online Witch wars to come. Unfortunately, this smear campaign continues to affect the California line to this day—including many of whom were never connected to the Protean coven, and whose participation or descent from the California line predates that great schism.

The uproar over the California line is of particular interest to me since it is one of the lines carried by my elders, and I have had the chance to interview Initiates from this and others of the Olwen lines in my research of the issue. What I find most disheartening about the Protean schism is the massive pain that has been caused to so many, with Gardnerians persecuting Gardnerians over who is more Gardnerian. Some of these attacks have even reached the level of oath-breaking in the way that they have been played out across the public forums of the Internet. When I first came out of the cyber broom closet—after decades of private practice—I actually had one Gardnerian priestess publicly call me a fraud on my own Facebook group, insisting that I was a Protean. Well, I was not and am not a Protean, as my California lineage predates the Protean schism. More to the point, I do not consider myself Gardnerian at all, and only posted the authentic lineage that I actually carry simply because it is part of my Witch DNA, so to speak. However, I do not practice and do not have training in the California line—just the lineage—which only further proves how the liturgy of the Craft can be passed on without training, which contributes to the egregious dissolution of the integrity of our ways.

Despite its turmoil and trials, the California line must be given credit for its perseverance and progressive attitudes. Although I do not agree with all of the innovations proposed or adopted by this branch of Lady Olwen's tree, it is unquestionably a trailblazing lineage that seeks to embrace the mores and customs of the modern age. In many ways, I look at the California line as the American Gardnerian version of Alexandrian Craft as both lines proved to be problematic for their local cousins in that they often chose conscience over established edicts. After the rift and rejection by the east coast "Hard Gards," members of the California line have, in recent years, connected to their Craft brothers and sisters in the UK and continue to form Gardnerian covens across the United States.

The last branch of the Olwen lines that I'd like to mention is the Donna Cole line. This branch sprouted when Donna Cole received her first and Second-Degree initiations in the Whitecroft line in the UK. Later, she would receive her third degree from a priest in the Long Island line. However, Theos, the Witch Queen of the Long Island Line, had enacted a firm policy that every initiation circle must be cast by a high priestess or Witch Queen. Theos enforced this rule upon Donna Cole's third-degree elevation because the circle had been cast by a man. Donna Cole then chose to re-initiate, receiving Theos' blessing and became known for her own line. While the Donna Cole line is an offshoot of the

Long Island line, it is said to contain influences of its Whitecroft roots in the UK and so deserves special mention.

The Alexandrians

This book would be incomplete if I did not address my own lineage as an Alexandrian Witch., for I am proud to be downline from Alex Sanders, King of the Witches, and his rich magical legacy forms the basis of my practices. Born Orrell Alexander Carter, he would later change his name to Alex Sanders—perhaps, it is said, in honor of Alexander the Great. I do not believe that there has been a Witchcraft elder who has had more power, fame, controversy, or infamy than Alex Sanders. In fact, there is an ongoing smear campaign that has endured to this day—complete with a few cover-ups for good measure.

Alex Sanders burst onto the Witchcraft scene in the early 1960s. His first coven was known as the Egerton Road Coven—though it is now more commonly referred to as the Manchester Coven. Its origins are steeped in mystery but members of that coven are said to have included Pat Kasprzynski (also variously spelled Kopinski or Kopanski), a former maiden of Patricia Crowther's Sheffield Coven, and a woman known only as Sylvia—sometimes said to be Sylvia Tatham though this, too, has been called into question. Alex claimed to be initiated by a woman named "Medea." It is presumed that Medea was this individual's Craft name and rumors have swirled around her actual identity for decades. Medea has been potentially identified by some inquiring minds as either Pat Kasprzynski, the mysterious Sylvia, Eleanor Bone, or even Patricia Crowther herself. The truth remains a mystery that perplexes to this day.

Alex certainly had contact with Gardnerians Patricia and Arnold Crowther. A painting by Arnold Crowther appeared in a photograph with Alex in one of the latter's first media appearances—within the pages of the *Manchester Evening Chronicle*, September 15th, 1962.[2] One might wonder how Sanders was able to use this painting as part

---

[2] Jimahl Di Fiosa, *A Coin for the Ferryman, The Death and Life of Alex Sanders* (Boston: Logios, 2010), 54-55.

of his publicized ritual when one considers Patricia Crowther's story that she received but a single written letter from Alex, met him one time and refused his initiation.[3] How did Sanders come by a painting by Mr. Crowther that was never sold and was later included in Patricia Crowther's own published materials? Clearly, there was a falling out between Sanders and Patricia Crowther—perhaps based on something that felt very personal to her. This is not a critique of the Crowthers as it is not entirely unheard of for Witches to fall out and shun one another, disown knowledge of one another and even deny one's status as an Initiate, but it does provide a crucial piece to the fascinating puzzle behind the iconic Alex Sanders and his origins.

Sanders also had a somewhat mysterious connection to Gardnerian priestess Eleanor Bone who, while having publicly criticized some of Alex's media exploits, may privately have visited him in London on several occasions. Bone did live for a period in London at the same time as the Sanders, and I have personally heard from entirely credible sources on the subject of their interactions. Whether this means that Eleanor Bone had anything to do with Alex Sanders' entry into the Craft is, like so many things about him, a matter for speculation.

Mother of modern Witchcraft Doreen Valiente validated that Sanders obtained a copy of the Gardnerian *Book of Shadows* by comparing a copy of Sanders' book with Gerald Gardner's own[4], yet this has done nothing to stop the wild fantasies concocted by Sanders' detractors. Spiteful ne'er-do-wells variously claimed that Alex stole a copy of the *Book of Shadows* by asking an Initiate if he could borrow it (as if Witches loan it out like a library book!) or that he copied it from badly mangled snippets of the Book that were deceitfully distributed by notable Witchcraft antagonist Charles Cardell. Neither is likely to be true. While Doreen Valiente asserted her own belief that Sanders "went to see Gerald Gardner in the Isle of Man, and Gerald gave him or allowed him to copy the '*Book of*

---

[3] Doreen Valiente, *The Rebirth of Witchcraft*, 2017 E-book ed. (Wiltshire: Crowood Press, 1989), Loc: 2768-2772, Kindle.

[4] Ibid, Loc: 2747-2748, Kindle.

Shadows," the most likely of the stories surrounding Alex's procurement of the Book are that he received it via legitimate initiation and training. He clearly had both in abundance.[5]

One fascinating theory could be drawn from a passage by Maxine Sanders in her 2007 book, *Firechild: the Life and Magic of Maxine Sanders*, about a curse Alex had received on the day he was about to give a public talk about the Craft:

> *"The morning of the talk Alex received a package in the mail carrying a Scottish postmark. It contained a scroll of parchment bearing magical symbols inscribed in black ink. It did not take long to recognize that it was a rather malevolent curse! The accompanying draft commanded Alex not to speak publicly on the subject of the Craft lest he betray the solemn oath taken at his initiation. It went on, stating that to break his oath would endanger other Initiates. Should he fail to heed this warning he would suffer cancerous tumours of the throat and tongue from which he would die."*[6]

Alex did not cancel the talk, but this quote did have me wondering and cross-referencing with a passage in Jimahl Di Fiosa's 2010 book *A Coin for the Ferryman, the Death and Life of Alex Sanders* in which the author refers to a letter that resides in the Museum of Witchcraft at Boscastle in Cornwall, UK. Within that letter, the anonymous author (who is surmised to be E.W. Liddell, the much-maligned author of the controversial Pickingill Papers) claims that the aforementioned Sylvia Tatham became Alex's high priestess upon the departure of Pat Kasprzynski (allegedly because he wouldn't marry her). The author also claimed that this was prior to the arrival of his future wife Maxine Sanders, with whom Alex would become most associated. The letter claimed that Sylvia had received her third degree from Loric, high priest to Monique Wilson, more

---

[5] Ibid, Loc: 2771-2772, Kindle.

[6] Maxine Sanders, *Fire Child The Life and Magic of Maxine Sanders*, 2008 ed. (Oxford: Mandrake of Oxford, 2007), Loc: 1606-1612, Kindle.

commonly known as Lady Olwen, and that, at the time, Alex traced his initiatory line to Lady Olwen herself.[7]

When you cross-reference that anonymous letter with Maxine's story about the curse from Scotland, and add to that the fact that Lady Olwen was the most notable Witch of Scotland at the time, it would make sense that the curse sent to Alex—the text of which all but certainly acknowledges that he is, in fact, initiated—would actually have come from someone within his own Witchcraft upline or, at the very least, was from someone who knew he was an Initiate. Mind you, much of this depends on Liddell's credibility, which lies on somewhat shaky ground.

When you sift through the facts, the rumor, the innuendo, and the lore, the evidence honestly does suggest that Alex was initiated into Gardner's Witch Cult. I have heard from several Witches in the know that Patricia Crowther's coven held a requiem rite upon Alex's passing, something she'd never dream of doing if she didn't recognize him as one of her own. I've also been told that, upon Crowther's own death, some new truth will come to light. I won't be holding my breath. I think the mystery of Alex Sanders may remain one of the most enduring parts of his appeal. It is likely that the smear campaign will continue for years to come; as Alex himself would say, "Witches are a quarrelsome lot." This is a shame, as Alexandrian Witches are here to stay and on our own terms. The Craft is greater and more powerful than any of those in the black hand gang who would bring our ways low.

Alex was a brilliant showman, and so it wasn't long before he attracted the attention of the press. Appearing in newspapers, articles, films, documentaries, and books, Alex Sanders effortlessly wrenched the spotlight away from the other public Witches of his day. Perhaps more than any of his exploits, the massive publicity he received from the media was what most earned him the ire of other publicity-minded Witches and would spark one of the longest-running Witch wars of the Craft.

---

[7] Jimahl Di Fiosa, *A Coin for the Ferryman, The Death and Life of Alex Sanders* (Boston: Logios, 2010), 62-64.

Alex was ever the prankster and the trickster and, during the height of his publicity, he made a shocking claim that would haunt his spiritual descendants for decades to come. The story in question first appeared in a 1962 newspaper article [8] but was most notably detailed in the pages of June Johns' 1969 book *King of the Witches: the World of Alex Sanders*. Essentially, Alex claimed that he was initiated as a young boy of seven by his grandmother, Mary Bibby, in what appeared to be a lurid sexual rite on his grandmother's kitchen floor. Allegedly, this is how Alex became a Witch and how he received the *Book of Shadows* as well. [9]

This fantastical tale would go on to become Alex's single greatest controversy and result in a legacy that all within the Alexandrian tradition must continually revisit and explain. Thanks, Alex! Still, I imagine his spirit continues to get a good chuckle out of it every time someone brings it up, and it did manage to serve an essential purpose. Alex knew that he wasn't allowed to reveal his initiator and so the tale of his childhood initiation provided an opportunity to sensationalize the story and take aim at his detractors as well with the most powerful weapon he possessed—his relationship with the mass media. Alex placed his Gardnerian detractors in the most precarious situation: by insisting that he received the *Book of Shadows* from his grandmother, the only way for the Gardnerians to prove that Alex didn't receive the book as a child was also to admit that the *Book of Shadows* was itself, at least in part, a modern creation. Nobody in the Gardnerian camp was willing to go there; to do so could have potentially exposed that at least parts of the *Book of Shadows* weren't from antiquity. Alexandrian priestess Galatea, a member of Sanders' original London coven, speculates, "The story served its purpose well. When the story came about, the Gardnerians were trying to prove he had never been initiated. I think he came up with a story that solved the problem. He said, 'I was initiated when I was a child' and then they have to prove that he wasn't. Remember at

---

[8] Ibid, 40.

[9] June Johns, *King of the Witches: The World of Alex Sanders* (London and Edinburgh: Morrison and Gibb Limited, 1969), 10-14.

the time they were saying the *Book of Shadows* went back a long time, so if to disprove Alex's claim that he got the book from his grandmother they suddenly said it was contemporary, they would have shot themselves in the foot. Alex was very tactical. Alex told a lot of stories and would laugh when people believed them."[10]

While Maxine Sanders has expressed belief that Alex's grandmother did introduce him to the magical arts, she has questioned the more lurid aspects of the story. She notes that "Alex's showmanship made much of it and in retrospect it was probably more colourful yet less shocking than Alex described, although his telling of it in his biography written by June Johns, *King of the Witches*, was, in his mind, a means to an end."[11]

Moreover, if the Gardnerians challenged Alex's claims too forcefully, it would not only expose the *Book of Shadows* to scrutiny, but it would also potentially uncover Alex's true initiatory origins in Gardnerian Craft—something that many in those circles would still prefer not to come to light today. The mystery of Alex's initiation continues to perplex, but truths and rumors alike continue to bubble to the surface of the cauldron. It is rumored that Mary Bibby did indeed work magic and that there were psychic gifts and magical happenings within the family of Alex Sanders. Perhaps Alex flavored the soup a little—something many Witches have been known to do—when claiming Witchcraft within his family but, like all magical legacies, many truths are often woven into the more fantastical parts of the narrative. With the facts must come the flavor!

Alex truly hit his stride when he joined with his Initiate, Maxine Morris, to become what could only be called the first couple of modern Witchcraft. As solidly identified with one another as Sonny and Cher, this power couple of magic would go on to define Witchcraft for years to come. Alex initiated Maxine on Tuesday, November 10th, 1964, they were handfasted in 1965. Their daughter Maya was born in 1967, the

---

[10] Jimahl Di Fiosa, *A Coin for the Ferryman, The Death and Life of Alex Sanders* (Boston: Logios, 2010), 33.

[11] Maxine Sanders, *Fire Child The Life and Magic of Maxine Sanders*, 2008 ed. (Oxford: Mandrake of Oxford, 2007), Loc: 1548-1550, Kindle

same year that they moved to London and took the Witchcraft world—and the rest of the world—by storm. Alex and Maxine were officially married in a civil ceremony on May 1st, 1968. Their son Victor was born January 9th, 1972.[12]

It was in London where what we know as the Alexandrian tradition of Witchcraft was actually formed. The London Coven of Alex and Maxine Sanders would become the iconic stage upon which many Alexandrians were trained—a list of seekers that included everyone from hippies to professionals, rock stars to movie stars. The interest from those seeking initiation, the fascination of the media, and the criticisms from Witches jealous of all the attention they were getting reached a fever pitch during the five years that Alex and Maxine ran the London Coven. When one considers the decades it has taken some notable Witches to achieve prominence, it becomes that much more of an accomplishment that Alex and Maxine created a legacy that has lasted decades within a period of only five years.

While the Manchester coven had practiced very much like Gardnerians do—with skyclad, scourging, and all of the original components of the *Book of Shadows*—when the London Coven was established, Alex and Maxine began to make significant changes that would form the foundation of Alexandrian Witchcraft. Maxine Sanders has described the core concepts of Alexandrian Craft as consciousness, beauty, power, and freedom. Consciousness grants us the awareness to be fully in control of ourselves—and our magic—within every moment. Beauty is an act of love and devotion to the Gods. Power is that which we seek at the core of Witchcraft. And, finally, freedom is what has inspired so many of the changes within our tradition. Alexandrian Witches choose not to overuse the scourge, we only work in the nude when the magic calls for it, we do not bloody or retain the measure, and our high priests are equal to the priestess as a union of authentic polarity.

Alex and Maxine also created a strong emphasis on training. The teachings passed within our tradition are both highly developed and

---

[12] Maxine Sanders, "Dates", Email Correspondence with Brian Cain, June 23, 2019.

multifaceted. They include hermetic exercises, ritual theory, and discipline, kabbalistic and angelic practices, a broad spectrum of occult knowledge, and the wielding of power. Alex and Maxine's contribution to modern Witchcraft cannot be overstated. Without their perseverance, commitment, and love for the Arts Magical, I do not think that the practice of Witchcraft would be as widespread or as accepted as it is today. We would also not have many of the spectacular Initiates—Gardnerian or Alexandrian—who were inspired by the beacon that they lit.

After Maxine and Alex parted ways in May of 1973 (not actually divorcing until several years later) [13], Alex went on to live in Bexhill-on-Sea and formed a new coven there. Maxine continued with the London Coven, which eventually evolved into the Temple of the Mother. The Temple of the Mother further advanced the magical systems of the Alexandrian tradition, with more considerable attention given to the occult sciences, angelic magic, and hermetic practice. The Temple further honed the structure of Alexandrian ritual, and placed a stronger emphasis on the importance of training than ever before. A large part of the Temple of the Mother was their role in healing—including working with the poor and dying in the London community.

When Alex Sanders departed his mortal coil in 1988, he had named Maxine his next of kin, proving that their bond had never truly been broken. After Alex's passing, the Alexandrian tradition continued to grow and evolve through the work of both Maxine and the many Initiates who held steadfast to the legacy of Alexandrian Craft. Maxine Sanders has worked tirelessly as co-founder of our tradition to maintain the integrity and power of the practices she worked with Alex to usher into the world. She has helped train, teach, guide, and educate Alexandrians for the thirty years since Alex Sanders passed from this world. We would be in a rather sad state if it were not for her constant efforts.

Today, most Gardnerians admire Alex Sanders, and many even accept him as a valid Initiate regardless of how they perceive his initiation to have taken place. However, the age-old grudge inherited through specific

---

[13] Ibid.

Gardnerian lineages continues to this day, and the smear campaign goes on. Alex Sanders, King of the Witches, was a man and, like all men, was fallible. He was also a sincere and devout priest and a powerful Witch who has left us with a living legacy that continues to thrive today.

The development of Alexandrian lines is more recent and does not tend to take on the same importance as it does in Gardnerian Craft. Gardner had trained several high priestesses who each went on to represent their own branch of Witchcraft. In contrast, the priests and priestesses that worked with Alex and Maxine did not, at first, achieve high status in any formal way beyond elevation to the third degree. To my knowledge, only three Alexandrian strains defined us for the majority of our tradition's history: the London Coven (Alex and Maxine), the Bexhill Coven (Alex), and the Temple of the Mother (Maxine). These are technically not lines—though perhaps they should be as they are the main roads back to the source. All Alexandrians derive from these three original covens in some way.

In his later years, Alex did take a cue from Gerald Gardner and worked with other covens independently of his own; he would occasionally hand out grandiose and extravagant titles to those he worked with—perhaps in an attempt to further seed his work and legacy. Unfortunately, those who received these titles would sometimes take them more seriously and wield them more fervently than even Alex might have ever intended. Others have gone on to create legacies that continue to influence the Craft.

THE DBG LINE

One of the earliest branches of the Alexandrian tree to emerge in America was founded by Jim Baker, whose downline remains extensive—especially in the northeast United States. His story is a lot like Raymond Buckland's. He went to the UK to receive training by Alex Sanders, and started his own coven back home, named Du Bandia Grasail [14], with the limited resources available to American Initiates at the time. Still, Baker used

---

[14] James R. Lewis, *Witchcraft Today: An Encyclopedia of Wiccan and Neopagan Traditions* (Santa Barbara: ABC-CLIO, 1999), 6.

what he had and succeeded in creating a lasting downline—which is now referred to as the DBG line. Some within that sought reconnection with Alexandrians in the UK—pursuing more in-depth training than Baker himself received—so that they could pass this training onto others in America. Others have been content to continue what Baker himself established.

Algard

One of the more controversial Alexandrian "lines" was founded by American Initiate Mary Nesnick. Alex Sanders always had a dream of coming to America, so perhaps he saw an opportunity to fulfill that dream in Nesnick. Nesnick had worked with Theos, a Gardnerian high priestess in the Long Island branch of Lady Olwen's line, but she became dissatisfied and contacted Alex about joining Alexandrian craft. As Alexandrians do not re-initiate Gardnerians—believing them to already be valid Initiates of Witchcraft—Alex accepted Nesnick's request and arranged for her to receive Alexandrian training from an Initiate named Patrick Sumner. It is said that Alex granted Nesnick the vaunted title of "Witch Queen of New York" though some have documented this title as the even more extravagant "Grand High Priestess of the Americas."[15] In spite of her resplendent appellations, Nesnick soon tired of Alexandrian Witchcraft as well but, perhaps not wanting to give up any of the pieces of the Witchcraft pie she had tasted, she took what she had learned from both Gardnerian and Alexandrian traditions and created what she called the Algard tradition. It is not entirely clear how the Algards actually practiced, for Nesnick disappeared from the Craft scene by the end of the 1970s. However, mixing the two traditions would undoubtedly have required choosing between definitively conflicting practices. Did the Algards scourge for purification? Did they always work in the nude? Nesnick clearly would have picked and chosen elements of each tradition according to her personal tastes—watering down the practices of both. Perhaps this is why the assertion of the Algards that

---

[15] Ibid, 7.

the components of these traditions were entirely interchangeable was rejected by the established priesthoods of both traditions at the time and the tradition itself was looked upon as a failed social experiment. Ironically, this mix-and-match system has fallen into favor once again. No, no one has resurrected Nesnick's practices specifically, but her ideology that one can combine Gardnerian and Alexandrian practices into one threadbare patchwork has been making an unfortunate comeback. A number of today's Initiates fervently hold onto the idea that they can mix those drinks and, as far as I'm concerned, that makes them Algards. A rose by any other name is still a rose.

THE KENTISH LINE

Another priestess that Alex Sanders gave a high and mighty title to was Sally Taylor—upon whom Alex bestowed the mantle of the "Witch Queen of Kent." Sally used that title to establish what is now known as the Kentish line. That line was also my introduction to the Alexandrian tradition.

Sally Taylor was originally initiated into the Gardnerian tradition by Brian Hildreth in Otago Harbour, New Zealand. In the UK, she was initiated into Alexandrian Craft by a man named Franklin. She later worked with Alex Sanders—who went on to present Sally with her title of Witch Queen of Kent. I have Sally Taylor's *Book of Shadows* and, having compared it to the version of the Book I am now working with, I can say for sure that she received pure Alexandrian materials. However, I do not think that Sally ever entirely abandoned her Gardnerian roots as her training seemed to contain a number of Gardnerian elements not generally found within Alexandrian Craft. Sally also went on to develop her own system called Brown Witchcraft, and those teachings were mingled into her training of others as well. Sally's daughter Sara would later visit Maxine's Temple of the Mother coven for further Alexandrian training, which is something several Kentish descendants have gone on to do, including me. Despite mixing her drinks, Sally remained an Alexandrian Witch until her death and is responsible for a thriving downline in America.

The Kentish line was the line I was initiated into by High Priestess Sandra Mariah Wright, a prominent Salem Witch. I am ever grateful to Sandra for being my initiator and for shepherding me through the inevitable critiques that came from coming out as a public Witch—especially one connected to someone as controversial as my husband, Christian Day. A number of those with axes to grind questioned my validity and, as I had spent the previous twenty-five years ensconced in the obscurity of a private coven in the Northwest, Sandra guided me through the insanity that often accompanies being in the public eye.

Not long after my initiation, Maxine Sanders herself stressed the importance of training to me and suggested that I reach out to Val Hughes of the Oswestry coven on the border of Wales. While the Kentish line gave me a solid foundation in Craft, I felt strongly that it was essential to build on that foundation by connecting to Witchcraft at the source—and that would be Britain. So began several years of extensive correspondence and many visits both to and from Oswestry and New Orleans with Val Hughes. I now trace my lineage through Val back to the Temple of the Mother.

The Farrar Line

The most notable Alexandrian Witches outside of Alex and Maxine Sanders are Stewart and Janet Farrar. A journalist but not yet a Witch, Stewart met Alex and Maxine and made them the basis for Stewart's pivotal book, *What Witches Do*. This showcased the Alexandrian tradition and further cemented the legacy of both Alex and Maxine—with Maxine featured prominently on the covers of both the UK and US editions. Alex was there too, albeit masked alongside Maxine on the UK cover and kneeling with his back to the camera on the US cover—so this was the first book in which Maxine took center stage.

Many believe, falsely, that Maxine herself had initiated Stewart, but he was, in fact, initiated within the London Coven by a Scottish Witch by the name of Muriel, a truth that is being released to the public for the first time in this book. Stewart was not long for the London Coven, however, and, without sanction from either Alex or Maxine, he started his own coven, with his partner Janet, with only his first degree. This rebellious act may have been the reason that Alex granted Stewart his second and, later, his third degree. While Gardnerians perform their second and third initiation rites separately, Maxine and Alex performed both rites together as a standard practice—one of the significant distinctions in our tradition. This remains one of the few occasions that Alex separated the second and third degrees. I surmise that Alex may have given Stewart his higher degrees in hopes that Stewart would complete his training.

Stewart and Janet Farrar would go on to collaborate with Doreen Valiente and, with Doreen's assistance, published components of her *Book of Shadows* in their books, *Eight Sabbats for Witches* and *The Witches' Way*. Many Initiates were appalled that Stewart and Janet would do this and considered it to be breaking their oaths to the Craft. Their defenders argued that what Stewart published was the Gardnerian version of the Book and not the Alexandrian variation. Some may say this is splitting hairs.

As an aside, some also considered Doreen to be breaking her oaths as well while others argued that, because Doreen contributed poetry and rituals to the *Book of Shadows*, that she had every right to publish whatever materials she pleased. Doreen may have contributed significantly to the works that she and Gerald Gardner compiled together, but they were not entirely her creation (or, for that fact, Gerald's) and, even if you make an oath to your Gods not to release something that you wrote yourself just yesterday, you are violating that oath if you release it. Witches take their oaths very seriously. While both *Eight Sabbats for Witches* and *The Witches' Way* brought many fine people into the Craft, this act of Stewart, Janet, and Doreen remains controversial to this day.

Stewart and Janet's downlines include the Connecticut line in America and the Hibernian line in Ireland. Stewart and Janet themselves, however, would later leave the Alexandrian tradition entirely in favor of their own form of Progressive Witchcraft, which Janet continues to practice in Ireland today.

SILVER'S LINE

The Silver's line was established by Gerry Greenslade. His initiation was one of three times in which Alex allowed the second and third degrees to be taken separately—a practice now standard in Greenslade's line. The most controversial aspect of the Silver's line is that only romantic couples are elevated to the third degree and allowed to hive off to new covens, which excludes both gay people and those whose spouses are not Initiates. This practice is not found in any other Craft line—much less in the Alexandrian tradition. Regardless of these changes, the Silver's line is extensively represented in both the UK and in the US and thus remains a considerable swath of the Witchcraft tapestry.

I am grateful to those Initiates who have allowed me to interview them about the various lines. Without their help, this chapter would not have been possible. While I may have a critique here and there, I genuinely admire all of the initiatory lines of Witchcraft. Each lineage is unique and contributes in its own way to the Great Work. I have my preference towards rebellious freedom; I am Alexandrian, after all! That being said, I would have been initiated into any of the modern branches of the Craft if any one of them were the only path available. The Goddess guides us all to what we need and to what is required. May the Gods ever preserve the Craft!

In each of the Craft lineages above, you may follow the bread crumb trail of one's training. You have a historical record of priesthood who did their best to carry on what they have learned—and that dedication is a beautiful thing to remember and celebrate. Even when our teachers are fallible, we can still stand upon their shoulders and learn from their journeys. Discovered truths can often pave the road toward further learning and discipline. Cherish the mistakes of your teachers and your own mistakes as well. The training style that I was most drawn to comes down from the Temple of the Mother passed to me by my teacher, Val Hughes. However, while my lineage is Alexandrian, my lineage is also Witchcraft.

All of these lines of the Craft should be celebrated for the perseverance, preservation, and creativity of their priesthoods. We may come from a single source only to be split amongst the icons who helped to blaze the trails, but we carry their wisdom forward, and this is the golden chain of initiation.

Chapter 5

The Flame of Initiation

I have made much mention of initiation so far. It's even in the book's title. It's also one of the most controversial subjects in the Craft and has been the subject of intense debate for decades, especially amongst those who want the ways of the Witch without the work. The Oxford Dictionary defines initiation as:

1. The action of admitting someone into a secret or obscure society or group, typically with a ritual.
   'rituals of initiation'
   1.1 The introduction of someone to a particular activity or skill.
   'his initiation into the world of martial arts'

2. The action of beginning something.
   'the initiation of criminal proceedings'[1]

---

[1] "Initiation," Oxford Living Dictionaries, accessed October 2, 2018, https://en.oxforddictionaries.com/definition/initiation.

You will often hear that second definition, "the action of beginning something," offered by some would-be practitioners as justification for beginning Witchcraft in much the same way that they'd press the button on a microwave oven. However, that secondary definition is clearly not talking about the kind of initiation involved in Witchcraft. The first definition of the "secret or obscure society" makes far more sense when you think back on the stories of Witches and other magical orders through the ages, especially when you consider such rites of passage are typically done both communally and through ritual, as Oxford also makes clear. Moreover, the first definition goes the extra mile to include initiation as one's introduction to "an activity or skill"—the word "skill" being synonymous with the word "craft." In other words, even if Witchcraft wasn't a priesthood but was simply a skilled craft, you still wouldn't be very good at it without the kind of initiation and training that makes one a true master of their art. While you surely might be able to dabble in a priesthood or a skill, you cannot initiate yourself into either.

The very idea of self-initiation was manufactured for the masses by reckless occult publishing houses seeking to propagate modern paganism and to sell books. It is not real nor is it logically effective. The authors who have promoted self-dedication rites in their books had far more integrity and wisdom in understanding that dedication can allow someone to profess intent while refusing to cave to the idea that self-initiation is even possible. There is simply no such thing as self-initiation in Witchcraft just as there's no such thing as self-initiation in Freemasonry, the Rosicrucian Orders, the Golden Dawn, the Ordo Templi Orientis, or any of the other mystery traditions. Witchcraft is not something beneath the dignity of the rest of Western occultism. We have many of the same standards, origins, and practices, a commonality we will continue to explore in this chapter.

You do not have to be an Initiate to practice magic or worship the old gods. You can dedicate yourselves to them and to the old ways without permission. You can also use whatever labels you desire as words are free to use, whether used correctly or not. However, without initiation you cannot reach the pinnacle of modern Witchcraft. Without initiation, you will not have the full knowledge or power of the Witch—regardless of what anyone tells you. You simply cannot gain access to our Gods, our spirits, our literature or our training without proper initiation. How can you call on a goddess when her name is hidden from you? How can you cast a circle when you really have no idea how it's properly cast? The entire uninitiated Craft movement is guessing, imitating, and appropriating our ways. That may be a hard pill for some to swallow, but it is the truth. Some would say that this free-for-all is a sign of the Craft evolving, but it isn't, not any more than the cheapening bastardizations happening to so many other sacred cultural traditions. The Craft is still the Craft, and we continue to bring in new Initiates every day.

I respect everyone who is on a magical journey. None of us began as Initiates. I called myself a Witch, wore a pentacle, and cast spells at the age of fifteen. We all started out somewhere, and that includes the well-trained Initiates you might meet today.

Initiation is deeply rooted in the fabric of mankind's earliest magical experiences. It is the very foundation of magic, religion, and our eternal quest to be one with the Gods. Shamanic practices are often cited as examples by solitary practitioners looking for justification for do-it-yourself Witchcraft. The image of the witch doctor toiling away in their cloistered hut may bolster the idea of the Witch alone, but it hardly tells the real story of how the shaman got to that point. If you actually study aboriginal people, both in modern times and in ancient tales, they still learned their craft, magic, and teachings from their elders—from the shamans of the tribe who came before them. And, at a certain point in their development, they would undergo their own initiation, which would often employ hallucinogenic plants in a ritual that would all but require the guidance of one who had already experienced such altered states. With the approving nod of the elders, the tribe would then look to the new shaman as trustworthy and wise.

Initiation has haunted the human experience for millennia. Every culture has continued to create essential rites of passage to mark the significant milestones along the journey of life. Although such rites vary, and they're not always religious in nature, they're crucial in keeping the fabric of society woven together. Human beings measure things by time and events. Birthdays, christenings, bar mitzvahs, graduations, weddings, and even funerals are all traditional ways of processing life's landmark moments as well as major personal transformations. Initiation comes in many forms, including tribal ritual customs, rites of adulthood, and even the first hunt. In England, there was the custom of the first kill in a fox hunt where the faces of participants were bloodied.[2] A barbaric ritual, but once again, an initiation of sorts.

Initiations were once always religious and powerful in nature. We have lost much of this essence in the West as today's rites of passage become more secular and dispensable, so it is only natural that those of us with respect for the old ways continue to uphold, desire, pursue, and develop magical initiations for the modern world. Those of us truly in tune with the magic of life's rhythms inherently know that initiation is the key to embrace them. Without it, you will not experience the transformation necessary to transcend to your full potential.

There will always be those who feel they do not need initiation. Perhaps these individuals believe that they were born into Witchcraft. Maybe they do not like working with others. Or, it is possible that they are still learning the lessons that humility requires. Convince them not, for the path of initiation is not for everyone. When you step onto this path, you are playing with fire. You are asking the Gods, the universe, and the powers of the unseen to change you at the very core of your being. If that request is granted, that change *will* occur, not only within your mundane life but on the inner planes as well. A warning: one cannot climb the pillars of magic without being challenged. Initiation invokes obstacles, puzzles, and sometimes destruction and chaos into your life, all so that you may receive the change that you've asked for. To remove

---

[2] Victoria Williams, *Celebrating Life Customs around the World: From Baby Showers to Funerals, vol. 1* (Santa Barbara: ABC-CLIO, 2017), 53.

the blindfolds and the mundane ego, and truly gain the sight, can be a perilous adventure for some.

The ultimate goal, of course, is to come out of the other side of initiation improved and empowered. The old saying, "to rise you must fall," comes to mind. The experiences, obstacles, and challenges are different for each individual. They are not to be feared. This is why Initiates are told from the very beginning that they cannot fear that which they invoke into manifestation. My own experience of initiation is that its challenges do play out in the mundane as much as they do the spiritual. For instance, I have often had the experience of being thrown into public controversy following any of my initiations with people who have no bearing on my life suddenly interested in every detail of how and why I was initiated. This has been a part of my journey and something that I believe was given to me to help with my personal development and growth.

Others have had their love lives fall apart, while still others were obliged to move long distances. I know of one priestess who, every time she's undergone an initiation, has been required by her company to move to a new state. I've known individuals to be hit by cars, injured, or to receive a multitude of blessings right out of the gate.

This is why I was taught that if someone asks you if they should be initiated, you should reply, "No. Run away. Don't do it. Only an insane person would seek initiation." That being said, I would become initiated again in a heartbeat, and so would most Initiates I know because, once you get to that other side—if you survive—you will be more powerful. You will be wiser. You will be more in control of your life and your destiny. You will be a Witch in more than just name.

Initiation is a deep and layered process. It is not simply the mere theatrics of waving a wand accompanied by some colorful words. The rituals themselves impact the mind in profound ways. I've seen Initiates go through the rites with utter joy, and I've seen Initiates go through the rites with significant emotional or physical difficulty. Each person experiences the trials of initiation in their own unique way. This is why we have certain taboos. We do not initiate people who suffer from mental illness unless they are able to manage their condition because these rites can make even the sanest person unstable. To do otherwise would be cruel and could be very destructive to the individual in question. The eagerly offended enjoy being outraged by such things, but I would probably also avoid teaching a blind person how to shoot a gun. This is Witchcraft and it can be dangerous. Any initiation rite should be approached with great thought and care. A schizophrenic person may not be capable of processing what happens during initiation. In this incarnation, working through their mental illness might be the only initiation required of them.

This is also the reason why the wise will not initiate people who lack stability in their life, such as the perpetually unemployed or those who suffer from addictions or other imbalances. One should be gainfully employed and have a stable home life if you expect to also maintain stability in the Craft. If you cannot control your own reliance on substances, how will you control your ability to wield magical power? You must be capable of fulfilling the duties of priesthood, which can include a great deal of time and effort, so your personal life should not become an impediment to that work.

Initiation produces a psychological impact that is necessary for personal development in the Craft. This happens through ritual and training. Initiation is also a magical spell—an invocation that puts you in contact with the entities of Witchcraft. These entities and our Gods have always worked with Initiates and this will always be the true and proper way in which they will receive humanity. Initiation is also a community—the priesthood. Only in this way can you receive the rights, privileges, and teachings contained within the Craft.

Yes, initiation is necessary for those who would rise to the heights and penetrate the depths of the occult world, but it has many benefits. Initiation gives you the keys to the kingdom. You are introduced to the great powers of the hidden world. Witchcraft is a living spirit—a force unto itself and has developed its own egregore over the centuries. It is steeped in secrecy and much of its wisdom resides in the hidden realms of reality. When you are initiated, these unseen forces become your guides, guardians, protectors, teachers, and familiar spirits. These beings are known as the Mighty Ones, although they do have other names. These forces, in truth, are a legion of entities that exist within the inner planes of Witchcraft. They are custodians of magic and the natural world, yet they also traverse the astral planes and all the magical dimensions imagined and unknown. The primary purpose of the Mighty Ones is to aid Initiates and to guard against outsiders from entering in without the proper keys. The Mighty Ones allow only Initiates to penetrate the Mysteries, to learn the words of power, to meet the secret gods, and to perform the great work with your brethren, for we can truly say, "ye may not be a Witch alone."

The reason that the practice of initiation into a magical sect or priesthood is so universal and has withstood the test of time is that it works. From the dawn of human awareness right up to the present day, this ancient magical technique was employed by the Sumerians, Phoenicians, Babylonians, Egyptians, Druids, Greeks, Romans, and nearly all pre-Christian peoples.

Initiation in the British Isles

Initiation within ancient Britain is a subject mired in obscurity, for much of their history and lore were unwritten. When we think about the early British people, we most often think of the Celts—an enigmatic culture that emerged around 800 BCE and dominated the British Isles for centuries—and their mysterious priesthood, the Druids. Like the Witches of today, the rituals and training of the Druids were a secret and hidden process. The Druids practiced an oral tradition so we are unlikely to ever discover a lost, forbidden manuscript that will articulate the full spectrum of their practices. Our knowledge of the ancient British people is limited to a few scarce sources, including folklore, the writings of Roman leaders and historians, the records of the early Church, and archaeological discoveries and the theories that accompany them. While the practices of the Druids were shrouded in mystery and thus we haven't any records of actual Druidic initiations, we do know that Celtic culture was filled with initiatory rites of passage and that such rituals marked the training of warriors, poets, musicians and even the making of kings.

Archaeology provides a window into the past, for we can look to ancient sacred British sites like the Isle of Anglesey's Bryn Celli Ddu and Barclodiad y Gawres, Ireland's Newgrange, and even Stonehenge to learn of the spiritual practices of old. Such ancient sites are said to have had a link with the otherworld and thus would almost certainly have been used as places for sacred rites of initiation by whoever built them. All of these Neolithic and prehistoric sites mentioned existed before the Celts or the Druids, who likely saw such places as having been left by the Gods. The Celts would have seen these mounds as doorways to the underworld—the land of the fairy Sidhe folk, and they are likely to have used them for initiation as well. I have been to all of these locations, and Stonehenge, in particular, reminded me of the Temple of Eleusis, which I visited while in Greece. I imagine great pilgrimages would have been made—often but once in a lifetime.

Within early Celtic Christianity, there are tales of those who made pilgrimages to sacred caves such as St. Patrick's Purgatory at Lough Derg, County Donegal, Ireland.[3] Devoted pilgrims would undergo purification and prayer before taking vigil in the cave—often overnight. This echoes back to the ancient Celtic custom of descent into the Sidhe mounds—places they saw as portals to the underworld—a common theme in initiation rites. It is likely that sacred sites like Newgrange once functioned in just such a manner—a destination for the Celtic peoples to descend into the otherworld much like the later Celtic Christians would enter into caves.

The Romans gave us the most detailed accounts of the Druids. Many scholars are skeptical of these writings because the Romans were at war with the Celts and trying to conquer them. However, much can be gleaned from their words, even if one must sometimes read between the lines. Julius Caesar, in his *Commentarii de Bello Gallico* (circa 58 – 49

---

[3] 1. W.Y. Evans Wentz, *The Fairy-Faith in Celtic Countries* (London, New York, Toronto and Melbourne: Oxford University Press, 1911), 442-452.

BCE), remarked that it could take up to 20 years to complete the course of study in Druidry.[4]

The Greek philosopher, geographer, and historian Strabo wrote that amongst the Gauls, three priest castes were the most honored. The first were the bards, who were singers and poets. Next was the *vates* (more commonly known as ovates), who practiced divination and were skilled in the ways of the natural worlds. Finally, there were the Druids themselves, who were chief among the priesthoods and acted not just as philosophical and spiritual guides but were tasked with the role of judge—settling disputes among the people.[5]

The accounts of Julius Caesar and Strabo give us a small glimpse into the structure of the Druid priesthood in Gaul. It was rigorous training, and the three castes might possibly even be likened to the Witches' system of degrees if those divisions were in any way connected sequentially. It would make sense that the high-ranking Druids would also have had to have been able to conduct the works of both bard and vote. Druids have been seen as keepers of wisdom, gifted in prophecy, and knowledgeable in the ways of the natural worlds.

There is no written account of a Druid initiation within the priesthood. There wouldn't be, as the Druidic rites were secret and initiation would have been among the most guarded of those secrets. However, elements of these rituals may have survived through myth and poetry. The most considerable wealth of Celtic knowledge came from Christian monks, who wrote down the oral lore and myths that they inherited from their Druidic predecessors and gleaned from the folk tales and songs they likely grew up with.

One such outstanding collection of lore is the *Mabinogi*. This mysterious anthology of tales, known more commonly as the *Mabinogion*, is a treasure trove of Welsh mythology. There are four primary books, but other Welsh tales are often included in their publications. Within these

---

[4] Julius Caesar, *"De Bello Gallico" and Other Commentaries of Caius Julius Caesar*, ed. Ernest Rhys, trans. W. A. Macdevitt (New York: J. M. Dent, 1915), 119.

[5] Leslie Ellen Jones, *Druid, Shaman, Priest: Metaphors of Celtic Paganism* (Enfield Lock, England: Hisarlik, 1998), 20.

pages are accounts that closely resemble what, as a Witch, can only see as the elements of initiation.

In one such story, the Welsh god Gwydion presents his sister, the Goddess Arianrhod, with a son she never knew she had. Arianrhod bitterly rejects her son by casting three terrible curses upon him. With the first, Arianrhod refuses her son a name lest she be the one to bestow him with one. With the help of his uncle, Gwydion, the young boy tricks Arianrhod into granting him the name Lleu Llaw Gyffes—the fair-haired one with the skillful hand. Not to be outdone, Arianrhod curses Lleu again that he may receive no weaponry unless she herself were to arm him. Gwydion aids Lleu again in manipulating the Goddess into arming her son. With the third curse, the most egregious, Arianrhod then declares that Lleu shall never marry a mortal wife, yet, Gwydion and the powerful wizard Math craft for Lleu a wife made of flowers and name her Blodeuwedd, thus tricking Arianrhod again by granting Lleu an immortal goddess for his bride. Sadly, Blodeuwedd later tries to kill Lleu and is turned into an owl, so the element of sacrifice upon initiation is introduced into the story and perhaps it was the Goddess Arianrhod who is in control of the process all along.[6]

There are parallels to the initiatory journey found hidden within the story of Lleu Llaw Gyffes. One might perceive the curses of Arianrhod to be initiatory challenges—ordeals that one must face along the path within. You can also find direct correlations to Witchcraft. To progress to the Third Degree of the Craft, one must be presented with the weapons of magic; one must be granted a new name; and, finally, one must discover the ecstasy that is the sacred marriage of Goddess and God. So, perhaps in the truth behind the layers of misogyny that the monks who first wrote these tales down likely infused into the story, Arianrhod was initiatrix all along, and this was the path to enlightenment that Lleu Llaw Gyffes was destined to follow.

---

[6] Patrick K. Ford, ed., *The Mabinogi and Other Medieval Welsh Tales*, trans. Patrick K. Ford (Berkeley and Los Angeles, California: University of California Press, 1977), 99 - 103.

Another ancient Welsh story often included along with the four books of the *Mabinogi* is the "Tale of Gwion Bach," which tells of how a young boy becomes the famed bard Taliesin—a poet whose work has survived to this day and who has often been associated with the wizard Merlin. The story tells of the Goddess Ceridwen, the Witch of the Celtic gods, and how she used her knowledge of magical herbs to brew a special potion of inspiration in her cauldron that she may grant wisdom to her loathsome son Afagddu in hopes that he would gain social acceptance. On gathering the herbs for her brew, Ceridwen tasked a young boy named Gwion Bach to tend the cauldron for a year and a day that she may produce the three drops of potion necessary for her purpose. Alas, Ceridwen fell asleep for the appointed time of the potion's completion, and three drops sprung from the cauldron onto Gwion who, in turn, obtained the inspiration contained therein. At that moment, he receives all knowledge, including the knowledge that Ceridwen would destroy him once she found out. Sure enough, the now furious Witch Goddess pursues a terrified Gwion Bach to exact her revenge. Having now gained the magical power to shapeshift, Gwion transforms into a hare to escape her while the Witch pursues him as a black greyhound. He then changes into a fish, while she hunts him as an otter. The boy then becomes a bird while Ceridwen becomes a hawk to catch him. Finally, Gwion Bach hides within a barn of wheat disguised as a single, golden grain and the Goddess changes herself into a black hen and devours him. However, nine months later, Ceridwen gives birth to a son. Not able to bear killing the boy again, she places him into a basket and casts him away upon the waters of a lake. The newborn is soon found, is given the name Taliesin for his radiant brow, and, in time, he becomes chief amongst bards, renowned for his poetic wisdom.[7]

This is, perhaps, the most compelling tale of initiation in all the Welsh myths. It is filled with symbols common to Witchcraft. One often hears of the journey of initiation taking a "year and a day," a duration oft-found in Celtic lore. The cauldron itself has long been a symbol of death, re-

---

[7] Ibid, 159 - 165.

birth, and transformation and shares a lengthy association with Witches as well. So too does the black dog and black hen (and black animals in general), and such dark pursuits of the light may be seen as the nocturnal forces of night chasing the bright son of day—as Taliesin's very name means "radiant brow." The Witches of folklore have long been said to be shapeshifters much like Gwion and Ceridwen.

However, it is Gwion Bach's transformations that are perhaps most closely paralleled with the transformation of initiation. As he shifts from shape to shape, Gwion traverses through the classical elements of earth, water, fire, and air. Like the hare that descends into the ground in so many stories of Witch folklore and the underworlds of the Celtic Sidhe, Gwion delves into the element of earth. He swims the streams of the element water as the fish and takes flight into the element of air as the bird. Finally, Gwion explores fire as he becomes the golden grain of wheat, which could easily be associated with the element of fire as the benevolence of the sun was so depended on by early agricultural societies. Once Ceridwen consumes Gwion Bach, he achieves the true initiation of death and rebirth. What is even more fascinating about the transformations of Gwion Bach is the sequence of the elements themselves. By transforming into earth, water, air, fire, and, finally, the spirit of death and resurrection, in that order, Gwion is following the exact path of the invoking pentagram of earth found in both Witchcraft and ceremonial magic.

The Invoking Pentagram of Earth

This is such a startling correlation that it seems unlikely to be a coincidence, and helps show us just how much wisdom the ancient Celts possessed.

The Cult of Dionysus

The cult of Dionysus may have been one of the oldest mystery cults in Greek civilization, and it continued to be spread across the world into Roman times, where the God was called Bacchus. The cult evolved over many centuries and through the various cultures and regions with which the God was associated. While many scholars suggest the cult's origins to be in the Mycenaean period of the 14th century BCE[8], scholar Karl Kerényi makes a strong case for Dionysus having ties to the Minoan culture of Crete which would bring him into a culture that dates as far back as 2700 BCE. The bull, so strongly associated with Cretan religion, is also a symbol of Dionysus, as are their shared symbols of wine, ivy, and the serpent.[9] The Minoan culture had centuries of its own initiatory mystery cults so it's not unthinkable that we may find the origins of the Cult of Dionysus there.

The classical art of ancient times often depicts Dionysus as surrounded by wild half-goat satyrs and woodland nymphs. In time, his followers came to include frenzied female maenads hungry for raw flesh, showing how the perceptions of the wild and ecstatic rites may have come to be more feared over time.[10] The Cult of Dionysus stirs the imagination: a mysterious god surrounded by unbridled women, satyrs, fauns, and nymphs taking part in rituals filled with darkness, orgies, and fevered madness, with devotees in the midst of it all performing acts of supernatural power and prophecy. It rather sounds like the kind of Witch's Sabbath described by the Church!

---

[8] Mark Cartwright, "Dionysos," *Ancient History Encyclopedia*, September 16, 2012, accessed February 27, 2019, https://www.ancient.eu/Dionysos.

[9] Karl Kerényi, *Dionysos: Archetypal Image of Indestructible Life* (Princeton, New Jersey: Princeton University Press, 1976), 26, 52, 113, 119.

[10] Mark Cartwright, "Dionysos," *Ancient History Encyclopedia*, September 16, 2012, accessed February 27, 2019, https://www.ancient.eu/Dionysos.

In time, the practices of the Cult of Dionysus were enveloped into the Eleusinian Mysteries, perhaps the most famous mystery cult of all—centered in the temple of Eleusis near Athens, Greece.[11] This merging of the wild, fertile rites of Dionysus with the more established and conventional rites of Eleusis may have been an attempt by Athenian authorities to exert control over an unruly cult that could be considered a threat to law and order. Or perhaps, they did it simply because the popularity of the God had grown to such enormous proportions.

Eleusis became a center of the Mysteries in the Greco-Roman world for about two millennia—performing the rites of initiation throughout that time. The first settlement there was dated c. 1900 BCE and, in circa 1500 BCE, the first temple to Demeter and Persephone was constructed. Eleusis remained in operation until it was destroyed in 395 CE by Germanic invaders.[12]

The magic of Eleusis was accessible to any who sought initiation into the cult. The only rules that barred induction were that you could not be a murderer, you were required to speak Greek, and you had to take an oath of secrecy on pain of death. This was a mystery cult, not an ethnic faith. Greek was required so that you could understand the rituals. Initiation at Eleusis was greatly valued in the ancient world and included many kings and emperors such as the Roman emperor Hadrian. Those of high and often divine status still desired initiation for it was considered a requirement for the development of the soul.

Beyond Eleusis, the Dionysia became one of the most important annual festivals of Athens and surrounding rural areas with ritualistic theatrical performances both tragic and comedic. In the rural areas, the Cult of Dionysus continued to maintain much of its hedonistic wickedness.

Eventually, the Cult of Dionysus found its way to the Roman Empire where the equivalent to the Greek Dionysia become the more well-known Bacchanalia, which spread secretly throughout Europe until the Empire

---

[11] Rosemarie Taylor-Perry, *The God Who Comes: Dionysian Mysteries Reclaimed* (New York: Algora, 2003), 109.

[12] Mark Cartwright, "Eleusis," *Ancient History Encyclopedia*, January 14, 2015, accessed February 27, 2019, https://www.ancient.eu/Eleusis.

actively suppressed it in 186 CE, most likely due to its association with unbridled freedom.[13] Like the Craft and other sorcerous faiths, mystery cults represented a force that those in power could not easily control.

The conquests of Alexander the Great caused several western and eastern cults to merge, helping to spread their practices and philosophies. These cults were of Greek, Egyptian, Persian, and Asian origin. The mystery cults are, in a sense, the first world religions. The Greeks already had the foundation for these types of widely-sought cults at Eleusis. The exchange of occult knowledge in this new Hellenistic world would give rise to other secret sects, such as the cult of Isis Serapis—which was born in Alexandria, Egypt during the rule of the Ptolemies, and the Persian cult of Mithra. These cults were exotic, clandestine, and promised secret knowledge to those who dared to pass through the gates of wisdom.

Christianity finds roots within the cult of Dionysus as well, It has been speculated that the Arthurian mysteries of the Holy Grail—the cup that was said to have held the blood of Christ and which absolutely finds compelling parallels to the chalice of Witchcraft—may have its origin in the sacred wine of the Dionysian rites.[14] Agricultural communities would have been very attracted to a god that mirrored their local deities and such peoples were able to recognize their own customs within the rites of other cults. Did the Celts identify Dionysus as a god of mead? Did the grail mysteries resonate with this agricultural cult that spread across the world? One must wonder. Such vegetation rites would have been disguised as Christianity gained in power throughout Europe and so the blood of Dionysus becomes the blood of Christ, held within the sacred chalice long associated with Witches.

Being one of the oldest and most widespread cults in the world, the Cult of Dionysus traversed ancient Greece, Egypt, and the Empire of Rome. It is hard to conceive just how far-reaching the impact of this

---

[13] Sarah Iles Johnston, ed., *Religions of the Ancient World: A Guide* (Cambridge, MA: Belknap Press, 2004), 311

[14] Juliette Wood, "Folklore Studies at the Celtic Dawn: The Role of Alfred Nutt as Publisher and Scholar," *Folklore*, 1999.

vegetation wine cult and its mysteries on western civilization actually are, but it is considerable indeed.

The Cult of Isis

While the Cult of Dionysus was undoubtedly widespread, there is one faith whose worship would span nearly every area of the known world—establishing an enduring legacy that continues to influence many of the world's religions today—the Mysteries of Isis. While Isis is best known for her beginnings as an ancient Egyptian goddess, she eventually became the Queen of Heaven to people the world over. It should be no surprise, as one of her symbols is the throne, which is clearly seen in her hieroglyphic imagery. Within a temple in the ancient Egyptian town of Sais, Plutarch describes a statue of Athena—who the author points out both Greeks and Egyptians alike identified with Isis—upon which is inscribed, "I am all that has been, and is, and shall be, and my robe no mortal has yet uncovered."[15] This singular proclamation would become the foundation of the very concept of the veil of Isis that continues to permeate so many occult and mystery traditions into the present day. The temple (and the town) was originally dedicated to the Goddess Neith, though like many goddesses, the attributes of Neith were absorbed into those of Isis. This declaration by the Goddess speaks to the deep mysteries of initiation and to the powerful legacy that the Cult of Isis has wrought upon the world. After all, if she's all that was, is, and shall be, what else is there?

While Isis was the throne, her sect as it grew in Egypt could also be said to have been the power behind the throne: the pharaoh. Perhaps we can call it the Cult of the Pharaoh as her spiritual role in influencing affairs of state would continue to gain importance over thousands of years.

The ancient Osirian myth begins her tale: Isis and the God Osiris were brother and sister (though some have speculated that they may have been the first actual king and queen of ancient Egypt). Isis plays the

---

[15] Plutarch, *Moralia*, trans. Frank Cole Babbitt, Loeb Classical Library (2003) ed., vol. Volume V (Cambridge, Massachusetts and London: Harvard University Press, 1936), 25.

dominant role and holds all the power with Osiris becoming submissive and reliant upon her. Osiris is then killed off by his brother, Set, who cuts his body into pieces and throws them into the Nile river. Isis then seeks to restore her beloved husband, lover, and brother and traverses the Nile in search of all the parts of Osiris, which she finds all except for his penis, which was eaten by a crocodile. Isis magically forges a new member for Osiris out of gold, hence establishing herself as the creator of life. She then resurrects the God, making love to him. Osiris, now having traversed the realms of the dead, becomes the Egyptian god of the underworld. Isis then gives birth to Horus, son of Osiris, who avenges his father's murderer by striking down his uncle Set and becoming chief amongst the Gods; thus the pharaoh was called the Living Horus—or Osiris Risen.

Isis would continue to be the creator of kings, gods, and mysteries. In the Greek world, she absorbed many goddesses and cults, and in Alexandria, she became, in essence, a monotheistic goddess. She was the Goddess of all mysteries and magic, and her cults held the core matrix of both Egyptian and Greek myth.[16]

You might be wondering why we are focusing on mystery cults so far beyond Britain. It's quite simple. They are not beyond Britain at all. Archaeological evidence has been discovered pointing to the presence of a temple of Isis in London itself.[17] While we do not know what direct spiritual connections there may have been between the Roman Cult of Isis and the Celtic Druids, we do know that the Celtic migrations spanned great distances and that the Celts had mingled with both the Egyptians and the Greeks. In either event, Isis and her mysterious veil have been woven into the landscape of esoteric and occult orders in Britain for at least several hundred years, and modern Witchcraft is as intimately intertwined with the veil of Isis as it is with either Celtic or Saxon beliefs.

---

[16] R.E. Witt, *Isis in the Ancient World*, Johns Hopkins Paperback Edition, 1997 ed. (Baltimore and London: Johns Hopkins University Press, 1971), 146,147,151, 153.

[17] Ibid, 138.

The Mysteries of Isis were absorbed into the rites of Eleusis, Dionysus, and other cults, leaving a significant and lasting impact on both world religion and western civilization. Isis would become a synthesis of all goddesses, and through the might of the Roman Empire, her cult had temples from Asia to Britain, and she was beloved by emperors and common folk alike.

The priesthood of Isis engaged in practices often associated with Witches both modern and ancient. They practiced the arts of healing and magic. They worked at times in the nude. They held nocturnal gatherings. And, they had three degrees of initiation.[18] A reliable connection between the Cult of Isis and the lore of Witches can be found in the southern Italian town of Benevento. It is there that one of Italy's temples of Isis was known to have been in use since 80 CE, during the reign of Domitian[19]. What makes the Benevento connection so interesting is that the town would later come to be strongly associated with both Witches and the Witch Goddess Diana—herself having shared attributes with Isis. According to local lore, the walnut tree of Benevento, from whose branches the serpent would hang, was a gathering place for the Witches' Sabbath, where alleged practitioners were said to worship both a vegetational god and the Goddess Diana. The stories of Witches in Benevento come from both centuries of regional folklore as well as the confessions of those accused in Witch trials. Belief in Witches endures to this day in that land where Isis, the Goddess of magic, once held sway. In fact, the presence of Isis can still be felt in the Piazza Papiniano of Benevento, where an ancient obelisk still stands in her honor.[20]

"In the old days, when witchdom extended far, we were free and worshiped in all the greater temples."[21]

---

[18] Ibid, 158, 159, 161, 162, 222.

[19] Birgitte Bøgh, "The Graeco-Roman Cult of Isis," in *The Handbook of Religions in Ancient Europe*, ed. Lisbeth Bredholt Christensen, Olav Hammer, and David Warburton (New York: Routledge, 2014).

[20] Andrea Romanazzi, *Guida Alle Streghe in Italia* (Rome: Venexia, 2009), 118, 121.

[21] June Johns, *King of the Witches: The World of Alex Sanders* (London and Edinburgh: Morrison and Gibb Limited, 1969), 154.

The author of the passage above is said to be old Gerald himself. Regardless, the choice of the phrase "greater temples" brings to mind the classical age before Christ—not Stonehenge or other stone circles of the British Isles but rather the sacred temples dedicated to the Great Goddess and tended to by devoted priests. Did the Witches of the New Forest hold such mysteries, or was this merely a creative occultist with pen in hand?

The initiatory mystery cults continued to evolve and thrive and were often combined. The Cult of Isis nurtured this syncretism from the city where she reigned as patroness—Alexandria, which held the vastest store of wisdom in the ancient world: the Great Library. Like Queen Cleopatra, Isis seduced both Roman emperors and citizens alike. It may very well be that she posed the greatest divine feminine threat against the rising tide of Christianity. When Rome receded in the West and eventually succumbed to the Christians, the Cult of Isis seemingly disappeared into the shades of memory. Did her cult of initiation go underground? Did it evolve into something new? Could its practices have, like those of Diana, come to be those of the beings we now call Witches? We may never know, but there are many curious possibilities. Let us not forget, that while the worship of Isis may have faded, just as the symbols and attributes of so many goddesses before her become her own, so too did the symbols and characteristics of Isis come to be associated with the Great Mother of Christianity: the Blessed Virgin Mary.

The Cult of Diana

Another widely revered incarnation of the Great Goddess—and one who has also been equated to Isis—is the Roman Diana. Diana may find her origins in the pre-Roman Etruscan peoples but was undoubtedly influenced by older myths of the Greek Artemis and Egyptian Isis as well, synthesized as they were within the Hellenized mind.

The Roman Diana emerged from her origins in an obscure cult along the shores of Lake Nemi on the outskirts of Rome to become one of the twelve major Roman gods, absorbing many of the qualities of the renowned goddesses who preceded her. To the Romans, she was the virgin goddess of the moon, the hunt, and nature—worshiped as part of the official state religion. Within the Empire, priests of the temples were usually elected from noble families.[22] We do not have full accounts of the initiatory rites practiced therein, but we know from archaeological sites like Pompeii that such rituals did exist. Rome preferred to keep religion controlled under the might and authority of the state, and so they were often wary of the more secretive mystery cults, leading to conflicts, such as those with the cults of Bacchus and Isis as well as the Druids. And so, like other gods before her, Diana became absorbed into the approved pantheon of the Roman Empire.

Legend tells that the birthplace of Diana's worship was in a grove along the shores of Lake Nemi—a name that derives from a Latin word meaning "holy wood." The area remains strongly associated with the Goddess today. Lake Nemi is known as Diana's mirror. The high priest at Nemi was called the Rex Nemorensis, which means "king of the sacred grove," and was tasked with watching over the tree sacred to Diana. The ritual strongly resembles the old myths of the divine king's ritual combat and sacrifice, which would traditionally be associated with seasonal rites, and this may hint at an earlier agricultural association for Diana. The station of the Rex Nemorensis was open only to runaway slaves, and the winner would be "free" to take the place of his slain predecessor. To claim the position, the seeker would first have to collect a stem of mistletoe from the sacred tree, known as "the golden bough," and a plant also known to be holy to the Celtic Druids. The mistletoe would be presented to the high priest as a challenge, then the two would fight to the death in ritual combat. The victor would either continue to be Diana's high priest or become her new one. Lake Nemi continued to play a role in goddess worship long after Diana became a staple of the Roman pantheons. Emperor Caligula himself kept barges on the lake upon which

---

[22] "There was no cast of Roman priests," *The Romans*, accessed June 4, 2019, http://www.the-romans.eu/society/Roman-priests.php.

he conducted rituals to Isis, showing the roots of Diana's absorption of aspects of her Egyptian counterpart. The emperor also took an interest in the combat rituals that defined the cult, even meddling in the game by offering stronger opponents when he'd felt that the high priest had been in his role too long. But his annoyance was not unfounded. It was said that the Rex Nemorensis should be at the "height of his powers," neither ill nor to die of old age. The myth of the sacrificial king who gives up his station for the sake of the land appears again and again in Witchcraft. [23][24]

The gradual acceptance and assimilation of the mystery cults in Rome—coupled with the Hellenized mindset that propelled them to integrate the characteristics of deities into one another—had a significant influence on the Goddess Diana. She had already absorbed Artemis, Selene, and Hecate, and so Caligula adding Isis to the mix was par for the course. With the fall of paganism and the eventual crumbling of the Empire, Diana may have taken on a new incarnation, one that represented the last goddess of the ancient mysteries—one that would eventually come to be feared and associated with sorcery, magic, and debaucherous acts. Traces of her worship were found in what is now Margut, France as late as the 6th century when Christianity was already taking hold. [25] Diana is also the only ancient goddess mentioned in the biblical New Testament, so she became a clear target of the Church's attempts to wipe out pre-Christian cults.

As the centuries of Christian oppression wore on, the Cult of Diana became absorbed into ideas about witchcraft, which came to reach their peak at the dawn of the Renaissance. Could this be a backlash to the emerging enlightenment, or is it possible that the old mystery cult of Diana was having a renaissance of its own?

---

[23] James George Frazer, *The Golden Bough: A Study in Magic and Religion*, Abridged ed. (New York: Macmillan, 1963), 1 - 7, 349 - 350, 815 - 816.

[24] John M. McManamon, *Caligula's Barges and the Renaissance Origins of Nautical Archaeology under Water*, Ed Rachal Foundation Nautical Archaeology Series (College Station, TX: Texas A&M University Press, 2016), 47

[25] Gregory, Bishop of Tours, *History of the Franks* (591), Book VIII, 195, https://archive.org/stream/historyoffranks00greguoft/historyoffranks00greguoft_djvu.txt.

Perhaps the most significant evidence that a secret cult to Diana not only existed but was perceived as a threat to the Church can be found in the early 10th-century Catholic document, *Canon Episcopi:*

> *It is also not to be omitted that some wicked women, turning back to Satan, seduced by illusions and phantasms of demons, believe and claim that in the hours of night they ride on certain beasts with Diana, goddess of the pagans, and an innumerable multitude of women.* [26]

A century later, Bishop Burchard of Worms (c. 950–1025) added the phrase, "Or with Herodias" to the passage, which not only merges a biblical New Testament figure with the Diana myth but plays into another, more mysterious Witch Goddess I mention further on.

Reginald Scot, in his classic exploration of the Witch, *The Discoverie of Witchcraft*, written in 1584, gives descriptions of the Sabbath, in which the Witches revel with fairies, Diana and the devil. It must be noted that Scot's work was written from the perspective of a skeptic who was trying to prove that Witchcraft was merely a fantasy and that supposed witches were being accused unjustly. Still, his book remains a window into the deep fears of Witchcraft and the ideas of its practice at the dawn of the enlightened age.

Scot describes assemblies at which the Witches bring forth new disciples, called novices. The novice must swear fidelity and by certain rituals, such as denouncing Christianity, making a pact, or an oath, will receive instruction in magic and receive their Witch's mark. The disciple would then be declared a Witch and promised long life and prosperity. The pact itself, associated as it is with the taking of oaths and induction into secrets, is reminiscent of the initiations of old.

Reginald Scot also mentions that the order of the bargain or oath is twofold, with one being public and one being private and secret. Perhaps this suggests two separate rituals or degrees, one held more secret than the

---

[26] Martha Rampton, ed., *European Magic and Witchcraft: A Reader* (Toronto: University of Toronto Press, 2018), 155.

other. Clearly, the use of the word "public" referred to the public activity of witches as they cavort with one another at the sabbath since any real public witchcraft activity would have gotten the oath taker tortured and put to death. Therefore, the reference to "private" seems to imply the idea of a secret inner circle among Witches. Moreover, the use of the word "novice" suggests that there are yet higher levels to attain. [27]

Diana and her secret cult have been a powerful myth in ideas about Witchcraft for centuries, and this became even stronger at the dawn of the twentieth century. Two publications have been primarily responsible for this: *Aradia: Gospel of the Witches*, compiled by folklorist Charles Godfrey Leland and published in 1899; and *The Witch-Cult in Western Europe* by anthropologist Margaret Murray, published in 1921.

Leland was a folklorist who claimed to obtain a manuscript from an Italian Witch named Maddalena. The book is presented as a work of folklore and weaves a story of an Italian cult of Dianic Witches that survived, hidden and persecuted, within Christianized Italy. The most authentic part of this text may be in the mixing of Christian and pre-Christian archetypes to create a cult that is uniquely both.

In the gospel, Diana is a creator moon goddess. With the help of her brother Lucifer, a sun god who is an unmistakable mixture between the attributes of Apollo and the Christian devil, Diana gives birth to a daughter named Aradia, who becomes the first Witch on earth, and teaches Witchcraft to both men and women alike. Consider Burchard's addition of "Herodias" alongside the Goddess Diana in his 11th-century addition of the *Canon Episcopi* and consider what the silent 'h' and 's' of Latin might make that word sound like and suddenly the connection between Diana and the Witches becomes even stronger.

Aradia is considered a savior to the people during times of persecution. The triad of Diana, Lucifer, and Aradia mirrors the triads of the old mystery cults, perhaps something that is manifesting once again in a new sect.

---

[27] Reginald Scot, *The Discoverie of Witchcraft* (New York: Dover Publications, 1972), 23 - 25.

The gospel does not tell us how this alleged cult initiated its members, but it does emphasize the teaching and worship, the secrecy and sorcery, and other elements that would be expected in a cult of Witchcraft. There is also a strong emphasis on wine, and through the wine, hearkens back to the agricultural nature of more ancient mystery cults. Unlike the virginal Diana of old, the Diana in this work has a daughter like Demeter, is strongly associated with wine like Dionysus, and, like Isis, is not only a great creator and mistress of magic but mates with her brother in a sacred triad as well. [28]

If Leland was creating a hoax, or if he was bamboozled by Maddalena—who was proven in other writings of Leland to have actually existed—the book was woven together ingeniously, and without any apparent personal motive. Leland neither claimed to practice Witchcraft like Gerald Gardner nor was he trying to present a theory within the scientific community like Margaret Murray. He was a folklorist. Folklorists collect folklore. Folklore does not necessarily have to be true or untrue as its authenticity is evaluated according to its continued appearance within the culture being studied. The subject of this chapter is initiation and, unfortunately, Maddalena's gospel does not give us information on this, but it does show how the initiatory cult of Diana may have survived the ages.

Controversial scholar Margaret Murray writes little of Diana in her book though she does acknowledge in *The Witch Cult of Western Europe* that Diana is the female deity of Witches found across Europe and refers to Witchcraft as a "Dianic cult." While Murray's theory of the cult being widespread across Europe may be a reach, the elements and symbolism she uncovered in her research do suggest the survival of ancient mystery religion, including initiation itself. Murray goes in-depth into the "admission ceremonies" of Witches, including vows, covenant, baptism, and the infamous Witch's mark. In her 1931 work, *God of the Witches*, Murray makes reference to a 17th-century witch bearing three

---

[28] Charles Goldfrey Leland, *Aradia, or the Gospel of the Witches* (Edinburgh, London: Ballantyne, Hanson & Co., 1899), 18 - 20, 45 - 50, 101 - 103.

blue marks [29], suggesting a degree system of some kind. While we must take the information gained under torture with a grain of salt, patterns continue to emerge throughout each of these works cited that paint a picture of the survival of ancient rites.

While Murray was celebrated in her day, she was never entirely accepted among scholars of Witchcraft and, by the 1970s, academia had become universally critical of her work. But, in 1989, another scholar's work began to open eyes to the idea that, while Murray might have reached far beyond what could be proven, she had definitely uncovered evidence of the survival of the ancient cult of Diana. Italian historian Carlo Ginzburg released his seminal work, *Ecstasies: Deciphering the Witches' Sabbath*.

In *Ecstasies*, Ginzburg delves into both trial records and the practices of the cults of old to show that what we call Witchcraft may have been the practice of shamanistic techniques—ecstatic methods that survive from the ages of the revelries of Dionysus, Diana, and other gods and goddesses of the ancient world. While *Ecstasies* could be a tool to explore so many aspects of both the operative and religious Witchcraft posited by Murray, for this section I'd like to zero in on a particular commentary by Ginzburg on Diana's cult itself. [30]

We have Witch trial records from 1384 and 1390 of accused Milanese Witches Sibillia and Pierina. What we can gather, collectively, from the two trials, with their often overlapping details, is that both girls claimed to have been members of a society under the leadership of a "Modona Horiente," who was described as "the mistress of the 'society', just as Christ is the master of the world," which certainly sounds like a goddess figure. Modona Horiente is said to have taught the society herbalism, the breaking of spells, divination, communion with animals, and other magical arts. Horiente herself was even said to have been able to restore life to the dead. Ginzburg notes that the friars who recorded the trials

---

[29] Margaret A. Murray, *The God of the Witches* (London, Oxford, New York: Oxford University Press, 1970), 101.

[30] Carlo Ginzburg, *Ecstasies: Deciphering The Witches' Sabbath*, trans. Raymond Rosenthal (New York: Pantheon Books, 1991), 92 - 93.

may have suggested Diana's involvement and Herodias' as well, which, in Latin, sounds quite close to "Aradia," since the girls themselves referred only to Horiente. However, even that shows the role that the Church itself thought Diana played in the works of Witchcraft. Pierina is written to have confessed to "having given herself to a spirit named Lucifello," but Ginzburg speculates that this may have been under torture. I'm not sure I agree on that point. I think what we see here is the Goddess with her consort leading their coven in the ways of magic. At first, both Sibillia and Pierina insisted that what they were doing was not a sin, only later begging for their souls to be saved under the pains of torture, so those details were not merely the delusions of the tortured. Is it possible we have an example of the Cult of Diana at work here? And, as this was referred to as a society, was initiation involved as well? [31]

Over time Diana's recorded role diminished from the annals of Witchcraft, having been replaced entirely by the Devil, but we do have occasional references to the Queen of Elphame or the fairies, perhaps as a memory of the last great goddess of the pagans.

A Path to Modern Magic

The pre-Christian world and its powerful mystery cults vanished from the world for thousands of years. Replacing them were the great cathedrals of the Church and a doctrine served by its new appointed shepherds. The personal empowerment of initiation, and all the doorways into the realms of magic, were closed and locked. Did any of it survive? Was magic passed down in secret? Did cults still thrive in remote regions, or in individual families? Did Witches still move in the woods by the cover of night? These are questions still being asked and debated today. The magical arts survived in manuscripts retained among the educated elite, and even at times, in the Church. We can also be thankful that the Egyptians and Greeks documented many of their rituals, spells, and songs. Many of us learned about the gods of the ancient Greek, Roman, and Egyptian pantheons in our early educations.

---

[31] Ibid, 92 - 93.

The Western magical arts endured in different capacities over the centuries, even through periods when they seemed most buried, suppressed, or lost to the world. If by chance the mystery cults survived in any formal way, I would think it was within the upper class of urban European society. Educated men began to rediscover Hellenistic philosophy and the esoteric sciences during the Renaissance and peaking at various times right through to the occult renaissance of the Victorian era. Some members of the elite even practiced the Arts, though they generally cloaked their practice with their own expertly blended shrouds of Christianity, secrecy, and mystery. It is only logical to deduce that those with money, power, and status would be both better suited and better able to keep and preserve diabolical secrets, preventing them from being lost to time even under the most oppressive circumstances of religious persecution.

However, it wasn't just the urban elite who held onto magical elements of the past. Rural areas long ago syncretized folk customs and traditions with agricultural life, and we still see evidence of these customs in the countless folk festivals still held in Britain today. We can conclude then, that even though they may have fully converted to Christianity, the rural people still kept the knowledge of the land and its old customs alive, and passed this knowledge down the subsequent generations.

Families were also vital in passing down the traditions of old. Many people who were not Witches, but devout Christians, passed down their customs regarding folklore, medicine, and magic. To them, this was just all they knew of the way things had always been done. They were not worshiping old gods or the devil, but sometimes they recognized familiar spirits, who appeared to them like strange ghosts from the past—usually feared, but almost always respected.

The fairy faith is an example of a series of long-held and deeply-rooted traditions. Understandably, because it was the sort of practice kept up and passed on within both cultures and communities. It may be the most authentic form of religious magic to have retained continuity in Britain. Though not officially a religion or a cult, the fairy, or Sidhe, were honored and placated with requests and offerings. Even today, people still go to the fairy trees and tie colored ribbons around them to heal the sick, find love, or petition for general blessings, much like one does when throwing a coin into a wishing well.

The old fairy sites are still visited today with gifts of cream, honey, cakes, and other sugary gifts to appease the fairies. Fairy mounds, or wrath mounds, have a long history in the fairy faith and we now know that many of these are actually pre-Celtic burial mounds. The reverence for these mounds dates back to the druids, who called them Sidhe mounds and believed them to be entrances to the realms of the Gods. This belief was passed on to the present day, and it is said that if one intentionally knocks on the mounds at certain times, they may be granted entrance within, to the world of the fairies. Upon entry into this realm, if one is to eat, drink, dance, or sleep there, they will remain there as a fairy for all time.

Even if the true beliefs of the Sidhe worshipers have been partially swept away, the old mound stories still bear an echo of their magic. The tale of the mounds is an example of the survival of magic in our stories and music, but it is also a story of initiation. After all, once you cross over entirely into the people of the Sidhe, you are one of them forever. Here, initiation is presented as frightening and the description of the fairy troop revelry, although enticing, invokes the image of a Witches' Sabbat in the popular mind. It speaks of a time when magical peoples gathered in secret places filled with mirth and reverence, but the only way to join the party was to become one of them. It is easy to imagine that many would have willingly drunk the mead and danced the dance to be forever free with the fairy people. People naturally wish to escape control and oppression even when they have been conditioned to accept it for generations. Initiation is the key to unlocking the door that was once closed. A door that leads to enlightenment. And it is this same desire that has led so many to the gates of Witchcraft—because Witchcraft offers freedom, power, joy, and personal transformation.

The path to modern Witchcraft may have been heralded with the return of initiation to the West, but the Renaissance, the age of reason and free-thinking, would bring about a multitude of movements and organizations, new ideas, and cultural exploration.

The Secret Orders

In 1717, the order known as Freemasonry became a formal, centralized organization within the ranks of upper-class British society under the umbrella of the Grand Lodge of England. Freemasonry was not a religion—it was a secret society for gentlemen that focused on personal development, intellect, and brotherhood—all aspects that kept it safe from the scorn of the Church.[32] Yet that is not to say it did not have secrets or those mystical elements found only in the art of ritual, for Freemasonry also offered initiation—three degrees, in fact, and each degree was meant to bring the Initiate deeper into the teachings and empower them with new rituals.[33] Although some might speculate on its success, Freemasonry was well-received and is still practiced today.

The origins of the Masonic lodges are obscure, but one of the oldest Masonic documents may hold a clue. An old poem from 1390, known as "The Regis Poem," appears to attribute Masonry to Egypt: "In Egypt, he taught it full wide, in divers lands on every side. Many years afterward, I understand, ere that the craft came into this land. This craft came to England, as you say, in time of good king Athelstane's day."[34] If this poem is accurate in a historical context, Masonry could have pre-Christian origins going all the way back to the time of Euclid in Egypt. Books and documents available for study today on the subject of masonry highlight the Masonic interest in the ancient world, its gods, and the occult sciences. Albert Pike, the sovereign grand commander of the Scottish Rite for 32 years, wrote a hugely influential book on masonry called *Morals and Dogma*, which was once unavailable to the public. Pike states that

---

[32] "History of Freemasonry," *Masonic Service Association of North America*, accessed June 4, 2019, http://www.msana.com/historyfm.asp.

[33] "Freemasonry and Initiation," *Pietre-Stone's Review of Freemasonry*, accessed June 4, 2019, http://www.freemasons-freemasonry.com/Freemasonry_and_Initiation.html.

[34] "The Regius Poem," *Pietre-Stone's Review of Freemasonry*, accessed June 4, 2019, http://www.freemasons-freemasonry.com/regius.html.

Masonry was the successor of the Mysteries, and that it still teaches in the same manner—through initiation.[35]

Pike also explains that the Abrahamic God is the sun, and he likened the moon to a vessel such as those of archetypal Goddess of old.[36] Interestingly enough, in this book, Pike references many pre-Christian gods and goddesses. He mentions Isis approximately 200 times, which is a fascinating connection to the early mystery cults. There is clearly mysticism within Freemasonry, as it offers men initiation and a chance to connect to their occult natures through ritual. The goal of the Masons is self-development and enlightenment, which for a very long time, were not available to the common man in the West. Yet, Freemasonry was only the beginning. Some Freemasons desired to delve further into the depths of the past, and even into the Arts Magical. Over the next several hundred years, many new orders were founded by Masons. Some of the more well-known organizations included the Druid fraternities, the Golden Dawn, the Ordo Templi Orientis, and the Hellfire Club. By then, a new age of magic had returned to the world and the old mystery cults of the Goddess were about to rise again, not with the grand opulence of Roman and Egyptian temples, but with the wild abandon of the more rural cults of Hecate and Dionysus.

Initiation within Witchcraft

The degree system of initiation has existed throughout the ancient and occult world and is also prevalent in modern Witchcraft. When Gerald Gardner referenced his initiation into the New Forest Coven in 1939, he only ever mentions one ritual—that of the First-Degree.[37]

The next account of initiation from Gardner can be found in his book *High Magic's Aid*, published in 1949. Here, he gives us a basic format of the first- and Second-Degree initiation rituals. He then briefly alludes

---

[35] Albert Pike, *Morals and Dogma of the Ancient and Accepted Scottish Rite of Freemasonry*, 2011 E-book ed. (Richmond, VA: Jenkins, Inc., 1944) Loc: 325, Kindle.

[36] Ibid, Loc: 239, Kindle.

[37] Philip Heselton, *Witchfather: A Life of Gerald Gardner, Volume 2 – From Witch Cult to Wicca* (Loughborough: Thoth Publications, 2012), 650.

to a higher degree by having the Witch of the story, Morven, say, "Of the last degree, and I quote, all who have taken the Second Degree are qualified to work it, but 'tis the quintessence of magic, and 'tis not to be used lightly. And then only with one whom you love and are loved by. May it be done. All else were sin."[38]

Did Gardner perform the rite with one he loved, and whom he loved? Or had he been told about this ritual, without having undergone it himself? Of course, *High Magic's Aid* is also a work of fiction, so he may have been properly veiling the higher degree. Regardless, it is clearly stated that the first two degrees are qualifiers for an optional rite. I speculate that the two degrees of Eleusis were the same. The First Degree offered entrance into the Mysteries. The Second Degree brought one further into their depths. And I believe the Third Degree existed for the full-time priesthood of the site. After all, there had to be someone to operate and organize the rituals.

We will most likely never know if the New Forest Coven operated within a three-degree system, though it is very likely. Both Philip Heselton and Doreen Valiente researched and put forth their theories as to who the members of the New Forest Coven may have been and who may have initiated Gerald Gardner. Some of the suggestions they offered included Edith Woodford Grimes, Bernie and Susie Mason, and individuals known only as Rosetta, Fudge, Rosamund, Sabine, and, of course, the oft-mentioned Dorothy Clutterbuck.[39] All of these people have been referenced within research into the New Forest Coven, and all of them seem to have been connected with each other in one way or another. Besides, they all lived in the same approximate area and during the same time period. All of these individuals, who may or may not have been members of the New Forest Coven, were Co-Masons or Rosicrucians, and at least one of them was a ceremonial magician from an offshoot of the Golden Dawn. If the New Forest Coven was a newly

---

[38] Ibid, 388-389.

[39] Philip Heselton, *Witchfather: A Life of Gerald Gardner, Volume 1 – Into the Witch Cult* (Loughborough: Thoth Publications, 2012), 214-215, 218.

established coven, a mere reconstruction of the past, it is possible that its members used their former initiation systems.

In the Masonic initiation systems, there is recognition of one's ranking between the various jurisdictions. For example, if you were initiated within one system or offshoot of the Masonic degrees, but you went to join a new lodge or order, the new organization would often accept you at your current rank within your prior group so long as your previous group gave blessing to your transfer. For example, Aleister Crowley recognized Gerald Gardner's Masonic degrees as being equivalent to the same degrees within Crowley's Ordo Templi Orientis (OTO), and thus Gardner was seen as having achieved the Third Degree in both organizations. This was a common occurrence among magical orders that had branched off from the Masons.[40]

This process was also utilized by Alex Sanders within Witchcraft. Sanders did not re initiate Gardnerians who wished to become Alexandrian, as he deemed it unnecessary. Instead, after they were trained, he considered them Alexandrian. Alex was an occultist, so it seems likely that he would have been aware of the old Masonic practice of recognizing rank within other jurisdictional bodies. Gerald Gardner was also a Third Degree in both Masonry and the OTO so it may be possible that Gardener saw his initiation into the New Forest Coven through the same lens, especially since initiation within secret societies was almost certainly rooted in the mystery cults of old.[41]

Degree-based initiation systems, particularly those with three degrees, were firmly established in all areas of the occult and it is transparent that the founders of the old orders adopted or inherited them from the mystery cults. This might beg the question, are Witchcraft degrees also Masonic? I doubt a non-Witch Mason would believe so, but the Witches I know who happen to be Freemasons accept the connection between the roots of both. Was there a cross-pollination occurring within the New

---

[40] Philip Heselton, *Witchfather: A Life of Gerald Gardner, Volume 2 – From Witch Cult to Wicca* (Loughborough: Thoth Publications, 2012), 350-351.

[41] Philip Heselton, *Witchfather: A Life of Gerald Gardner, Volume I – Into the Witch Cult*, (Loughborough: Thoth Publications, 2012), 67.

Forest Coven? Or is this a case of Gerald Gardner dusting off what he believed was already there?

In mythology, folklore, and trial records related to Witchcraft, the number three comes up frequently. To become a Witch, walk around the Church backward three times at midnight. Receive three marks from the devil. Knock on a wrath mound three times to gain entrance. The number three is ingrained in magic throughout history, so it is not entirely shocking to imagine that it might have also been influential in Witchcraft. Whether as the result of cross-pollination between the various occult orders and Witchcraft traditions or because of their use at specific points in history, a three-degree initiation system continues to be the standard in most covens and magical systems.

When Gerald Gardner established his first covens, the three degrees were at the core of his *Book of Shadows*. All Initiates of Witchcraft accepted the degrees as standard practice, but how Gardner initially distributed them seems to have been a matter of choice and circumstance. Some Initiates were given all degrees at once. Others, he gave the second and third at the same time, and this became his common practice for initiating new high priestesses. Recalling his book *High Magic's Aid*, we know that Gardner discusses the first- and Second-Degree initiations as the keys of entry into Witchcraft, and the third rite as an optional act undertaken by Second Degrees.

The common standard practiced by most Gardnerian Witches today is to separate each degree, usually by a year and a day at minimum. In Gardnerian Witchcraft, the First-Degree initiation inducts you into the cult as a priestess and Witch. With this degree, you are allowed to copy the *Book of Shadows*, attend regular meetings, and receive secret instructions in the arts of Witchcraft. With the Second Degree, you essentially become a coven elder, a privilege which may include an office, such as Coven Maiden or Lieutenant, or assistant to the high priestess or high priest. Members of this grade assist with the training and general operations of the coven and often lead rituals. Different craft lineages may vary regarding the rights and privileges of each degree. At times, Second

Degrees are allowed to form a maiden coven, though this is generally only done for geographic reasons. These maiden covens are extensions of the original coven. They are allowed to operate for the most part independently, but under the guidance of a coven that has an established high priesthood, until the leaders of the maiden coven receive their Third Degree, or the group is disbanded. The Third-Degree initiation is what bestows the title high priest or high priestess, and Third Degrees have the right to form their own autonomous coven for any reason. It is this autonomy of the Third Degree that is most essential and should not be forgotten in the Craft, as I believe it is the one thing that keeps us fertile. A Third-Degree initiate may, however, choose not to hive off and establish their own coven, but instead to remain within the original group as a valuable elder and teacher.

In Alexandrian Witchcraft, we have the same three degrees of initiation as Gardnerians, as we both work from the original *Book of Shadows*. Our second book, however, is further developed and contains additional techniques and invocations not used in Gardnerian rituals. We also have an approach that is different than that of most Gardnerians. We generally perform the second- and Third-Degree initiation rites at the same time, which was the common practice of Alex and Maxine Sanders and their students. The first-degree initiation is one's entry into the Witch Cult itself; the Second Degree is penetration into the Mysteries, and the Third Degree is the celebration of the former two: a seal of power. I am not sure if Alex was taught this practice or if he developed it for himself, but it is interesting that it mirrors the instructions given by Morven in Gerald Gardner's book, *High Magic's Aid*. It is also reminiscent of how Gardner conducted his original initiations, but regardless, it is the Alexandrian method. I was taught that the reason the Second and Third Degrees are kept together is that in truth, there are two sides to every coin: student and teacher, God and Goddess, darkness and light. The third is the seal of power only possible at the right moment. The First Degree brings the Initiate into contact with the fertilizing powers of the Craft, and the second introduces them to the underworld powers. As Alexandrians, we do not see the benefit of leaving our priests of the light captive in the underworld, but there is another philosophical reason. The two sides of the coin approach limits the use of the Second Degree as a carrot on a stick, as Alex felt that this could become a control mechanism rather than a teaching tool. There is no benefit to either the Initiate or the Craft in initiating someone to the Second Degree who will not also receive the third. Keeping the Second and Third Degrees together also keeps pure the boundary between teacher and student. Some covens find it beneficial to give greater responsibilities to their Second Degrees and allow for milestones to be given to the student, but I prefer the cut and dry approach. Another aspect that may enlighten some Initiates is that First Degree Alexandrians can do everything Third Degrees can do, save for initiating to the higher degrees or founding their own covens. For this reason, a Third-Degree can easily start a new coven with a First Degree of the opposite sex. We have many First Degrees who are incredibly proficient in their occult workings and may simply not wish to teach or run a coven. But despite different points of view, all covens Gardnerian and Alexandrian agree that the three rites are necessary in the Craft and that they are all full of potent power.

Witchcraft is a religion. It is a priesthood. And despite the views of modern eclectic Wiccans, park pagans, do-it-yourself roadkill witches, "hereditary" witches, liars, and the Christian opposition, Witchcraft requires initiation and training. We Witches have a legacy that goes back not only to Gerald Gardner and the New Forest Coven, but to the entire golden chain of initiation that has been transferred from western occultism. Ours is the story of humanity's initiation into the realms of magic. It is a story of persistence and survival. It is the true story of Witchcraft. We are firmly established and here to stay, and today there are thousands of Witches around the world sharing in the goal of the Great Work.

A Collection of Coven Photos

Witch Carie Ewers

Witches Carie Ewers and Renaldo Head

Altar Photo

Witches at the Sabbat

High Priest Levi Rowland Hailing the Mighty Ones

Witch Austin Shippey Working the Censer

Witches Elie Barnes and Christian Day Blessing the Wine

Alexandrian Witches Working the Power

High Priestess Christine Stephens at the Mirror of Diana

High Priestess Christine Stephens at an Old Occult House at Nemi, Italy.

High Priest Brian Cain at the Heraklion Archaeological Museum with the statue of Persephone-Isis and Pluto-Serapis with the three-headed dog Cerberus. Found in the Sanctuary of the Egyptian Gods at Gortyn on Crete (Mid-2nd century CE)[1]

---

[1] Carole Raddato, "Statue Group of Persephone-Isis and Pluto-Serapis with Cerberus," *Ancient History Encyclopedia*, May 18, 2019, accessed June 25, 2019, https://www.ancient.eu/image/10673/statue-group-of-persephone-isis-and-pluto-serapis-/

High Priest Brian Cain in a Tribute Photo to Alex and Maxine Sanders

CHAPTER 6

The Goddess of the Witches

You find yourself in a wooded forest. Is this a dream? Did you imagine the flight that brought you here or have you been here all your life? You do know this place; these woods are familiar. The scent of sweet flowers and pine hang in the summer air and soft music echoes in the distance. You are drawn to its melody—a melody of a serene song. You begin to walk through the woods hearing the animal noises and other sounds, following the music until you reach a clearing.

You realize you are not alone. There are many others with you. In silence, you follow the others moving towards a figure in the center of the clearing. The figure is shrouded in white gossamer, shining with the light of the moon that hangs overhead. As you get closer, you hear the haunting voice of an older woman saying, "I am the Queen of all Witches." Yes, you remember, and you know. These are Witches, and you are one of them. The woman before you is veiled. Her voice begins to soften into the sweetness of a young girl. It continues to flow like music. It was her words that brought you here—words filled with both power and beauty.

She continues, "I will teach you things yet unknown." Yes, you think. "Yes," escapes your lips. This is why you have come here—to learns the Arts Magical from this Witch queen.

Her voice turns to a stern boldness as she proclaims, "And ye shall be free from slavery." The shimmering gossamer gown seems to fall away, and before you stands not a crone, not a young girl, not a Witch of your imaginings, but a goddess: ancient, strong, and bold. She is naked, yet even without her gown, the moonlight dances on her skin. She wears a silver crown shaped like a crescent moon, and a jeweled necklace. Her hair is as dark as midnight and the soft locks flow over her shoulders. You catch her gaze, and her deep, piercing eyes startle your heart. You are looking into the eternal. These are not mortal eyes. She is ancient. Images of this goddess once adorned the most magnificent temples in the world. Her palace is set among the stars. The kings of the Earth once bowed before her and she had priests to carry out her daily worship. How did this great ancient queen find herself here in the woods as a forbidden mistress of Witches?

She says to you, "I have been with thee from the beginning." Her eyes are filled with love and compassion, like those of a caring mother, and you begin to well up with tears of joy and happiness, for you know she is the mother of all living things. This is the Goddess of Witchcraft. She exists in the depths of history, myth, and folklore. In some periods she was the Queen of Heaven, in others a demoness. The Church strove to erase all memory of her from the world, and for a time, she seemed to slip away into some forgotten fairy realm.

Our goddess was introduced to the modern world alongside the religion of Witchcraft by Gerald Gardner in his first nonfiction book, *Witchcraft Today*. This was her débutante ball, if you will. Up until this point, ideas of Witches and goddesses were often dismissed as products of myth and superstition, but through Gardner's work, the Witches' Goddess was reintroduced into Western society as its first modern pre-Christian image of the divine feminine. The Goddess of Witchcraft was worshiped in the ancient world and remains a powerful presence today because this primordial force was resurrected and made relevant again. The modern Witch cult had emerged—stepping out of the shadows of the Church ready to reclaim its station at the right hand of the great Goddess.

Witchcraft and its Goddess were breaking news in the 1950s. Both emerged from their relative anonymity at precisely the right time—just as the people of a Christianized Europe felt desperately in need of a divine feminine to empower them, free them, awaken their sexuality, and root them in the natural world. At the time, this was a revelation, and it would draw the attention of thrill seekers, occultists, skeptics, rivals, and those on the path of initiation. Today, formal Witchcraft exists throughout western civilization and has manifested covens in most European and English-speaking countries.

The Craft has its own culture, and our Goddess has secret names and core qualities. She is the Goddess of magic, fertility, sacred marriage, motherhood, sexuality, and the Mysteries, but more than anything, she is Goddess of the moon, which serves as her primary symbol. To Witches, the Goddess appears young and beautiful, as she is the embodiment of eternal life and fertility. However, she also controls the ebbing tides and the waxing and waning forces of nature. In this role, she sometimes assumes the form of the great sow and terrible hag queen.

A Witch priestess dresses in different manners to represent the Goddess during ritual. Sometimes, she might be crowned like Diana, veiled like Isis, wear jewels like Ishtar, or even wear nothing at all. Symbols more secret, and known only to Initiates, are used in her worship. The modern Witchcraft priesthood originates in Britain; therefore, its cultural roots are British and not purely Celtic, Saxon, or Roman. Witchcraft is also a mystery cult. Our Goddess is a Goddess of Initiates, not a goddess of a long-lost tribe or extinct people.

From an occult point of view, the Goddess of Witches is a monotheistic one. We can find her face in the divine feminine in every form. For example, she is Athena, and she is Demeter. Neither of these goddesses would strictly be considered goddesses of Witchcraft. However, they do share commonalities with her. Because of her monotheistic nature, our Goddess is all-encompassing.

The Moon Goddess

The moon has always been the primary symbol for the Goddess of Witchcraft, and it is by the moon that you will often discover her face in pre-Christian peoples. Isis, Diana, Artemis, Astarte, Hecate, Selene, and Luna are just a few examples of moon goddesses who remain popular among Witches and magicians today.

The moon is associated with both magic and the occult, and it symbolizes the inner planes and the spiritual matters of man. It is a nocturnal light that we see in the sky. From our earliest primal roots, Witchcraft (and religion in general) would have been primarily explored at night. Daylight hours were too precious and necessary for survival, especially when winter was right around the corner. During the daylight, you were able to gather, hunt, and eventually plant and harvest. You were very busy working so that you could eat and live. The evening hours would be the natural time you had to reflect, to commune, to celebrate, and to work magic. This is why the sun is the physical manifestation, and the moon is the spiritual manifestation in Witchcraft.

Women's menstrual cycles also last approximately 28 days, linking them to the moon by those early peoples who made such a connection to the moon's own monthly cycles. The association may also explain the moon's early association with fertility. As the full moon resembles the womb of a pregnant mother, it is easy to imagine the sympathetic link associated between the moon and the Goddess as a life-force.

It was also by the moon that we developed some of the earliest calendars as a way of measuring time and marking the seasons. These calendars were oriented to the moon, as evidenced by their 28-day cycles. This is where the word "month" originates. The lunar calendar had 13 moons, or months, and it was only when we switched to a solar-based calendar that twelve months occurred. Now, we occasionally have what is called a blue moon: a time in which a twelve-month year has an inescapable thirteenth moon cycle.

Witchcraft is a lunar cult, and our Goddess is and always has been the moon. The coven traditionally consists of a number between three and thirteen Witches, in honor of the three phases of the moon and the thirteen moons of the old lunar calendar.

The Triple-fold Goddess

The triple-fold or three-fold goddess is a trinity made prevalent within the practice of modern Witchcraft and Goddess worship. In Witchcraft, she is synonymous with the moon goddess, represented in her three aspects of a maiden, a mother, and a crone. The Maiden is represented by the waxing moon, the Mother the full moon, and the Crone the waning moon. The terminology of maiden, mother, and crone is in part a modern construct; however, the archetypes themselves are found deep within antiquity.

The current theory put forth by would-be occult historians is that the triple Goddess is simply an invention of Robert Graves in his book *The White Goddess*, but this is a reductive viewpoint. The Triple Goddess did not always assume roles associated with a woman's aging process, although this is not entirely unheard of. Isis, in her part as a trickster, comes to the aide of her son Horus to secure his throne during a divine tribunal of the gods, but Set tries to keep her from attending and forbids her from coming onto an island.[1] In this myth, she transforms into both a crone and a beautiful maiden to make her entrance.

The goddess Hera had three temples at Stymphalus--one each for Hera the child, Hera the wife, and Hera the widow.[2] In Sparta, Hera's three aspects were war, sovereignty, and cultivation.[3] Homer called her

---

[1] "Isis the Trickster Goddess," *Isiopolis*, accessed June 10, 2019, https://isiopolis.com/2012/09/01/isis-the-trickster-goddess/.

[2] Adam McLean, *The Triple Goddess: An Exploration of the Archetypal Feminine* (Grand Rapids, MI: Phanes Press, 1989), 72.

[3] Joan V. O'Brien, *The Transformation of Hera: A Study of Ritual, Hero, and the Goddess in the Iliad* (Lanham, MD: Rowman & Littlefield, 1993), 130.

golden-throned Hera, white-armed Hera, and Hera the wife or sister.[4] Clearly, Homer was talking about Hera the queen, Hera the warrior, and Hera the wife or sister of Zeus. We can see in Hera's transformation that she had, through the course of time, slowly lost some of the ancient roots that likely originated in the old lunar cults and contained trinity goddess elements, but Hera is not the only Triple Goddess found within the Hellenistic world. Hecate and the later Trivia were often depicted with three-faced statues called *Hecataea* or at times appeared with the heads of dogs, snakes, and lions.[5]

Mythologically, the Triple Goddess is also linked with other goddesses forming trinities such as Demeter, Persephone, and Hecate. In this example, Hecate serves as the wise counsel, advice giver, and initiator who helps guide Demeter into the underworld to aid in the rescue of her daughter Persephone from Hades. Persephone is the Maiden, Demeter the Mother, and Hecate can easily be linked to the modern-day Crone archetype. Other examples of triune goddesses are Selene in heaven, Artemis on Earth and Hecate in the underworld. In this trinity, Selene represents the celestial world, Artemis the natural world, and Hecate the underworld.[6]

In all artwork from the ancient world, Hecate is depicted as young and beautiful in all her aspects. She was, however, unquestionably associated with the underworld, which has led to her more modern association with the crone or dark goddess.

Some of our most exceptional examples of triune goddesses can be found in Celtic lands. In the Irish invasion stories, Amergin the bard encounters the three goddesses of the land of Ireland. These goddesses are called Ériu, Banba and, Fódla, who decreed that they would bless Amergin if the land itself would be named after them. Ériu is still the origin of the name Ireland that we use today, and means the "land of

---

[4] Ibid, 135.

[5] Adam McLean, *The Triple Goddess: An Exploration of the Archetypal Feminine* (Grand Rapids, MI: Phanes Press, 1989), 67.

[6] Ibid, 62-63, 67.

abundance."[7] Another triune goddess found in Ireland is the Morrígan, whose name means "great queen." She is described often as three collective goddesses named Badb, Nemain, and Macha. These goddesses are associated with both battle and magic.

The most popular Celtic triple goddess is, without a doubt, the Druid goddess Brigid. Brigid was clearly a Witchcraft goddess in her creative aspects of poet, healer, and smith, all of which were seen by the Druids as part of the magical arts. In the Celtic world, these aspects covered the full range of the true magician. The poet possessed memory and a creative process from which could flow forth spells, songs, invocations, and even curses. Only the smith knew the arts of the elements necessary to arm the tribes by creating weapons and jewelry, and therefore represented manifestation. The healer, who carried the knowledge of the often-elusive properties of plants and medicine, represented the life-giver.

In one Scottish myth, Brigid is held hostage as the personification of spring by an old goddess of winter known as the Cailleach, who is one of the few goddesses actually depicted as a hag or crone. Cailleach's son Angus falls in love with Brigid and eventually rescues her.[8] Although this is a seasonal tale and similar to that of the myth of Hades and Persephone, it also serves as an example of the triple nature of the Goddess in that Brigid plays the role of both maiden and queen while the Cailleach represents the withered crone.

At the Roman baths in the English city of Bath, carvings were discovered representing the three goddesses known as the three matres or matronae, an image found throughout Europe and dating as early as the first century CE[9] This triune goddess may be an earlier depiction of the Celtic goddess Sulis before she was Romanized as Sulis Minerva. Sulis shares attributes with the Goddess Coventina, both being goddesses

---

[7] T. W. Rolleston, *Celtic Myths and Legends*, 1990 ed. (New York, NY: Dover Publications, 1990), 132.

[8] "Brigit," *Druidry*, accessed June 3, 2019, https://www.druidry.org/library/gods-goddesses/brigit.

[9] "Bath—Aquae Sulis," *Cornwall School of Mystery and Magic*, accessed June 11, 2019, http://cornwallschoolmysteryandmagick.uk/bath-aquae-sulis.

of place and both being patrons of "both eye ailments and female disorders."[10] Coventina has often been depicted as three nymphs, which helps strengthen the case that Sulis is the Goddess in the carvings. Sulis was the local Goddess of Bath and its surrounding landscape and held associations with healing as well as the darker aspects of retribution. Many curse tablets, the majority of which were addressed to Sulis, have been discovered at the site of the ancient spring found within the complex.[11] Perhaps the three aspects of Sulis were nature, healing, and justice.

Mythology and folklore around the world are filled with examples of ancient trinities of female power, such as the three fates, the Norns, the Gorgons, and the three Marys of the Bible. I speculate that this trinity had its origins with the moon goddess of the old lunar cults and she continues to be worshiped today as the Goddess of the Witches.

The Goddess of Magic

Another vital marker of the Witches' goddess is magic. This is often forgotten. She is the queen of all Witchery, the great magician, a sorceress in her mythology whose stories highlight a proficiency for spell casting that is also reflected in her priesthood, which often comprises skilled magicians. Examples include the priests and priestesses of Isis who were known for spell-craft and healing, the Druids who invoked Brigid, and the Welsh bards who sought the cauldron of Ceridwen for the magic of inspiration. In Norse mythology, she is Freyja, the rune mistress and enchantress, patron of healers and seers.

Witches today still assemble for Hecate at the crossroads and take flight at night with Diana—not just for worship or to bow down before the Goddess of the ancient world, but also for the magical powers which she bestows upon those who serve her. We invoke the Goddess in part to bring down power into our circles and in part to penetrate the secrets she offers those seekers who would know her magic. This connection

---

[10] James MacKillop, *Myths and Legends of the Celts* (New York, NY: Penguin Books, 2005), 126 - 127.

[11] Ibid, 127.

with magic is vitally important for it is the gift the Goddess has given to all mankind.

For example, in one folktale, the Goddess Diana grants her daughter Aradia the ability to gift those who conjure her the magical powers to curse, bless, heal, see the future, and manipulate spirits, animals, and the weather.[12] Diana was also associated with the Queen of the Fairies (who is referred to as the Queen of Elphame in Scottish witch trial documents). People still make pacts with the fairies and their queen to manipulate the events in their world. One must simply traverse modern-day Wales or Ireland to discover that the magic of the Fairy Queen is alive and well.

The Goddess in Polytheism

Witchcraft is directly responsible for the emergence of modern Neo-Paganism, women's spirituality, and the Goddess movement's rise in popularity today. The published works and many media appearances of the early Initiates inspired many non-Initiates to create their own groups, but it was Initiatory Witchcraft that was and is at the core of this entire counterculture revival of the divine feminine.

It is a bit ironic that the divine feminine has reclaimed her throne in the West through Witchcraft. Before modern Witches, the West had been left only with the Virgin Mary and a few female saints. Today, polytheism has had a revival in Western society, and people worship many goddesses. Many people have reconnected to European religion and have begun to reconstruct its ancient practices inspired by either their ancestral roots or a culture they feel an affinity toward, such as Celtic, Germanic, Greek, Roman, and Saxon.

As a result of this cultural reclamation, specific goddesses such as Freya, Lilith, or the Morrigan might have devotees who are not Witches. These people often consider themselves pagan. Some of them do practice magic and also identify as Witches or Wiccans. However, Neo-Pagan may be a more suitable term for them. Polytheism is not the Craft, for

---

[12] Charles Godfrey Leland, *Aradia, or the Gospel of the Witches* (Edinburgh, London: Ballantyne, Hanson & Co., 1899), 14-15.

the polytheist sees each god and goddess as unique and separate while the Initiate understands that all goddesses and all gods are but visages of the core divine feminine and masculine.

Moreover, unlike many polytheist groups, we are not an ethnic faith. I personally think that ethnically-rooted religions can sometimes be a bit dangerous. They have a tendency to breed nationalism, racism, and other forms of bigotry. If you are a part of something simply because of your skin color, your ethnic makeup, or your cultural identity, you may come to see everyone else as an outsider. The Craft teaches reincarnation, and so it does not give preference based on ancestry; our ancestors are spiritual, and all Initiates may tap into them.

Witchcraft is a scavenger religion. We use what works. And yes, we do at times go down the rabbit hole of polytheism in our work with Gods outside of our traditional practices because Witches know these gods to be manifestations of the original primordial duality. But we also know that when you're working intently with a specific aspect of deity, that face becomes very real to you and those specific aspects become crucial to the work and worship at hand. The God and Goddess play different roles through the many faces they wear just as we do in our own lives. You might be someone's mother or sister, lover, student, employer, or friend. We each play different roles to different people, but those who are truly close to you see you in all your complexity and are able to discern the core within you.

Those devoted to a goddess or even many goddesses are not necessarily worshiping our Goddess of the Craft because their idea of that goddess is different from our framework and relationship. The Goddess of Witchcraft is not in their heart or mind. From our point of view, they are blindly working with one of her many faces, but to an initiate, she is all things and wears all faces. We must remember that this is not true for everyone. Some non-Initiates do seek to work with the Witch's goddess because of her magical nature or because they are already on the path of initiation and have just not arrived home yet. The Witches' Goddess will make contact on the inner planes when the time is right. Those who seek to work Witchcraft, yet have not received initiation or training, will often just refer to our deities as simply the God and Goddess, Lord and Lady, or they will work with one of her more popular public faces such as Diana, Hecate, or Isis.

The Goddess in the Stone Age

Sewing together the quilt of our goddess' history is no small task. One might call it impossible. Her sources are ancient, with roots as far back as the Stone Age. Discovered in approximately 22,000 BCE, the Venus of Willendorf is one of the oldest female forms ever noted. Archaeologists found this artifact in 1908 and suggested that it was a fertility figure or a goddess of hunter-gatherer tribes.[13] Hundreds of these types of female images have been discovered throughout the ancient world, which makes it clear that the female form was directly linked to fertility and that the earliest known prominent deity of mankind was most likely a Goddess.[14]

Early peoples understood the role of the fertile female as essential for their survival. Since our Gods are Stone Age in origin, we call Witchcraft "the Old Religion." It is not because we suffer from a delusion that our religion has an unbroken continuity, but because we worship the oldest gods in the world, the divine at the heart of every faith.

With the evolution of religion, and as time went on, more and more gods and goddesses were interpreted by the human mind. While most religious people turn to officiants to learn the will of the Gods, in Witchcraft we penetrate to the very heart of the divine to meet our own spiritual and mundane needs and to truly understand the requirements put in place by the Gods and our role in fulfilling the Great Work. The Goddess represents life and the God represents death and in them are revealed all the cycles of nature. This is why the early Goddess was based on fertility and the reproduction of animals, plants, and humankind,

---

[13] "Venus of Willendorf," *Great Discoveries in Archaeology*, accessed June 12, 2019, http://anthropology.msu.edu/anp264-ss13/2013/03/28/venus-of-willendorf/.

[14] "Paleolithic Art," *The Columbia Encyclopedia*, 6th ed. (Columbia University Press, 2018).

while the God was based on hunting and embodied qualities of both protector and provider as necessary.

Magic was the first element of religion and, like love, the Goddess gave it to us because she wants us to be both abundant and happy. The worship of magic continued throughout the ages, and those who could wield it have always been revered and feared. Such reverence for magic gave rise to the first Witches. The magician priests of the stone age mother and the old gods they worked with share DNA with the Goddess of the Witches we worship today.

The Goddess in Early Civilization

Our record of the Goddess prior to the birth of civilization is limited to the evidence of archaeological digs and cave paintings. The cradle of civilization, also known as the fertile crescent, includes civilizations that sprung up around the three great rivers in Africa and the middle east—the Nile, the Euphrates, and the Tigris. This region contains Upper and Lower Egypt and Mesopotamia, and in these great cultures, the Goddess took on several forms which all share a common thread. Nut, Aset (Isis), Ishtar, Inanna, and Astarte are the oldest goddesses associated with magic, love, fertility, the moon and female sovereignty. They belonged to the Egyptians, Sumerians, Akkadians, Assyrians, Babylonians, and Phoenicians who greatly influenced the religions of Persia, Greece, and Rome, and it was these mighty cultures who then, in turn, spread the mystery cults of the old Goddess around the world.

The Goddess of the Tribes

While the Goddess was well established in the cradle of civilization, Mesopotamia, and Egypt, she was just as crucial to the migrating Indo-European peoples and tribes. This migration took place about 1800 BCE and began with the Greeks, Germans, Italics, and Celts, then later included the Slavs and Scythians. The waves of these tribal migrations are in truth not easily separated, for in reality they once intermingled and overlapped, eventually settling in their respective locations and evolving into distinct cultures and language groups. The Greeks were greatly influenced by the Phoenicians from Mesopotamia and the Egyptians. They then, in turn, influenced the Romans, who would go on to influence the world.

While some tribal peoples have left little in the way of written records, we do know that the last of the tribes in the West consisted of Celtic and Germanic groups. The Celtic tribes developed complex religious systems and a sophisticated priesthood: the Druids. We have limited knowledge of the Druids, but we do know they worshiped goddesses and that matriarchy held some prominence in the Celtic family and pantheons. The Celts revered major goddesses such as Don, Danu, Brigid, Epona, and the Morrigan. Ireland bears the name of a Goddess, according to legend, and Britain would eventually be personified as Britannia, a female form of power and a representation of the nation. Like the Greeks, the Celts associated the land and the moon with the divine feminine by virtue of their naming. Did the Druids also have the heart of the Mysteries that would be celebrated within a Greek understanding at Eleusis, or was it something introduced at a later period? We will probably never know. What we do know is that both the nomadic Celts and their Druid priests exchanged wisdom with the Greeks and other cultures and that they originated somewhere in the east.

Rather than following a matriarchal and lunar religion, the Germanic and Norse tribes developed a more warlike patriarchy in which the gods were mostly warriors, and the most rewarding afterlife of Valhalla was reserved only for those who died in battle. However, this is not to say that they were entirely male-oriented, as they did feature such goddesses as Frigg and Freya, but they were capable warriors as well.

When the Roman Empire finally encroached upon the tribes and began conquering the Germanic and Celtic areas, they brought with them the syncretically-minded approach of Hellenistic religion, which led them to merge the tribal gods with their own. Despite the distortion that comes from so many centuries of the syncretization of gods and goddesses by so many cultures, the core concepts of the ancient and primordial God and Goddess remain. Our great mother still retains her core fertile, lunar, and magical qualities today.

The goddesses of the tribes were often localized, often named in some way for the land that a tribe occupied. A goddess may even be named after a particular hill or river. But regardless of her many names, it is not difficult to discover her visage still cloaked in the ancient magic that is her gift to humanity. Every tribe had its magical people who also worked with the Gods and spirits of the ancient Craft, even if they called them by their own chosen names and clothed them in the vestments of their respective cultures.

Iconic Witch Goddesses

I have mentioned many goddesses in this chapter, and though I cannot do them all justice, I am going to explore several of the more influential goddesses in-depth, chosen because they share many of the archetypal virtues necessary to be considered a Witch Goddess.

Ishtar

Ishtar began as an Akkadian goddess identified with the Sumerian goddess, Inanna.[15] Ishtar, like Isis, would later absorb other goddesses and take on new names, eventually becoming the most important goddess in Mesopotamia and Babylon. Ishtar was worshiped as a goddess of the new moon, but she has also been called the Queen of Heaven who ruled over the sun, stars and other luminaries.

Ishtar was also syncretized with the planet Venus, which gave her dominion over love. Being a goddess of the new moon, love, war, and magic, she was unique in that no other goddess of this period fits the many-faced archetype of the Witches' Goddess quite like Ishtar. She was depicted as naked, jeweled, and wearing a crescent moon on her head. Her symbol was an eight-pointed star, and her animals were the lion and scorpion, which also links her to the Egyptian goddesses Bast, Sekhmet, Hathor,

---

[15] Henk Dijkstra, *History of the Ancient and Medieval World*, vol. 2 (New York: Marshall Cavendish, 1996), 225.

and Isis.[16] However, her most crucial link to the Craft can be found in the myth of her descent into the underworld. In the myth, Ishtar's lover Tammuz had died and was taken by the Gods into the underworld. In her grief and mourning, Ishtar descended to the land of the dead and at the gates, demanded entrance, seeking to free Tammuz. Ereshkigal, queen of that domain, denied her entrance, yet Ishtar persisted, threatening to break down its gates and raise the dead to feast upon the living. Thus, the queen of the underworld bid let her enter.

Once inside, Ishtar had to pass through seven portals, and at each portal, she had to remove her jewels and another garment until she was completely naked.[17] She thought that after she passed through each of the seven portals, she'd be able to free Tammuz, but instead, the Goddess of the underworld cursed her and Ishtar was trapped, helpless in the underworld. Since she was the Goddess of fertility and love, her absence from the world was problematic. If she remained in the underworld, it would mean winter and despair would reign forever in the world above. The high gods desired to restore the balance, so the waters of life were sprinkled upon her and her lover, Tammuz, allowing them to leave the realm of the dead through the seven portals and reclaim each of Ishtar's garments and jewels until she was completely restored in time to enter the world once more.[18]

Ishtar's initiation into the seven portals of the underworld—which undoubtedly represented the seven planets—truly cemented her role as both Queen of Heaven and Queen of Hell. There is also obvious agricultural symbolism represented here, given Tammuz's identity as a sacrificial god of both death and resurrection. Their story mirrors that of Isis and Osiris and is a powerful myth that emerges within all mystery cults. We find it again with Persephone and Hades, and even in Celtic

---

[16] Louise Pryke, "Ishtar," *Ancient History Encyclopedia*, May 10, 2019, accessed June 17, 2019, https://www.ancient.eu/ishtar/.

[17] Louise Pryke, *Ishtar*, 2017 E-book ed. (New York and London: Routledge, 2017), Loc: 2123, Kindle.

[18] Ibid, Loc: 2236, Kindle.

countries with the tales of Brigid and Cailleach. Modern Initiates have their own myth descended from these same stories.

Ishtar might have simply faded away if not for her Phoenician incarnation, Astarte, who was also called Asherah by the Hebrews and Ashteroth by the Canaanites, and she retained all the qualities of Ishtar.[19] After Alexander the Great defeated the Persians and liberated Phoenicia, Ishtar's successor Astarte became Hellenized and was henceforth strongly syncretized with both Artemis and Aphrodite. When Alexander died, Phoenicia fell under Ptolemaic rule, and the Alexandrians associated the Goddess with Isis-Aphrodite.[20] The Cult of Astarte did not spread into Europe (save for a slight romance with Greece and Italy), but it was quite popular in the Mediterranean world, having temples as far as the island of Malta.[21]

I think it is essential to realize that the archetype of the Witches' goddess once prevailed as the Goddess herself in ancient civilizations: not obscured, not hidden, but as the overarching, supreme goddess of those civilizations. Ishtar is the earliest example of a goddess associated with both the moon and the planet Venus, a concept which would go on to influence Western occultism and Witchcraft up to the present day.[22]

Isis

Isis has been actively worshiped for over 4,000 years. The daughter of Geb and Nut, and sister to Osiris, Set, and Nephthys, she has been called the first queen of Egypt, the wife of Osiris, mother of Horus and mother or stepmother to Anubis. Her ancient Egyptian names were Aset, Eset, Iset, Au-set, Aut, Anqet, Hent, and Heqet. Isis has long been a goddess of Eg

---

[19] Morris Jastrow, Jr. and George A. Barton, "Astarte Worship Among the Hebrews," *Jewish Encyclopedia*, accessed June 20, 2019, http://jewishencyclopedia.com/articles/2048-astarte-worship-among-the-hebrews.

[20] "Isis," *Center for Hellenic Studies, Harvard University*, accessed June 19, 2019, https://chs.harvard.edu/CHS/article/display/6542.6-isis.

[21] John Day, *Yahweh and the Gods and Goddesses of Canaan* (London and New York: Sheffield Academic Press Ltd, 2000), 129.

[22] Janet & Stewart Farrar, *The Witches' Goddess* (Custer, WA: Phoenix Publishing, 1987), 104-105.

ypt, with stories reaching so far back that one of her many early names was "Africa."[23] Her symbol was the throne, and it was said you could not rule without her; for this reason, she was of continued importance to the pharaohs and Roman emperors.

It was in the city of Alexandria (built by Alexander the Great and his lover Hephaestion), that the pharaoh Ptolemy the First would raise Isis above all the other gods and create a new Hellenistic Egyptian empire in which the Goddess ruled supreme. Alexandria was a Greek city on Egyptian soil, and Ptolemy was its second Greek pharaoh, following Alexander the Great, who liberated Egypt from Persian oppression and was crowned pharaoh as a result. Ptolemy, in his efforts to merge his people, needed to find a way to Hellenize the gods of the Nile. This proved to be problematic, as the chief god of Egypt had for thousands of years been Ra, a sun god, and the Greek equivalent to Ra was Apollo, but Apollo was not the chief of the Greek gods. That role was claimed by Zeus, whose Egyptian equivalent was Amun.

Ptolemy found a faithful friend in the Goddess Isis, for as pharaoh she was his divine mother, so he set up Isis as the chief goddess, and most of the Egyptian pantheon was swept under her figure in Alexandria. This was not a problem for local Egyptians, as Isis was the mother of all and had always been popular amongst the people.

To the Greeks, Isis was Hellenized as the new Athena, Aphrodite, and Demeter. Her husband Osiris was transformed into Serapis and given a unique Hellenistic appearance for people of a Greek mind. Serapis may not have gained popularity in native Egypt (as the Egyptians preferred Osiris proper), but among the Greek empires, the cult of Isis and Serapis seemed to flourish. Serapis was an exotic Zeus, but Isis gave the Greeks something they may have found lacking in their native goddesses—a universal woman, lover, mother, queen, warrior, healer, and magician. She offered true goddess power without bending the knee to her husband.

---

[23] deTraci Regula, *The Mysteries of Isis: Her Worship and Magick* (St. Paul, MN: Llewellyn Publications, 1995), 74.

Isis also enshrouded her own mysteries behind her famed veil, and some believed that the rites of Demeter centered in the Eleusinian Mysteries originated in Egypt. Isis was also the Goddess of Magic and magic was openly practiced and sought out at her temples. This would have been of particularly great interest for would-be magicians and healers in the European world, which was how the Isiac cult was born as one of the world's first cross-culture religions. In Alexandria, Isis would become the Goddess of 10,000 names. She absorbed Maat, Hathor, Bast, Aphrodite, Athena, Dea, Hera, Demeter, Hestia, Astarte, Pelagia, Fortuna, Inanna, Nike, Tyche, Maia, Nanaia, Persephone, and Selene, and these other goddesses became acceptable names of Isis in her Isiac cult.[24]

It was common in the Hellenistic world to erect temples to hybrid gods, such as Isis-Aphrodite or Athena-Nike. In Alexandria, the Isiac cult centered at the Great Library which was the mainstay of the city and was presided over by Isis and Serapis. In the Greek world, Isiac temples held statues to Isis, Serapis, Horus/Harpocrates, and the guide Anubis/Hermanubis. Anubis curiously held onto his ancient role in the Isiac cult, instead of being absorbed. This may be in part because Isis was at times said to be his mother or foster mother.

The Ptolemies contributed to the expanding worship of Isis by making her a monotheistic goddess in Egypt. All goddesses were Isis, and all lands equally belonged to her. It is said that Initiates who had to travel back to foreign lands were instructed to worship Isis by the name in which she was known to the local people. If this is true, it means that in the Isiac teachings, the spreading of their message was more important than the persona or recognition of Isis.

The last Ptolemy, and last pharaoh of Egypt, was Cleopatra. No other person contributed more substantially to the worship of Isis than Cleopatra, who was believed to be the living incarnation of the Goddess. She called herself "New Isis" and her lover Julius Caesar, father of her firstborn son, was Osiris or Serapis. Her other lover, Marc Antony,

---

[24] Ibid, 74-79.

was likened unto Dionysus,[25] and their two children were Alexander Helios and Cleopatra Selene.[26] In the Hellenized Egyptian mythology, Dionysus was one of the consorts of Isis, and they were the parents of Helios or Apollo and Selene or Artemis.

It is imperative to understand that Cleopatra, Marc Antony, Julius Caesar, and Augustus were the celebrities of their time in the Roman world, as Rome was a vast empire. After the murder of Julius Caesar and the ensuing civil war and death of Marc Antony and Cleopatra, Augustus became Rome's first official emperor. At this time, the Republic of Rome had fallen, and for the very first time in hundreds of years, Rome had a king of its own. The Republic was founded on overthrowing a tyrannical king, so this must have been a worrying course of events for most people.

Imagine being a free citizen of Rome, ruled over by a senate. Freedom is a virtue of your culture. You are taught from a young age that Romans are not meant to have kings or emperors, yet suddenly you have one in Augustus. Julius Caesar (who, ironically, and unknown to the common people, actually helped lay the foundation for the Empire), and Marc Antony are celebrated heroes to your people, and both have just been brutally assassinated by the Senate. Then you start to wonder—were Julius Caesar, his great friend Marc Antony, and their exotic lover-queen Cleopatra, all murdered by this new emperor?

We must remember that many of the inhabitants of Rome witnessed the parade-like celebrations of these individuals. They knew them and loved them, and admiration of Greece and Egypt was also very cosmopolitan in Roman society. Caesar erected the first temple of Isis in Rome and within that temple was a statue of Isis in the image of Cleopatra. The famed queen is said to have ended her own life, and the new Roman Empire later destroyed the Temple of Isis in Rome and banned the cult of Isis entirely. The cult of Isis and the Goddess Isis herself began to be suppressed. Isis, the Goddess of 10,000 names, the goddess worshiped in Egypt, Greece, and then Rome, was now the figurehead of a banned cult.

---

[25] Stacy Schiff, *Cleopatra: A Life* (New York, NY: Hachette, 2010), 169.
[26] Ibid, 193.

But the cult continued meeting in secret among Roman Initiates. By taking her own life, Cleopatra may have snatched victory from Augustus, but she also entered the hearts of his own people as Isis.

Eventually, Augustus died, and future emperors who favored the cult of Isis restored her temples and built new ones all over the world. Emperors such as Caligula and Hadrian became Initiates and active devotees of Isis. Caligula saw her as Isis-Diana. At Lake Nemi, called the mirror of Diana, he sailed great barges and held ceremonies to Isis.[27] The Temple of Pantheon supported by Hadrian had statues of all the Gods, and it was rumored that the statue of Venus wore earrings cut from a pearl that once belonged to Cleopatra.

How did Isis manage to seduce so many emperors? The answer is actually quite simple. She justified their status not only as kings but as god-kings—something she had done for pharaohs for thousands of years.[28] The Goddess whose mysteries were sparked in the cradle of civilization, who was worshiped for thousands of years in the ancient lands of Africa, made seafaring by the Greeks, and had her throne set in Delos, Delphi, Eleusis, Athens, and Alexandria, was fully embraced as the new Mother of Rome.[29] As a Roman goddess, Isis became monotheistic and went on to spread her wings all over the world.

The cult of Isis remained powerful in Alexandria, parts of Greece, and all over the Roman Empire. In harbors, you can find evidence of her influence from the Arabian Gulf to the Black Sea. She had followers in Gaul, Spain, Pannonia, and even Germany. She was worshiped in Arabia, Asia Minor, Portugal, and Britain.[30] There is even remote evidence that

---

[27] John M. McManamon, *Caligula's Barges and the Renaissance Origins of Nautical Archaeology under Water*, Ed Rachal Foundation Nautical Archaeology Series (College Station, TX: Texas A&M University Press, 2016), 47.

[28] R.E. Witt, *Isis in the Ancient World*, Johns Hopkins Paperback Edition, 1997 ed. (Baltimore and London: Johns Hopkins University Press, 1971), 50.

[29] Ibid, 20-21, 50.

[30] Ibid, 21.

she may have been worshiped by the Viking tribes, where Isis replaced or was equated with Freya by a tribe called the Rus.[31]

The Isiac cult of Alexandria established priesthoods and temples in all of the major capitals of the world. It was a flourishing mystery religion offering many people a new way of life. The priests of Isis brought with them to their temples water from the Nile, sacred cats, language, art, knowledge of medicine and magic, female empowerment, and a foreign mystery cult that increasingly became cross-cultural. Isis was for everyone. Interestingly, it is even theorized by some that we owe the widespread domestication of cats to the temples of Isis. Whether or not this is true, it is without question that the Isiac movement had a lasting effect on Europe.

It is said that when Christianity was rising in the Roman Empire, its only real competition was Isis and evidence of this can be found in her Christian syncretization with the Blessed Virgin Mary. The symbols of Mary still mirror those of Isis today: Images of Mary enthroned with the baby Jesus, Mary standing on the moon, Mary with serpents, and Mary decorated with stars are all prominent symbols shared by the mothers of Horus/Jesus. Isis, Goddess of 10,000 names, is also Mary.[32]

Isis remains the great Queen of Magic. She is Queen of Egypt, Greece, and Rome. She is Isis of every land and people. She holds all the attributes of the Witches' Goddess. She is Moon Goddess, nocturnal sorceress, fertile mother, nurturing healer, naked lover, majestic queen, and persecuted Witch.

HECATE

Hecata, or Hecate, has been translated to mean "worker from afar."[33] She was an obscure Greek goddess of magic, the underworld, and initi-

---

[31] deTraci Regula, *The Mysteries of Isis: Her Worship and Magick* (St. Paul, MN: Llewellyn Publications, 1995), 146.

[32] R.E. Witt, *Isis in the Ancient World*, Johns Hopkins Paperback Edition, 1997 ed. (Baltimore and London: Johns Hopkins University Press, 1971), 216-217.

[33] "Hekate," *Theoi Greek Mythology*, accessed June 14, 2019, https://www.theoi.com/Khthonios/Hekate.html.

ation. She was also a goddess of the moon, doorways, crossroads, ghosts, fairies, and otherworldly spirits. Hecate was at times descended from titans, and like most of the gods, existed before the pantheon of Olympus.

Like many goddesses associated with the moon, Hecate is depicted as a triple-fold or triune goddess. As mentioned earlier in this book, moon goddesses were often portrayed as triple-fold to represent the waxing and waning cycles of nature or the transformative power of the divine feminine. Having six hands, four torches, and sometimes other items such as pitchers, bowls, knives, and keys, Hecate's images hint at her archetypal properties. We know she was historically invoked for magic, divination, and unearthly communion with spirits.[34] She was also a guide not only for travelers and the dead but also for Initiates into the Mysteries.

Hecate's original aspects may have become obscure over time, as her imagery is often merely shown as three identical women without explanation, but her aspects may be hidden in her depiction as having three animal heads: that of a horse, a dog, and a lion—the three types of beast. The horse is a domestic herd animal, and in Greek mythology the moon goddess Selene drives a chariot drawn by horses. It represents nobility, travel, and triumph. The horse can be seen as a symbol of community by tribes and early civilizations. The dog represents the underworld, hunting, and magic, and is often depicted alongside the Greek goddess Artemis. The dog is both a scavenger and a faithful companion. The lion is an ancient goddess symbol representing power, wealth, and dominion, and its pelt was worn by both Hercules and Alexander the Great.

Whatever Hecate's original aspects might have been, they were often conflated to become triune with other Greek and sometimes Roman goddesses. Hecate, or Trivia in Rome, was associated with Artemis,

---

[34] Arthur Fairbanks, *The Mythology of Greece and Rome* (New York: D. Appleton, 1907), 138-139.

Selene, Demeter, Persephone, and Diana.[35] In Rome, she was fused with Diana, as Diana Triformis.[36]

Hecate was a goddess of fringe places, as were Pan and Dionysus. She was sometimes even feared for her moonlit spectral haunts and wild, ghostly hunts. To the Greeks, she was likened to the dark side of Artemis and associated with the new moon. Yet, she was also held in the highest regard by those who wished to work the magical arts and she was often invoked for spells of love, power, and destruction.[37] Some of Hecate's more popular devotees were the sorceress Medea and the courtesan Simaetha, and she is a central figure in the *Chaldean Oracles*, all of whom invoked her for their spells, rituals, and prophetic works.[38][39]

Hecate certainly had a magical following in the ancient world, but what I find most remarkable is not her shadowy presence in the Mysteries of Eleusis, nor her high-profile magical patrons, nor am I bedazzled by her modern witchy aesthetic. What I find most powerful and potent about Hecate is that she is still relevant today. Modern Witches from all over the world incorporate her into their rituals, worship, and spells. At present, Hecate may have a broader world stage than any of her Olympian counterparts. Even in this book, she has risen far above her ancient station. Hecate is no longer a Greek goddess or a titan, but a goddess of Witchcraft to the world.

Today, Hecate's roles differ from those of her past incarnations. She is often depicted as a crone, an archetype less relevant in the ancient world when she was portrayed by the Greeks as a beautiful virgin or maiden. Yet, when conflated with other goddesses such as Persephone and Demeter,

---

[35] Matthew W. Dickie, *Magic and Magicians in the Greco-Roman World* (London: Routledge, 2001), 100, 104.

[36] Janet & Stewart Farrar, *The Witches' Goddess* (Custer, WA: Phoenix Publishing, 1987), 125.

[37] Arthur Fairbanks, *The Mythology of Greece and Rome* (New York: D. Appleton, 1907), 139.

[38] Matthew W. Dickie, *Magic and Magicians in the Greco-Roman World* (London: Routledge, 2001), 104, 107.

[39] Ruth Majercik, *The Chaldean Oracles* (Leiden: Prometheus Trust, 2013).

and viewed through the lens of modern traditions, the image of Hecate as the hag of the underworld is not so farfetched.

Like Isis, she is a goddess of many faces worshiped today as a representative of the Goddess by Witches, invoked by magicians, and called on by those drawn to the necromantic persuasion. She continues to shine at crossroads as a beacon for those who dare penetrate the darkest of mysteries.

Brigid

A Celtic goddess and Catholic saint of Kildare, Brigid is a goddess of fertility, agriculture, livestock, smithcraft, poetry, inspiration, music, healing, light, fire, heavenly luminaries, magic, sacred wells, and fairies. The goddess Brigid's origin first appears in the stories of the Tuatha Dé Danann, the people of the fairy mounds. Her father was their last king, the Dagda, whose name means "good god," and her mother was the Morrigan, whose name means "queen" or "great queen." (The Morrigan was, incidentally, also a three-formed goddess, and it is speculated that her name may have been a title.) [40]

Originally a Druid goddess, Brigid's aspects centered around magical skills, smithing, poetry, and healing—which were all sciences and arts essential in Druid craft. But she was also a magical goddess and even as a saint, stories of her life contained narratives of people going to her and asking her for spells, specifically love spells. [41]

Brigid may have been one of the Druids' primary goddesses, but her original name is lost to time. "Brigid" means "high one," which may have been commonly used as a title just like "the Morrigan." The Druids followed an oral tradition, so they had secret names for many things including the Gods, and Brigid was likely the common name used among non-Initiates, much like Adonai is used by Jewish people to represent their god. There are many variations of her name found across the Celtic

---

[40] Brian Wright, *Brigid: Goddess, Druidess and Saint*, 2011 E-book ed. (Gloucestershire: The History Press, 2009), Loc: 484-501, Kindle.
[41] Ibid, 2397, Kindle.

regions of Europe, though it is without question that the final seat of her cult rests in Kildare, Ireland. It is from Kildare and its many legends that we acquire much of the information we know about her. She has been called throughout Europe Brigit, Bríg, Bride, Bricta, Brixta, Brigindona, and Brigantia. By the Romans, she was called Britannia, which shares the same root word as the name Britain.[42]

Brigid has strong associations with fire, light, and dairy. Her Celtic festival of Imbolc or Oimelc ("ewe's milk") is the time when the sheep's milk comes. This festival occurred traditionally around February 1st and was transferred to her saintly incarnation as Brigid's Day.[43] This was the first Celtic spring festival, and modern Witches have come to associate it with their Sabbat of Candlemas, with Candlemas also being the name of a Catholic holiday. Modern Witches share many feast days with the Church, as they are pre-Christian in origin, with Brigid's day being a perfect example. The Witches' Sabbat inspired renewed interest in Brigid as a goddess and not just a saint. Today, many Witches celebrate the folk customs of Brigid in their rites.

Brigid is a very magical goddess, and like other modern incarnation of the Witches' goddess is triple-fold, something that typically is identified with deities of the moon. However, many folklorists and students of the subject believe that Brigid was a sun goddess and not a moon Goddess, though, in truth, there is proof of neither. I believe the assumption that Brigid was a sun goddess is based on her association with the Druids and with fire and light. The Druids have been typically labeled a sun cult, although in truth they were equally focused on all heavenly bodies. The Druids understood the course of the sun and the moon as well as other visible luminaries.

While many of Brigid's more obvious attributes may be connected to the sun via her association with other gods and with the radiant solar light so often associated with Christian saints, I believe that there are

---

[42] Sumathi Ramaswamy, *The Goddess and the Nation, Mapping Mother India* (Durham and London: Duke University Press, 2010), 93-94.

[43] Brian Wright, *Brigid: Goddess, Druidess and Saint*, 2011 E-book ed. (Gloucestershire: The History Press, 2009), Loc: 2112, 2125, Kindle.

also clues to Brigid's role as a lunar goddess as well. Directly associating her with either the moon or the sun requires a bit of speculation, but she is without question, a goddess of light and luminaries. Out of the five primary goddesses I focus on in this book, Brigid is the only one whose lunar association can be called into question. As I have mentioned, Witchcraft has its origins as a lunar fertility cult, so it is of importance to find these connections when defining a Witchcraft goddess.

In the end, we may never truly know for sure whether Brigid was a lunar goddess, but I will present the following clues to the reader to help determine whether they have any substantial merit. Either way, I have chosen to include Brigid the High One, because I believe she was a Witchcraft Goddess to the Gaelic-speaking world. There are many prayers and folk spells that invoke Brigid, and they help shed some light on how people once viewed or worked with the Goddess. For example, one such spell for churning butter has a line that reads, "She who puts beam in moon and sun."[44]

Another curious custom is that of the moon board. On Brigid's Day, pieces of the feast, made in the shapes of the moon, the sun, and the stars, were placed on the board, and the board itself was put over a doorway with prayers said over it. The origin of this folk spell is unknown, but it demonstrates a link to the heavens. Whether or not this was celestial or just symbolizing the Christian heaven, we do not know.

The most compelling evidence of Brigid's lunar association comes from her nocturnal vigils held by nuns. Legend says that in Kildare, a perpetual flame was kept burning. The flame was surrounded by a circular hedge of willows. Willow happened to be the Druids' moon tree. No male was allowed entrance into this hedge.[45] One night, every 20 days, the flame would be left unattended after offering the words, "Brigid, tend that fire of thine, for this is thy night."[46] The nuns were keeping a faded practice alive, one that had belonged to their predeces-

---

[44] Ibid, Loc: 2944, Kindle.
[45] Ibid, Loc: 1695, Kindle.
[46] Ibid, Loc: 1687, Kindle.

sors, the priestesses of Kildare. Was this in memory of the moon cycles? We must remember that these nuns were Catholics. What night did they not hold vigil? Was it the new moon or the full moon, or was it a remnant of some long distant memory? The nuns of Kildare have been numbered to include seven, nine, or nineteen women, which may also bear significance.[47]

My husband Christian and I had the pleasure of visiting Ireland and Kildare and whilst there, we made it a point to visit sacred sites whenever possible. All across Ireland, we visited as many stone circles, fairy mounds, and sacred groves as we could, with Kildare being one of our last stops on our journey. I can say Ireland is the most goddess-oriented place I've ever been, rivaling even Athens. If imagery was not of the Virgin Mary, it was of Brigid. I only remember seeing one Saint Patrick statue and I never saw any Jesus statues anywhere I went, not even of baby Jesus. In matriarchal Ireland, Mary seemed to be without her young companion.

Throughout Ireland, my husband and I visited several sacred groves, wells, and grottoes to Brigid. Often, there would be fairy trees near these places. One site had a beautiful, giant effigy of her within a glass shrine, around which people had inscribed the names of their dead loved ones on stones. Nearby, there was a grotto with a sacred wishing well featuring many lit candles, photos, mementos, and offerings to this goddess and saint. Kildare, in particular, felt like a pinnacle of the Goddess energy and without question, it still belonged to Brigid. I remember noticing in the middle of the town square there was a giant statue to Brigid, and nothing about it looked Catholic or Christian. She was a woman holding a flame, nondescript, and without crosses. Her iconography was all over the city, making it clear that Brigid is still the Goddess of Kildare and therefore, one of the most impressive living examples of a Western goddess.

She has never given up her seat of power, even after becoming veiled as a saint. She is worked with today by Witches, modern Celtic re-constructionists, Catholics, folk magicians, and even members of Voodoo communities. Witches have embraced HER as an icon of ancient female

---

[47] Ibid, Loc: 1687, 1697, Kindle.

power, and within HER, we see the ancient goddess of Witchcraft deeply entrenched into the landscape of the British Isles.

Diana

Diana, the virgin goddess of nature and the moon, whose temple was placed on the Aventine Roman hillside, is a daughter of Jupiter and Latona, a twin sister to Apollo, and a high goddess of Rome who is believed to have been Etruscan in origin. She may originally have been an older Indo-European goddess sharing roots with the Sumerian and Greek Danae and the Phoenician and Greek Dione, who was also a Titaness and mother of Aphrodite. The Celts also had variations of this early Indo-European goddess: Danu, Don, Damona, Damnu and Arduinna may all be variations or incarnations of the same goddess.

Diana means "divine" or "heavenly." The root can be found in the Indo-European word, "di," which means "bright" or "shining."[48] The Gaelic words *Dianna* or *Diona* mean "divine" or "brilliant," furthering the connection.[49] The Roman Goddess Diana was acquainted with many other goddesses in the Hellenistic world including Artemis, Selena, Luna, Astarte, Hecate, and even Isis. This evolution can be found in the Temple of Ephesus, one of the seven wonders of the world.

In the Temple at Ephesus, Diana replaced a hybrid of Artemis who had already merged with an early matriarchal fertility cult. In Greek culture, Artemis had previously been associated with Astarte and later, with Isis. There were temples to Isis-Artemis already established, and because of Diana's association with Artemis, she was also a face of Isis in the Roman mind.[50] In Ephesus, both Artemis and Diana were transformed from chaste virgins into sexual and fertile mothers. A separation began to occur between the pure and virginal official Roman state Goddess Diana and

---

[48] Doreen Valiente, *An ABC of Witchcraft Past and Present* (New York, NY: St. Martin's Press, 1973), 113.
[49] Janet & Stewart Farrar, *The Witches' Goddess* (Custer, WA: Phoenix Publishing, 1987), 215.
[50] R.E. Witt, *Isis in the Ancient World*, Johns Hopkins Paperback Edition, 1997 ed. (Baltimore and London: Johns Hopkins University Press, 1971), 150.

Diana, the more sexualized and fruitful mother Goddess. The dilemma was eventually solved by Roman emperors who became Initiates of the Cult of Isis and other mystery cults—and thus discovered the great mystery that all goddesses are one. Nero, Hadrian, and Caligula were all known devotees of the Mother Goddess Cult and significantly contributed to the syncretization of Isis with existing Roman goddesses such as Diana.

From her Indo-European roots to her status within the Empire, Diana had been firmly established in the Western world and was recognized and revered by the common folk. As Isis, she was worshiped and adored by Initiates of the Mysteries, but as Diana, she was the familiar face of the ancestral goddess of Europe. The most fascinating visage of Diana came to exist after the fall of the pagan world to the rising tide of Christianity. This was when the Medieval Diana and her mythic Witch cult emerged. She was called both a goddess of Witchcraft and the last pagan goddess by the early Christian Church (see "The Cult of Diana" in Chapter 5). Diana and her Medieval cult of Witches are obscure and difficult to trace over time. History paints the picture that pre-Christian religion vanished like the dinosaurs overnight and without fanfare. This is highly unlikely and illogical, but Church propaganda was not challenged until the present day.

References to a goddess implied that the Church was talking about a pagan sect, but it is even more telling that Diana was the first deity to be described by the Church as the leader of the witches, a role that would later be assumed by the Christian devil. This incarnation of Diana was a lady of forbidden diabolical gatherings. Even if one makes trial references to Diana out to be mere fantasy, it is clear she existed at least in the consciousness of Medieval and early-modern times. This suggests that whether the cult was current or fictitious, it was rooted in reality at least at one time or another. I am of the opinion that such a cult did exist and has since retained a level of subversive survival. Diana was the primary goddess to exist in Medieval literature about Witchcraft.[51]

---

[51] Carlo Ginzburg, *Ecstasies: Deciphering The Witches' Sabbath*, trans. Raymond Rosenthal (New York: Pantheon Books, 1991), 90-91.

Her character was a new Hecate and a shadow of her former Isiac glory. Her other names and associated titles included Herodiana, Herodias, and Abundia, or Queen of the Fairies.[52]

Diana was speculated to have once been worshiped throughout Western civilization as the Goddess of magic and Witchcraft. She was ingrained into medieval mythology—feared and, perhaps, also revered by those who still honor the old ways. At first, she was clearly demonized by the Church, but perhaps when those methods became ineffective, she was replaced by the Devil and transformed into an incarnation of the Blessed Virgin Mary. In this way, the Virgin Diana and Isis, the mother of god-kings, were officially merged into the mother of Christ. Today, Diana is not worshiped in the Roman way, but as a goddess of Witchcraft who has a unique history in the modern Witchcraft revival.

As a result of Charles Leland's book *Aradia, or the Gospel of the Witches*, which I explore more deeply in Chapter 5, Diana and her daughter Aradia—considered to be the first Witch within Leland's work—were connected to some of the early traditions of Witchcraft and its literature. Gerald Gardner and Doreen Valiente undoubtedly used Leland's work in the formation of the Witches' *Book of Shadows*. Today, many traditions work with either Diana or Aradia, and Aradia could even simply be another name for Diana. Today, Diana is invoked for all different kinds of magical petitions and her worship centers around the moon. In Witchcraft, she is not typically seen as a virgin, but as a mother archetype and as a goddess of the moon. In this way, she has retained aspects of her former incarnations of Isis and Hecate.

The Goddess of Witchcraft has secret names known only to Initiates, but she also has many names by which men have known her. She is Ishtar, Isis, Hecate, Brigit, Diana. She is the moon, the Earth, and the waiting sea. She is the great Initiator and the keeper of the Mysteries, and when

---

[52] Doreen Valiente, *An ABC of Witchcraft Past and Present* (New York, NY: St. Martin's Press, 1973), 114.

you work with the Goddess of Witchcraft, you are tapping into the primordial fountain of all magic.

CHAPTER 7

The God of the Witches

The God of the Witches conjures within many of our minds the horned, winged, and cloven-hoofed image of Baphomet made famous by 19th-century occultist Eliphas Levi. We see the mischievous devil in the woods worshiped by naked witches frolicking in savage revelry, the shadowy man in black at the crossroads, the black goat, the black dog, and Pan, the satyr-like lord of nature. The God of the Witches is all of these things and much, much more. He begins his journey in the Stone Age, prevails in the classical age, and exists within the darkest fringes of our primal natures. In Christian society, our God was the boogie man of its socially-unacceptable outskirts. Today, we might find him somewhere between the tales of folklore and the worship he receives at the hands of today's Witches. These Witches refer to him as the Horned One or the Horned God, and Witches teach that his iconography is shared with the Devil, and it is. But this is not the Devil or Satan as we know him from the Bible, but the folklore devil of Medieval Witchcraft who dances with his witches in a magical circle at the edge of the woods.

The God of the Witches is the other half of our Goddess. He represents the primal instincts within all of us—he is nature, he is all power, and he is all-powerful. Within Witchcraft, he has numerous names of power used by Initiates, however, he, like the Great Goddess, has worn many faces throughout the world. In this chapter, we are going to explore the journey of the God of the Witches and how he continues to manifest himself before Witches today.

The Horned God

It would be impossible to study the subject of Witchcraft and not encounter the Horned God, for he appears throughout the history and folklore of Witches, though he has often worn veils stitched together by the propaganda of other faiths. But who is this iconic deity and what are his origins? Why does his image still survive despite so many attempts to portray him as demonic and—worse—as a trivial parody? What story can history tell us of his transformation from a god of the hunt and nature into the malevolent red devil seen in countless kitschy illustrations today?

The story of the Horned God began in Paleolithic times, when humankind first learned to use tools to reason with the environment around them. They looked to the sky and to the Earth for answers to the age-old question: why am I here? And early peoples learned not only to survive but also to use magic—to employ the powers within to impact the world outside of themselves.

The hunt was an extremely essential ritual for the people who lived in this period, especially those in climates with harsh winter months. The hunt provided the people with food, clothing, tools, weapons, and even shelter. A successful hunt meant life would be good and that the god of the hunt had blessed the tribe; however, if the hunt failed, it could mean death and even the extinction of the people. Early peoples were primarily nomadic hunters and most of the animals they hunted had horns, so it makes sense that they would associate horns with concepts of the divine. They believed that they required the grace of the divine to ensure the success of the hunt. Combing through the stories of many early cultures gleans many examples of the Horned One emerging universally as a figure of importance. In *The Witches' God*, it is written that "Of the male god-forms of history, one predates agriculture by countless thousands of years; he has survived indestructibly in harmony with it, and in spite of monotheist attempts to banish him. That is the Horned God of Nature."[1] A number of early cave paintings feature images of beings adorned with animal skins and wearing horns. One such famous image was discovered in the Trois Frères, a cave in Ariège in southern France.[2] Such paintings depict the very earliest recorded Witchcraft rituals in which, using a form of sympathetic magic, a priest would become possessed by a spirit or god. His fellow hunters would then dance around him with weapons, chasing him, and eventually symbolically killing him. This act of ritual magic not only honored the spirit of the hunt, but also ensured a successful one.

The Horned One was one of the earliest faces of the male divine. He was the son, protector, and lover of the life-giving Goddess. In their original aspects, the God and Goddess represent the two sides of nature—life and death—which are both necessary for all fertile, flourishing life. When agriculture and pastoralism became prevalent and hunting lost some of its importance, the Horned One's role was not diminished, but it did shift in various ways. In some cultures, he appeared as a god of shepherds, taking on names like Pan or Faunus, and retaining his role as lord of animals. In this role, instead of ensuring the success of the hunt, he was responsible for blessing the herds with protection and fertility. In the ancient rituals of sympathetic magic, the hunter and the hunted became symbols of sacrifice and resurrection to pray for a good harvest, but in its later incarnations, the continued magic of life and death was adapted to evolving circumstances.[3] The Horned One transformed from the spirit of the slain animal to that of the shafted wheat and first fruits. Evidence of this transformation lies in the fact that many harvest gods

---

[1] Janet & Stewart Farrar, *The Witches' God* (Custer, WA: Phoenix Publishing, 1989), 32.
[2] Margaret A. Murray, *The God of the Witches* (Oxford: Oxford University Press, 1952), 23.
[3] Rene Alleau, *History of Occult Sciences* (London: Leisure Arts, 1967), 14.

often retained their horns, or at least, an association with horned animals. Gods like Dionysus, Bacchus, and the Green Man are all perfect examples of this.

Although the Horned One found new ways to present himself before a changing and evolving people, he retained aspects of his former self; these survived through the myths of the Wild Hunt found across Europe. Artemis, Diana, Apollo, Hecate, Odin, Woden, Gwyn ap Nudd, the Green Knight, Herne the Hunter and the archangel Gabriel have all been connected to spectral hunts that take place under cover of night. Once again, the old magic of the hunter and the hunted and of life and death had to take on a new shape—and it did, through a divine-led procession of the dead searching for lost souls to take back with them into the underworld. For example, in Windsor forest, Herne the Hunter is said to appear on a horse and wearing a crown of stag antlers.[4] He is accompanied by red-eared hounds, and sometimes even other riders. Legend has it that on long winter nights, one can hear him blow his hunting horn to a chorus of howls from the hounds of hell who accompany him. Some say he appears in times of national crisis, and to others, he is an omen of death.

In Wales and Glastonbury, there is a similar myth about the god Gwyn, or Gwyn ap Nudd. In the tale, he leads his Wild Hunt on Samhain, and on this night, he hunts for the lost spirits of the dead so he may guide them to the underworld.[5] The idea of the "wild hunt" is extremely fascinating because it has nothing to do with either survival or fertility. Rather, this hunt is about the spiritual journey of death—the passage between the worlds of the living and the dead—and how the Horned One becomes a psychopomp of this process.

In Celtic culture, the Horned One may have had countless names, as we do not know what most of the Celtic gods looked like. However, the most popular and well-known Celtic god is Cernunnos, which

---

[4] Margaret A. Murray, *The God of the Witches* (Oxford: Oxford University Press, 1952), 34.
[5] "Samhain at the Gates of Annwn," *Eagles and Dragons Publishing*, accessed June 19, 2019, https://eaglesanddragonspublishing.com/.

means "horned one." In Gaul, a single ancient altar preserved his name; images of this horned god have been found throughout Celtic Britain and Europe, with numerous artifacts and places retaining his image or variations of his name.[6] Other Celtic gods that may have had horns include Taranis, Camulus, Antenociticus and Oisin.

One of the most important artifacts depicting the Horned God is the Gundestrup Cauldron. This silver ritual object, discovered in a peat bog in Denmark, had depicted one of the Horned God's more famous images within; scholars typically identify it as Cernunnos.[7] The deity is sitting in the lotus position, crowned in antlers, and wears a Celtic torc round the neck with another in his right hand; a great horned serpent is in his left. He is shown next to a life-giving Goddess crowned and cupping her breasts. In images of a goddess associated with this Horned God at other sites, there are what appear to be pomegranates,[8] perhaps associating her with the Underworld—the land of the dead. This fruit is oft-associated with that realm, and their presence reinforces the connection with its horned god. The Gundestrup Cauldron clearly enshrines the Horned One as an important chthonic god. Julius Caesar remarked that the Gauls all claimed descent from Dispater, the Roman equivalent of Hades.[9] Although we cannot say for sure who this god actually was, he may have been the god found within the Gundestrup Cauldron.

In ancient Egypt, horned gods were widely prevalent; some of the animals most sacred to the culture were goats, rams, and bulls. Khnum was one of his earliest incarnations, and in Lower Egypt, he appeared

---

[6] Janet & Stewart Farrar, *The Witches' God* (Custer, WA: Phoenix Publishing, 1989), 97-99.

[7] "The Gundestrup Cauldron: Largest and Most Exquisite Iron Age Silver Work in Europe," *Ancient Origins*, accessed June 14, 2019, https://www.ancient-origins.net/artifacts-other-artifacts/gundestrup-cauldron-largest-and-most-exquisite-iron-age-silver-work-europe-020989.

[8] Miranda Green, *Animals in Celtic Life and Myth* (London and New York: Routledge, 1992), 227.

[9] Julius Caesar, *"De Bello Gallico" and Other Commentaries of Caius Julius Caesar*, ed. Ernest Rhys, trans. W. A. Macdevitt (New York: J. M. Dent, 1915), 121.

as Banebdjedet, the "Ram Lord of Djedet,"[10] who was later known as the Goat of Mendes.[11] Some occultists have even suggested that Banebdjedet may be the origin of Levi's Baphomet. Though the chief of these Egyptian horned gods was undoubtedly Amun—who later became Amun-Ra, a hybrid between Amun, the fertility god of Thebes, and the Sun God, Ra—the most important horned god in all of Egypt was Osiris, the lord of death and resurrection. Osiris played a highly significant role in Egyptian religion. He was king of the underworld and governed the afterlife, yet he was also the Apis bull associated with the fertility of the Nile River itself.

When Alexander the Great conquered Egypt, he further developed the narrative of the Horned One by creating a new cult and hybrid deity, Amun-Zeus, and like the pharaohs before him, Alexander assumed the role of a living god. He was often depicted wearing the ram horns of Amun, from whom he claimed descent. In the Koran, Alexander was called *Dhu'l Karnain*, "the Two-Horned."[12]

Eventually, the Horned God and all of his faces became demonized. Horns were once a symbol of holy power, but they began to take on a more sinister role when the popular image of the Biblical Devil and his association with Witchcraft entered the public consciousness. In time, the Old God would escape the clutches of the Church and once again reclaim his rightful place as the old God of Witchcraft. The Renaissance period marked a time of true rebirth. The philosophies of the Renaissance, which included humanism, naturalism, and neo-Platonism all sparked renewed interest in the ancient world within philosophers and fueled their early whispers of the Old Gods. Later, it inspired the occult revival of the 19th century, and it was here that the Horned God's cloven hoof took its first steps into a new world.

---

[10] Joshua J. Mark, "Egyptian Gods – The Complete List," *Ancient History Encyclopedia*, April 14, 2016, accessed June 20, 2019, https://www.ancient.eu/article/885/egyptian-gods---the-complete-list/.

[11] Eliphas Levi, *Dogme et rituel de la haute magie*, 2nd ed. (Paris : Germer Bailliere, 1861), 93-98.

[12] Margaret A. Murray, *The God of the Witches* (Oxford: Oxford University Press, 1952), 25.

In 1854, the occultist Eliphas Levi created the image of Baphomet that is still used today. It is important to note that even though this image is clearly a hermaphrodite (bearing traditionally male and female genitalia simultaneously), it is a modern-day example of the resurgence of not only Witchcraft but of the Horned God.

The Victorian era fostered a new love for nature. The Old Gods became the favorite subject of artists, poets, and theatrical performers. To this end, the gods found a place in pop culture, and a favorite of the period was Pan, who in many ways is the perfect herald of its magic, as he represents both nature and sexuality.

THE Gods are dead: no longer do we bring
To grey-eyed Pallas crowns of olive-leaves!
Demeter's child no more hath tithe of sheaves,
And in the noon the careless shepherds sing,
For Pan is dead, and all the wantoning
By secret glade and devious haunt is o'er:
Young Hylas seeks the water-springs no more;
Great Pan is dead, and Mary's Son is King.

And yet—perchance in this sea-trancèd isle,
Chewing the bitter fruit of memory,
Some God lies hidden in the asphodel.
Ah Love! if such there be then it were well
For us to fly his anger: nay, but see
The leaves are stirring: let us watch a-while.
~Oscar Wilde[13]

In 1931, Margaret A. Murray published her book, *The God of the Witches*. This thought-provoking work is in part responsible for the rebirth of the Horned God and has certainly influenced his presence in the modern-day

---

[13] Oscar Wilde, Complete Poetry, ed. Isobel B. Murray (Oxford, England: Oxford University Press, 1998), 29.

Craft. This is not to say that Mrs. Murray pulled Old Horny out of her hat, but she did put forth the idea that the Devil of the European witch hunts was a misrepresentation of the old God.

In 1951, Gerald B. Gardner published *Witchcraft Today*, and in doing so, launched the British Witch cult now known as the religion of Witchcraft. This modern cult of Witchcraft has become a recognized world religion by many, and the chief God in Witchcraft is the Horned One, so it seems as if this ancient God not only survived Christian Europe, but has experienced a rebirth as the world's most popular pre-Christian God.

The Sun God

In modern Witchcraft, the Sun God is merged with the Horned God and is perhaps best recognized in the form of Baphomet, and is symbolized by the Sabbatic goat with the candle or torch placed between its horns. These aspects of the God often seem very separate, but are at times quite unified. This may appear to be a concept unique to modern Witchcraft, but it is actually found in antiquity.

An early example can be found in stories of the God Amun-Ra. Amun was depicted as a ram, and he is the original goat of Mendes. Ra was the sun itself. At night, he was the nocturnal, hidden God Amun, but by day, he was the magnificent, glorious Sun God Ra.

Witchcraft is a lunar cult, and the primary companion to the moon goddess is the Horned God who is represented by the sun—her polar opposite in the sky. He is also often seen as her twin, or sometimes as her child. This ancient trinity of mother, lover, and child can also be found in Egypt through the story of Isis, Osiris, and Horus, in which Osiris is both the brother of Isis and the father of Horus. Osiris is a horned god of the underworld, but Horus is a god of the sun and resurrection—the solar form of Osiris Risen. This very much mirrors how Witches see their God today, even when he is cloaked in Celtic garb or that of whatever culture the witch is drawn to.

Throughout history, many cultures have viewed the moon and sun as lovers, siblings, or parent and child; these have included those of the

Greeks, Romans, Germanics, Celts and even certain Native American tribes, like the Choctaw Indians, who once lived in the area of New Orleans.

Some of the sun gods of old include Helios, Sol, and Apollo, among others. In Charles Godfrey Leland's *Aradia, or the Gospel of the Witches*, the Goddess Diana is the twin sister to Lucifer, a name generally associated with Satan or the Christian Devil.[14] In *Aradia*, reference is made to him being driven from Paradise. This would seem to insinuate that it is indeed the Devil that they are speaking of, but it also appears that Diana's original brother Apollo may have been merged or confused with the Devil of the Bible. *Aradia* compares Lucifer to a mouse being chased by the cat Diana. Interestingly enough, white mice were sacred to Apollo and kept in his temples. One of his titles was even *Apollo Smintheus*, or, "Apollo the Mouse."[15] Given that the only other brother Diana has ever had is Apollo, one can easily speculate that Lucifer is actually the more modern face for that ancient Apollo. Lucifer means "light bearer," and was the Roman term for the planet Venus—also known as the morning star—which is itself another name for the Devil. I don't think it would be much of a stretch to say that perhaps Lucifer was another name for or an aspect of Apollo, or a god that replaced him in Medieval Witchcraft and mythology.

Leland's *Aradia* is not the only source suggesting Lucifer's connection to Witchcraft. In some Italian witch trial records, a spirit (and possible sun god) called Lucifello presided over the game of Diana, suggesting that he may have been actively worshiped alongside Diana.[16] In the modern Craft, our god is the Horned One, although we do draw upon his aspects as the fiery god of the sun at certain seasonal rites. In our faith, he is born at the winter solstice and grows into manhood by the

---

[14] Charles Godfrey Leland, *Aradia, or the Gospel of the Witches* (Edinburgh, London: Ballantyne, Hanson & Co., 1899), 1-2.

[15] Doreen Valiente, *An ABC of Witchcraft Past and Present* (New York, NY: St. Martin's Press, 1973), 31.

[16] Carlo Ginzburg, *Ecstasies: Deciphering The Witches' Sabbath*, trans. Raymond Rosenthal (New York: Pantheon Books, 1991), 93.

summer solstice. These solar rites echo the ancient rituals of the sun gods and continue to be a window into his mysteries today.

Iconic Witch Gods

Just as I did in Chapter 6, I am going to explore some of the more noteworthy gods that embody the archetypal virtues of the Witches' god.

Amun-Serapis

Amun-Serapis is a deity I am pleased to include as a God of Witchcraft. His importance and his iconography have been overlooked for far too long, and he has been profoundly influential within the mystery cults, as one of its most magical horned gods. Amun-Serapis is actually a conjunction of three different gods: Amun, Osiris, and Apis.[17] Hybrid gods were widespread in the ancient world and represent how ideas about the gods evolved throughout various cult centers. "Amun" means "hidden one;" Osiris, "mighty one;" and Apis, "sacred," as in, "sacred bull," and all of these names have significant meaning in Witchcraft today.

Amun was one of the oldest and most important horned gods of ancient Egypt. He was a ram-headed god of reproduction, fertility, wind or air, agriculture, time, magic, and prophecy, whose cult was centered in Thebes.[18] Amun went on to merge with several gods but never lost his place at the head of the table. Over time, he was incarnated as Amun-Ra, Amun-Zeus, Amun-Jupiter, and Amun-Ra-Serapis, as well as, Amun-Serapis.

After the Persian Conquest, Egyptian religion was suppressed, but in 332 BCE Alexander the Great liberated Egypt from the Persians. The Greeks believed their gods and those of Egypt were the same, so they syncretized Amun with Zeus. The new Pharaoh, Alexander, was proclaimed the son of Amun and it was in his Egypt that Amun-Zeus

---

[17] Stefan Pfeiffer, "The God Serapis, His Cult and the Beginnings of the Ruler Cult in Ptolemaic Egypt," in *Ptolemy II Philadelphus and His World*, ed. Paul McKechnie and Phillipe Guillaume (Leiden: Brill, 2008), 390.

[18] Eleanor Harris, *Ancient Egyptian Magic* (Newburyport, MA: Weiser Books, 1998), 143.

was created, eventually becoming Amun-Jupiter in Rome.[19] When Pharaoh Ptolemy succeeded Alexander as ruler of Egypt, he wanted to continue to merge his Greek and Egyptian subjects by designating official patron deities of the city of Alexandria. Isis was the clear choice for the Goddess of Alexandria, as her worship was already popular among both the Egyptians and the Greeks, with the Greeks equating her with Athena, Aphrodite, Selene, Artemis, and Demeter. In Ptolemaic Egypt, Isis was the Goddess loved by all, but who would be her consort?

The chief of the gods was known to the Greeks as Zeus, while the Egyptian equivalent was Ra, or Amun-Ra. The Greeks already had a sun god—Apollo, who was entirely distinct from Zeus. Isis' most traditional consort was Osiris, who the Greeks equated with Hades, or sometimes Dionysus. Still not Zeus. The best answer seemed to be to somehow make Zeus and Ra one, but then how would one replace Osiris in the minds of the Egyptians? In Ptolemy's quest, I believe his attention must have been drawn to the cult of Osorapis. Here, Osiris—or Hades—had already been merged with the Apis, who had also at one time already been associated with Ra and the sun, as Apis-Atum.[20] This Apis also had an association with Alexander the Great, who paid homage to him during his reign. Osorapis had all the aspects required to be the ideal god of Alexandria, save for one—his image. The Greeks were unlikely to adopt a bull-headed god.

According to legend, while on a search for a patron god for his empire, Ptolemy received a vision of the God Serapis and thus embarked on a quest to discover a statue to represent this god and bring it back to Egypt. That statue was ultimately retrieved from Sinope in Asia Minor, and thus the God Serapis had emerged at last.[21] Images of Serapis often bore a considerable resemblance to both Zeus and Hades, though he was

---

[19] Joshua J. Mark, "Amun," *Ancient History Encyclopedia*, July 29, 2016, accessed June 16, 2019, https://www.ancient.eu/amun/.

[20] "Apis," *Encyclopedia Britannica*, accessed June 20, 2019, https://www.britannica.com/topic/Apis-Egyptian-deity.

[21] Stefan Pfeiffer, "The God Serapis, His Cult and the Beginnings of the Ruler Cult in Ptolemaic Egypt," in *Ptolemy II Philadelphus and His World*, ed. Paul McKechnie and Phillipe Guillaume (Leiden: Brill, 2008), 393-394.

often also portrayed with the ram horns of Amun. He held a pitchfork as Hades did, and was often accompanied by the three-headed dog, Cerberus. This newly-appointed God of Alexandria was now God of Heaven, Earth, and the Underworld. In some ways, Serapis was Osiris reformed and revitalized. The ancient God of the Nile was now not only the king of the dead, but he was also the king of the sun, the living, and of the gods.

Among the Greek empires, the cult of Isis and Serapis seemed to flourish. Serapis was an exotic Zeus, but Isis gave the Greeks something they may have found lacking in their native goddesses: a fully-realized woman, well rounded in the ways of sexuality, fertility, independence, and, most importantly, magic. Serapis, alongside Isis, became the patron god of Alexandria. He also gained devotees in other Greek territories throughout the Mediterranean. But unlike Isis, he never gained popularity among the native Egyptians, who still preferred Osiris.[22]

In Alexandria, priests of Serapis wore white linen robes and the insignia of their office, which was a seven-pointed star.[23] The star most likely represented the Seven Luminaries, as it still does today. The temples of Serapis were known for divination, dream interpretation, and healing and the Alexandrians came to equate Serapis with a variety of different gods, including: Hades, Pluto, Zeus, Osiris, Apis, Adonis, Dionysus, Amun, Pan, Ptah, Sokar, Ra, Helios, Asclepius, and Poseidon.[24] Like Isis, Serapis had taken on a sort of monotheism within the Mysteries. It is recorded that the God described himself thus: "My head is the firmament of heaven; My belly the ocean; My feet constitute the earth; My ears are set in the sky; And my far seeing eye is the bright light of the sun."[25]

Eventually, Amun-Serapis, the horned Serapis, as the consort of Isis, spread his influence across the Roman Empire. He was so popular that he

---

[22] Ibid, 392.

[23] Rollin Phipps, *A History of Alexandria* (Arlington, TX: The University of Texas at Arlington Press, 2004), 70-71.

[24] Ibid, 70-71.

[25] R.E. Witt, *Isis in the Ancient World*, Johns Hopkins Paperback Edition, 1997 ed. (Baltimore and London: Johns Hopkins University Press, 1971),53.

replaced Zeus and Jupiter as the patron god in some areas. In Dacia, he was called Jupiter-Sol.[26] In the Roman cult of Sol, Amun-Ra-Serapis was associated with the God in the festival, Sol Invictus.[27] And although Serapis was overshadowed by Isis, as a couple they were and remain powerful, pre-Christian symbols that are not easily erased from the subconscious mind. One can easily see this image of Serapis of the classical age, with his curled beard, protruding horns, and stang-like pitchfork in hand, enthroned at a Witches' Sabbat with the Moon Goddess and Queen of Magic, Isis, beside him. As Isis transformed to wear the face of Mary, Serapis had become the devil, something most necessary for a god once also called Serapis Christus. He needed to be demonized and forgotten, and he was for over a thousand years. Today Serapis, like his old incarnation Osiris, has been resurrected by modern-day devotees of Isis and practitioners of Witchcraft. The Craft today owes his image and magic a great deal, for he is the Horned God of the Underworld, God of Nature, and the Life-Giving Sun. He is also one of the few historic examples of a monotheistic and cross-continental horned god.

Pan

Pan is one of the oldest of the Greek gods, worshiped in caves and all sorts of wild places, with roots that reach as far back as the highlands of Arcadia. His name, in both ancient and modern Greek, means "all," although it is debated that it comes from the root "*paon*," which means "pasturer."[28] I believe both of these may be somewhat true, as Pan was a god of pastures and shepherds, yet in Alexandria, Egypt, he was also philosophically viewed as a cosmic force.[29] Pan gained a stronger following in Athens and eventually Delphi, because the Athenians credited him with their victory over the Persians in the Battle of Marathon. It is said that the armies of the Athenians entered the battle chanting, "Pan!

---

[26] Ibid, 147.
[27] Ibid, 213.
[28] Janet & Stewart Farrar, *The Witches' God* (Custer, WA: Phoenix Publishing, 1989), 75-76.
[29] Ibid, 76.

Pan! Pan!", instilling in the enemy the terror and panic often associated with the God.[30]

We do not know much about the actual worship of Pan, other than that shepherds made offerings and sacrifices to the God. He was strongly associated with nymphs, who were very similar to the maenads of Dionysus. Pan's worshipers were often called to assemble in the nude,[31] and his many festivals were no doubt sexual in nature. Sometimes, his statues were whipped to encourage the God to bestow fertility, abundance, protection, and purification upon his devotees.[32]

In Delphi and Arcadia, Pan was a god of prophecy, and it is said that his gifts may have also been bestowed upon Apollo. Though Pan was a sexual, wild God of nature, he also had a profoundly mystical side, particularly in his Roman incarnation. Pan was eventually absorbed into the cult of Dionysus, who took on the form of a younger Pan and shares many of his attributes. In this Roman incarnation, he was the old God his sevenfold pipe represented the music and movement of the heavens, and this Pan was the Goat of Mendes that we know today.

Pan's importance in the occult world and modern Witchcraft revival did not stem from the ancient world, but from Victorian England and the occult Renaissance. Poets like Byron, Keats, and Shelley—wove the Old God of Nature into the British popular mind and he began to take form once again in the British countryside. Occultists like Eliphas Levi, Aleister Crowley, and Dion Fortune enshrined the god, writing about him and carrying out new rituals in his name.

In Witchcraft, we worship the Horned One, who is often depicted in the likeness of Pan. For example, the early 17th-century woodcut of Robin Goodfellow depicts Puck, a horned and goat-footed devil of folklore, dancing with a broom and a lit candle and surrounded by a circle of

---

[30] "Pan Cult," *Theoi Greek Mythology*, accessed June 16, 2019, https://www.theoi.com/Cult/PanCult.html.

[31] Doreen Valiente, *An ABC of Witchcraft Past and Present* (New York, NY: St. Martin's Press, 1973), 304.

[32] "Pan (mythology)," *New World Encyclopedia*, accessed June 17, 2019, https://www.newworldencyclopedia.org/entry/Pan_(mythology)#cite_note-Borgeaud-5.

dancing witches.[33] Goat-horned, cloven-hoofed, and bearded, like the popular image of the devil, he is unquestionably rooted in the imagery of Pan. Pan was brought to Britain by the Romans, but the English word "Puck" is connected to the Irish *"pooka"*[34] or Welsh *"bucca"*—shape-shifting nature spirits of Celtic folklore—and *"poc,"* which described a male goat. Whether these old folk gods were already associated with the goat or merged with Pan is unknown, but in Ireland, the annual Puck Fair procession ends with a goat being crowned by a little girl called the Queen of Puck or Lady of the Laune. The goat is called the Puck King. The Puck Fair is one of Ireland's oldest modern festivals, taking place each year from the 10th to the 12th of August, in Killorglin.[35] Originally, it was called *Aonach an Phoic*, which means, "Fair of the He-Goat."[36] It is unknown how old the fair is, but it is at least 400 years in practice, and was recorded as early as 1603. The meaning of the fair is debated, but at its beginning, the young Puck Queen gives a proclamation that has been passed down from generation to generation. It reads, "Noble friends, we are gathered here once more to celebrate an ancient and cherished tradition, handed down to us from our forefathers and from their forefathers before them: a tradition without like or equal in the world today. It is a time of renewing old and dear friendships and making new ones. I offer you for the next three days the sincere welcome of the people and the freedom of the town of Killorglin under the patronage of his majesty, King Puck."[37] This opening passage, read year after year for generations, expresses the local belief that the festival is indeed ancient and though I am not suggesting that Pan and Puck are the same,

---

33 *"Robin Goodfellow, His Mad Pranks and Merry Jests, 1639,"* British Library Collection, accessed June 21, 2019, https://www.bl.uk/collection-items/robin-goodfellow-his-mad-pranks-and-merry-jests-1639.

34 Janet & Stewart Farrar, *The Witches' God* (Custer, WA: Phoenix Publishing, 1989), 219.

35 "History and Origins of Puck Fair," *Puck Fair*, accessed June 21, 2019, https://puckfair.ie/history.

36 "About Puck/Important Information," *Puck Fair*, accessed June 21, 2019, https://puckfair.ie/information.

37 Keelan Foley, "The History Of Puck Fair | Killorglin 1613-2013," YouTube video, 02:55, Posted July 2, 2013, accessed June 23, 2019, https://www.youtube.com/watch?v=-8slTCWkG0A.

but traditions like the Puck Fair may help to explain why the goat-footed god was so quickly embraced, or re-embraced, by British consciousness.

One of my favorite examples of Pan's emergence into modern pop culture is the devil of folklore in cult classic films. The 1968 movie, *The Devil Rides Out*, is an excellent example of this. At the Witches' Sabbat, the characters invoke the devil, whom they call the Goat of Mendes, and he appears in the form of Pan. This image has had a powerful impact on the subconscious mind and is utilized today by Satanists, Witches, and occultists alike. This imagery can be found in the depictions of Baphomet inspired by Eliphas Levi, as well as in tarot cards, medieval woodcuts, art, and folktales. When one mentions the God of the Witches, it is usually an image of Pan that is imagined.

The goat, which has long been associated with Witchcraft in Europe, when combined with Pan's occult British popularity made him an obvious choice to be associated with the Horned God of the Witches. Although Pan is not the official god of Initiates—Alexandrian or Gardnerian—he remains a potent symbol of our God in his manifestations as the great He-Goat of the Mysteries. Pan comes to us as Lord of the Sabbat in our visions of the inner planes. As a visage of the primordial Horned God, Pan does indeed come from the same source as our own hidden deity; he is by his very nature a true God of Witchcraft. By his devotees, he has been called *Pamphage* and *Pangenetor*, all-devourer and all-begetter. [38]

Today, Pan is great, and he is all. When you look into the face of Pan, he will look back at you. He is sex, chaos, and ecstatic pleasure; he is the primal force of man's carnal nature. Pan can be invoked for prophecy, dreamwork, protection, pleasure, joy, abundance, inspiration, lust, and even healing through dreams. He is a god of hunting, shepherds, fishermen, beekeepers, wild places, nature spirits, and fertility. Pan is no longer the simple god of Arcadia. He, like Hecate, has risen above his Olympian counterparts and remains a living occult force in the world today.

---

[38] Doreen Valiente, *An ABC of Witchcraft Past and Present* (New York, NY: St. Martin's Press, 1973), 304-305.

Dionysus

The official worship of Dionysus is approximated to date from 1500 BCE to 400 CE. One of the last of the Olympians, he replaced Hestia as the 12th god of the Olympians, demonstrating his later importance in Greek society, but his origins are obscure. He is said to have originated in Thrace, within the culture of the Mycenaeans, who were in fact greatly influenced and dominated by the Minoans. In Macedonia, Dionysus was the chief god, then called Dionis, or Dion. In that culture, he was the god of wine, fertility, and the sun.[39] The Ptolemies continued this solar association with Dionysus in Alexandria, Egypt, where he was particularly important. The Ptolemies even claimed descent from Dionysus, which cemented the divine status required for pharaohs. Because of this, Alexandria became a major center for the cult, and at times, the god was even worshiped as the consort of Isis.[40]

Dionysus had many names and absorbed many other gods. He was called Chthonios (he of the underworld), Soter (savior), Lysios (liberator), Phanes (illuminator), Deunysos, Zonnysos, Dithrambos (twice-born), Iacchus, Sabazius, Bassareus, and Zagreus.[41][42] He was known as the God who Comes, the Lord of Souls, the Bull-Horned God, Bacchus, Liber Pater, and Serapis. Dionysus was a shapeshifting god, capable of becoming the bull, the serpent, and the lion—an ability which associated him with the legacy of trickster gods. He is a god of sacrificial death and rebirth, so parallels can undoubtedly be drawn between the ancient rites of Dionysus and theological associations with Christ.[43] The parents of Dionysus are said to be Zeus and Semele, although, in other stories, his mother has been Demeter, Persephone, or Dion. His

---

[39] Basil Chulev, "The Gods of Macedon," *Ancient Macedonia*, 2016, accessed June 15, 2019. https://www.academia.edu/21627850/Ancient_Macedonia_-_The_Gods_of_Macedon.

[40] Rollin Phipps, *A History of Alexandria* (Arlington, TX: The University of Texas at Arlington Press, 2004), 74-75.

[41] Janet & Stewart Farrar, *The Witches' God* (Custer, WA: Phoenix Publishing, 1989), 172.

[42] "Dionysos Titles," *Theoi Greek Mythology*, accessed June 18, 2019, https://www.theoi.com/Cult/DionysosTitles.html.

[43] Rosemarie Taylor-Perry, *The God Who Comes: Dionysian Mysteries Reclaimed* (New York: Algora, 2003), 6, 12.

consorts have included Ariadne, Aura, Aphrodite, Isis, and the young satyr boy Ampelos.[44] He has had many mortal lovers, both male and female.

The cult of Dionysus should not be ignored in the history of modern Witchcraft. It influenced or was absorbed by most all the European cults. After all, his practices have held and continue to hold considerable influence over all those cults and religions for which wine plays a significant spiritual role. Wine is of great importance in the cults of Diana, Isis, and Serapis, as well as the religions of Christianity, Judaism, and modern Witchcraft. The stories of the Holy Grail—itself a sacred vessel of wine—and those brave souls who sought its mysteries, may be layered over the older myths of Dionysus. At Eleusis, his rites were called the Lesser Mysteries, and they were necessary to experience and understand if one wished to receive the greater mysteries of the cult.[45]

During one of our trips to the British Museum in London, my husband and I observed an Etruscan mirror from the 4th century BCE that bears the imagery of Dionysus and his consort Ariadne, named respectively on the mirror as Fufluns and Areatha. Areatha's name is inscribed in Etruscan as ΑΟΑΞΑΡΑ (see "Bronze Etruscan mirror" illustration below).

One might wonder what connections exist between this manifestation of Ariadne and the later Aradia of Leland's *Gospel of the Witches*. In either case, this image and others of Dionysus, Ariadne, and their cult bear more than a striking resemblance to the gods of Witchcraft today. Additionally, the ecstatic rites held in the God's name are virtually identical to descriptions of the Witches' Sabbats of Medieval and early to modern Europe. Initiates of Dionysos were both male and female; the priestesses were called maenads or Bacchantes, and were often referred to as the God's nurses or mothers. The priests were called "*thiasoi*," and dressed as satyrs and in other ritual garb, including the skins of animals

---

[44] "Dionysos Loves," *Theoi Greek Mythology*, accessed June 17, 2019, https://www.theoi.com/Olympios/DionysosLoves.html.

[45] Rosemarie Taylor-Perry, *The God Who Comes: Dionysian Mysteries Reclaimed* (New York: Algora, 2003), 81.

sacred to the god.[46] In Eleusis, the priests and priestesses alike were called *bacchoi*. It was believed that the God lived in his priesthood or possessed them, giving them supernatural powers. Channeling his power, they could heal, prophesy, charm snakes, suckle animals, and express feats of great strength

Bronze Etruscan mirror (350BC-325BC). Displayed in the British Museum.

The rituals of the Cult of Dionysus featured divine possession, drunkenness, ecstatic rites, initiation, blood sacrifice, orgies, and mystical ritual cries. His worship often took place in wild places, such as in forests or on mountaintops. In procession would come people carrying phallic images and torches, with others dressed as Pan, Sileni, or with women shouting, "*euoi*," and waving the thyrsus—a pinecone-tipped staff—to

---

[46] Ismene Lada-Richards, *Initiating Dionysus: Ritual and Theatre in Aristophanes' Frogs* (Oxford: Clarendon Press, 1999), 333.

the sound of drums and pipes, all culminating in a dance around the enthroned Horned God.

The Lesser Mysteries, or Rites of Dionysus, and its supernatural followers may indeed be a historical source of modern misconceptions about the Devil's Sabbat and diabolical witches. Even in the classical age, the Cult of Dionysus was at times feared and persecuted. Just when the cult faded away or transformed into something else is unknown, but I believe it left a powerful imprint that may have lingered on in folk practice and rituals up through and into Christianity. Indeed, as with all cults, we cannot really determine the date of its extinction with complete certainty.

Dionysus is a God of many things: wine, harvest, fertility, ecstasy, madness, prophecy, sex, initiation, pleasure, nature, sacred rites, theater, rebirth, regeneration, civilization, the Underworld, and even, sometimes, the sun. He has been depicted both as an older bearded man and as a beautiful youth. He is associated with goats and is sometimes shown with bull or ram horns, and wearing a crown of ivy. Also, Dionysus often carries a thyrsus and he sometimes rides a panther or a leopard—or wears their skins. His chthonic nature may have its origins in Knossos, veiled within the myths of Ariadne and the Minotaur, especially since the sacred bull is one of his images. In the tales, he also rescues several mortals and goddesses from the underworld, including Ariadne, Persephone, and his mother, Semele, and these stories are most likely another take on the life-cycle mysteries. Dionysus is connected to all the ancient mysteries, and to most of the gods enshrined by them. He lives on today through the wine consumed in every Catholic mass and at every Witches' Sabbat.

Dionysus, the God who Comes, still holds an essential place in Witchcraft today. I believe that given his connection to Pan, Isis, Osiris, Serapis, Amun, Zeus, and many other gods, Dionysus is a crucial component to the DNA of the old Horned God of the Stone Age, and to the modern Witchcraft God we worship today. Effectively, he bridges the gap between the old hunting god and the agricultural god of the harvest.

Cernunnos

Cernunnos means "horned one" and the name has become the umbrella title for all of the Celtic horned gods; it is also a popular name for the God of the Witches. In truth, though Initiates may have different names or pronunciations for the God depending on one's lineage, we all share the epithet, "the Horned One," in referring to our God. Though Gardnerians and Alexandrians may draw heavily from Celtic sources because of our British origins, we are a European mystery cult rather than a historical, tribal, or ethnic faith.

Celts, Germanics, Romans, and Greeks all share the same common ancestors who originate from the same language group, Proto-Indo European, and the Proto-Indo European word for horn is "*krnu*,"[47] with the word for one being "*oinos*,"[48] giving us "*Krnuoinos*," or "horned one," in Proto-Indo European. This not only helps us to understand his origins, but it also validates the Witches' belief that he has ancient Stone Age origins. His consistent image was indeed prevalent throughout Europe on statues, reliefs, cave paintings, coins, jewelry, and other artifacts, so it goes without question that Cernunnos not only existed, but was widely worshiped. He was often depicted with stag antlers, wearing or holding a torc, and surrounded by animals, particularly stags and a ram-horned serpent.[49]

His name varied in different regions, and it is from place names and on a few inscriptions that remain intact that we know some of those differences. It can also be found in folklore and even in Catholicism. The name Cernunnos is Latin, and is found on only one inscription upon a Gaulish altar which was discovered beneath the Cathedral of Notre Dame in Paris.[50] The altar, which now resides in the Cluny Museum,

---

[47] *Indo-European Language Dictionary*, entry: HORN, accessed June 21, 2019, https://in-do-european.info/dictionary-translator/translate/English/Indo-European/?q=Horn.

[48] *Indo-European Language Dictionary*, entry: OINOS, accessed June 21, 2019, https://in-do-european.info/dictionary-translator/translate/Indo-European/English/?q=Oinos.

[49] "Cernunnos," *Encyclopedia Brittanica*, accessed June 21, 2019, https://www.britannica.com/topic/Cernunnos.

[50] Margaret A. Murray, *The God of the Witches* (Oxford: Oxford University Press, 1952), 29.

contains the inscription below. The first letter is slightly worn, but it looks like a C and, based on evidence, it likely is a C. The Gaulish word *"cernan"* means antler or horn and two similar inscriptions support this: one in Luxembourg, *"Deo Ceruninco"*; and a Gaulish inscription in Greek, *"Karnonos."* [51]

The Celtic God Cernunnos, after a French-Roman sculpture discovered in the foundations of Notre Dame cathedral, Paris.

In Britain, he was called Herne of Windsor Forest and also Cerne, the Abbas giant in Dorset. Both Herne and Cerne have left marks of their influence on the names of many British places. With Herne, only a few folk tales have survived regarding the god. As previously stated, Herne is said to appear in times of national crisis, [52] a tale which harkens back to other stories of guardians of Britain such as Arthur and Bran the

---

[51] Alexa Duir, "Who is Cernunnos?", *Association of Polytheistic Traditions*, 2005, accessed June 21, 2019, http://www.manygods.org.uk/articles/essays/Cernunnos.shtml.

[52] Janet & Stewart Farrar, *The Witches' God* (Custer, WA: Phoenix Publishing, 1989), 99.

Blessed, both of whom have spirits that are said to protect the island should danger ever threaten. Herne also leads the wild hunt with his red-eared hounds. One might recall that the Wild Hunt is associated with the underworld, the dead, and witchcraft throughout Europe, but in Wales and Glastonbury, the wild hunt is led by Gwyn. Since we have very few images and descriptions of Celtic gods, it is possible that Gwyn and other hunter deities might have had horns as well, but we don't have the pictorial evidence to verify. Other names that most likely have an association with the god Cernunnos include Camulos, Grannos, Cernwn, Cernowain, Saint Ceraunos, Saint Kierán, Saint Korneli, King Ptolemy Keraunos, and Alexander's title of *Dhu'l Karnain*,[53] which means "the two-horned one" in the Koran.

Most of our knowledge regarding the antlered god derives from his images. Aside from the Gaulish altar, we have countless examples. In Val Camonica, a cave painting of the antlered god was discovered, where he is robed and holding torcs and a horned serpent while a naked man worships the deity in adoration.[54] And then there is the aforementioned Gundestrup Cauldron. On the outside of this famed vessel are eight different figures in a perfect circle: what appear to be four goddesses and four Gods. We do not know who these goddesses or gods are. On the inside of the cauldron, in the very center, are what appear to be slain animals and men, which I believe symbolize sacrifice. Along the inside of the cauldron are depictions of various heroes, warriors, and animals, along with an antlered god, the most popular image referred to as Cernunnos today. Although the cauldron has no such inscription, it shows an antlered god holding a torc in his right hand, wearing a torc around his neck, sitting in a cross-legged position, and with a horned serpent in his left hand. Around him are stags, goats, wolves, and various other animals.Right next to the god on the inside of the cauldron appears an unnamed goddess. She is surrounded by extremely exotic animals— mythical animals that appear to be dragons, cats, or griffins—and two

---

[53] Margaret A. Murray, *The God of the Witches* (Oxford: Oxford University Press, 1952), 25.
[54] Doreen Valiente, *Witchcraft for Tomorrow* (Custer, WA: Phoenix Publishing, 1978), 26.

elephants flanked by two six-pointed stars. It is fascinating to note that in Celtic society, the cauldron was a symbol not only of sustenance and regeneration but also of sacrifice and death. I believe that this cauldron is meant to symbolize the Underworld, or a place of death and rebirth. Here, Cernunnos and this unnamed goddess preside over life, death, and nature. The Gundestrup Cauldron tells a tale that is still told by Witches today—a story of an eight-spoked wheel with perfectly equaled gods and goddesses on the outside and an ordered universe. The cycles of nature echo the eight Sabbats of the witches and inside of this womb is all life and all death, the realm of the God, the kingdom of Cernunnos. Interestingly enough, in the images, Cernunnos looks very Celtic, while the goddesses seem to take on a more eastern, exotic flavor, which perhaps suggests that they originated from different places. There are other examples of him appearing with unnamed goddesses on other artifacts, as if they are, in some areas, a sacred pair.

In Sommerécourt, Saintes, and among the Aedui of Santosse, such depictions have been found of the pair generally surrounded by animals, and sometimes holding cornucopias or goblets.[55] In Sommerécourt, the goddess holds a pomegranate and feeds the horned serpent from a basket. Next to her is a smaller woman, perhaps meant to be her daughter or a priestess. In the regions of the Aedui of Santos, it is believed that the goddess may be Epona since she is surrounded by horses.[56] It is well known that both Cernunnos and Epona were venerated in the area, but without inscriptions to serve as evidence, we cannot be certain. However, the goddess of the pomegranate and of the cauldron both suggest underworld ties, which is not a common association for Epona. I am also not currently aware of a Celtic goddess associated with pomegranates, which supports my earlier theory that this goddess may be of exotic origins. It is also possible that Cernunnos' consorts in these depictions are all different goddesses.

---

[55] Miranda Green, *Symbol and Image in Celtic Religious* Art (London: Routledge, 1992), 71.
[56] Ibid, 72.

Cernunnos has been historically a Celtic god and a Druid god, but he is now worshiped by modern Witches. In Witchcraft, we have myths regarding the Horned One that are of unknown origin, but we believe him to be the first primordial god of man and the hunting god of the Stone Age associated with death, resurrection, winter, and the underworld. He is the other side of nature, the consort of the ancient moon mother of life and fertility. The Celtic Horned God embodies all of these concepts. He is strong, wild, free, and powerful. In antiquity, Cernunnos was invoked as a god of aggression, war, fertility, power, agricultural prosperity, justice, health, and death. When Julius Caesar said one of the primary gods of the Celts was Dis Pater, Lord of the Underworld, he might very well have been referring to Cernunnos.[57] The depictions of Cernunnos indeed support him as a Celtic Hades, as his stories include a sacred marriage, a connection to death, warriors, animals, resurrection, and a life-giving goddess. The Romans often depicted him with Apollo and Mercury and his favorite companion, the horned serpent, was also portrayed with Mercury and Mars. More interestingly still, the god Serapis was described as just such a horned serpent. All of these details seem to support my assertion that Serapis fits the archetype of the Witches' god. In truth, this god has no concrete legends, myths, priesthood, or even a name. His origins are obscure, as is his area of worship and though it seems unlikely that such a god should even have a modern day following, the same could be said about religious Witchcraft. A testimony to both truth and power, Cernunnos may have many names, but he is the consort of the Goddess of Witches, and he continues to be relevant in the world today.

THE DEVIL

One might be surprised to find that I have included the Devil in a chapter about the God of the Witches. The modern movement of religious Witchcraft has worked tirelessly to educate the general public

---

[57] Julius Caesar, *"De Bello Gallico" and Other Commentaries of Caius Julius Caesar*, ed. Ernest Rhys, trans. W. A. Macdevitt (New York: J. M. Dent, 1915), 121.

that Witches, despite centuries of persecution and propaganda, do not worship the Devil. The Devil and Satan are Christian concepts. Witches, and our Gods, predate these ideas. Our Witchcraft ancestors were pockets of people still practicing the old ways and cults of antiquity. We have also highlighted the fact that the popular image of the Devil is not found in the Bible. Nowhere in the Bible does it mention such a description. The cloven-hoofed, horned, pitchfork-wielding figure is not found anywhere in the scriptures, so conceptions of the Devil are without question drawing on pre-Christian mythology.

Early Christianity sought to destroy the old religions by demonizing their gods. Serapis—with his curled horns, pitchfork, hounds of hell, and ability to take on serpent form—as well as Pan, Faunus, Dionysus, Bacchus, and the many manifestations of Cernunnos found throughout the world, would have appeared to the early church as demons and devils because they were reminders of their own pagan past. The potent images of these old horned gods have been ingrained in art and culture from antiquity—as if the gods of the old always become the demons of the new.

Today, many people on solitary eclectic paths self-identify as practitioners of so-called "traditional witchcraft," which I personally find ridiculous because there's nothing traditional about it. In fact, it might be more accurate to refer to them as what I call "trial record witches". Such practitioners place far too many of their beliefs on the confessions found within the records of the European witch trials to the exclusion of other influences. Drawing on such trial records for insight is something both Margaret Murray and Reginald Scott included in their research and Gardner himself certainly would have been familiar with their methods, and there are definitely commonalities in records across Europe and spanning centuries, from which you can draw conclusions. However, you can't just stop there. You must also look at that information through the lens of folklore, mythology, and in particular contrast with the "trial record Witches," the influence and legacy of mystery cults on the imagery and ideas of the Witch.

Most importantly, we must take such confessions with a grain of salt because they were nearly always obtained as a result of savagely brutal torture, fear of execution, and the delusions that such methods would instill in the minds of the tortured. A true tradition must be measured over time. It must have a lasting impact and legacy, and this is why I have gone far beyond witch trial records to discover who Witches actually were.

Although I do not agree that real Witches work directly with the Devil as our God, it is my opinion that the old Horned God was at one point in time called the Devil. Whether or not his followers adopted the title, it did, in a very significant way, become one of his epithets.

In Old English, the word devil comes from "*deofol*," which originates from the Latin or Greek "*diabolos*," meaning accuser or slanderer.[58] This is a touch ironic because the Church and its adherents were indeed slandering the old gods and their followers. Another source for the word devil, however, is the Latin "*deus*," which means "god," and is related to the Sanskrit, "*deva*," a shining one or god.[59] So, in reality, when we say the word devil, we are actually talking about God.

I personally prefer restoring my God or Gods to their pre-Christian forms, however, completely dismissing the trials and folklore would be shortsighted. Although we are looking through a broken lens, I believe that real knowledge can be gleaned. After all, as they say, the devil is in the details. For the purpose of this work, we're exploring cases and examples of the old God being mingled, mixed into, or even outright called the Devil. Is this merely Christian propaganda, or was there an echo of the remains of ancient rituals still being enacted and confused with the Christian mythos of devils and devil worshipers?

As mentioned previously in this chapter, Leland's Lucifer and Lucifello of the trials are a perfect example of an old god being woven into Christian mythology and becoming a folk devil. Like Lucifer's association with Diana, the folk devil is often paired with a goddess or female represen-

---

[58] "Devil," *Online Etymology Dictionary*, accessed June, 22, 2019, https://www.etymonline.com/search?q=Devil.

[59] Doreen Valiente, *An ABC of Witchcraft Past and Present* (New York, NY: St. Martin's Press, 1973), 109.

tation, such as the queen of Elphame, Elffin or fairies, or sometimes a coven maiden. His followers are deemed to be witches. This folk devil has had many recorded names, many of which can be traced to possible pre-Christian gods. His imagery also seems to be fairly consistent, despite some regional variations. His predominant colors were black and red, and he was sometimes recorded as a black dog, a goat, or as a man dressed in black, often with a hood. In his more diabolical imaginings, the Devil looks like a monstrous version of Pan, sometimes with a tail or bat-like wings. At times, however, there is an association with light, though it is generally, but not always, hidden. One of my husband's favorite accounts comes from the Aberdeen trials of 1597. The name, in this case, is Christsonday.[60] Christsonday was the companion of the queen of Elfin and was described as an angel clad in white.

Here once again appears a cultural blending of religious ideas. Is it possible that among the lower classes who did not read or write that such an eclectic mix of Christianity and the old gods did emerge? We must remember that before the rise of Christianity, this mixing of gods and ideologies was commonplace. And after all, the Devil of the witch not only looked like the old Horned God, but shared many of his same qualities. Like the Horned God, the Devil offered sex, power, freedom, and rebellion against what had become an oppressive society. He echoed a memory of a time when one's worship burned with the passion of liberation and wild abandoning.

Another very popular name for the Devil, particularly in the British Isles, was Robin. The name is so prevalent in trial records and folklore that it is possible that Robin is the name of a forgotten pagan god. The robin bird, the red-breasted robin, and the Cock Robin feature heavily in British mythology. This Devil was believed to be the personification of spring, therefore seeing the robin each year was considered a sign that spring had actually arrived and the robin was never to be harmed for this

---

[60] "Marioun Grant (15/4/1597)," *Survey of Scottish Witchcraft Database*, accessed June 22, 2019, http://witches.shca.ed.ac.uk/index.cfm?fuseaction=home.caserecord&caseref=C%2FEGD%2F2141&search_type=searchpeople&search_string=lastname%3D%26firstname%3D%26residence%3D.

reason, lest one incur terribly bad luck. The robin and the wren, with the wren symbolizing winter, are said to battle at the winter solstice, where the robin is, of course, victorious. This symbolism is echoed in a poem out of Lancashire:

The robin and wren
Are God's cock and hen.
The spink and the sparrow
Are the devil's bow and arrow. [61]

There are many Christian myths and folktales about robins, but since these give them positive associations, how then did Robin become a widespread name for the principal evil?

Robin is a diminuitive of the name Robert and means "bright fame," or "bright with glory," [62][63] which means he can easily be seen as being solar in nature, much in the same way that Lucifer is. The folk God, Puck, is also called Robin Goodfellow, and is often portrayed as having Pan-like features.

In the trial of Dame Alice Kyteler, she calls the Devil "Robin Artisson." [64] And then, of course, there is the English folk hero Robin Hood. We are not discussing here the possibility of a real Robin Hood. Whether or not one believes the man actually ever existed is of no account. For the purpose of this work, I do not consider him a real person, but a mythical figure connected to the Robin of folklore.

Robin Hood was a very popular story amongst the people of England, so popular that he began to be grafted onto May Day celebrations

---

[61] William Henderson, *Notes on the Folk-Lore of the Northern Counties of England and the Borders* (London: W. Satchell, Peyton and Co., 1879), 123.

[62] "Robin," *Online Etymology Dictionary*, accessed June 22, 2019, https://www.etymonline.com/word/robin.

[63] "Robert," *Online Etymology Dictionary*, accessed June 22, 2019, https://www.etymonline.com/search?q=robert.

[64] Doreen Valiente, *An ABC of Witchcraft Past and Present* (New York, NY: St. Martin's Press, 1973), 252.

throughout England,[65] once again representing the old God or folk hero. Robin Hood was at odds with society and rebelled against the establishment, government, and Church. It has been noted that he had twelve followers, the twelve Merry Men, and with Robin himself that makes thirteen people—the same as the number of Witches in a Coven. Like other examples of the old God, Robin Hood also had an association with a female counterpart, Maid Marian.

Nick, another name for the devil, may be connected to the Anglo-Saxon, "*neck*," which means "spirit."[66] Farming communities often held rituals and games where a corn dolly would be called the neck, as it represented the spirit of the harvest. Old Nick can be connected to the name "Nik," which is also a title for the Anglo-Saxon god Woden.[67] Woden was often said to appear in all black, and while his favorite haunts were wild places and crossroads, he was known for roaming the countryside. Witches and the Devil have a longstanding association with such places, and with men in black and the crossroads. Might Old Nick be the Devil? Or is he, once again, a memory of an ancient, pre-Christian god?

The Devil has many more names in the trial records and folklore—Old Hornie, Barrabon, Hammerlin, Peterlin, Hou, and Old Scratch, just to name a few. I personally think Old Scratch may be another alias for the winter spirit, Krampus. Krampus means "claws" and his traditions come from Germanic custom. I would encourage everyone to look up the Krampus festivals that take place to this day in parts of Germany. Krampus can also be found on old Victorian postcards, as he was once a companion to Santa Claus. If you study the winter spirit Krampus and these festivals, he immediately conjures up the idea of the old, ancient Horned God, and the Devil. In fact, when you look at some of his modern-day festivals and the recordings we have of older ones, they look like they could have been taken right out of a Witches' Sabbat, complete with

---

[65] Margaret A. Murray, *The God of the Witches* (Oxford: Oxford University Press, 1952), 41.
[66] Ibid, 38.
[67] Doreen Valiente, *An ABC of Witchcraft Past and Present* (New York, NY: St. Martin's Press, 1973), 108.

fiery cauldrons and a birch-wielding horned creature dragging chains and bells. Krampus is most likely an old Horned God, one who was originally associated with the winter solstice. But once again, we have a curious example of an old god taking on the identity of a folk spirit or demon.

Most modern Witches do not work with the Devil and will refute any notion or stereotype that Witches ever did. We do not use the title to describe our beautiful god, but in a very real way, the folklore devil associated with Witchcraft was merged with old pagan gods and ideas. Perhaps Aleister Crowley pays the best tribute to the Devil of Witchcraft in his poem, *Hymn to Pan*. "Io Pan! Io Pan! Devil or god, to me, to me ... "[68]

The God of Witchcraft represents the carnal, raw, dark aspects within us and within nature—, the embodiment of Pan and Dionysus, qualities that some Christians would deem sinful and evil, and attributes they would bestow upon the Devil. Whether praised or vilified, the Horned God has held a continued presence among people and cultures across history. He originated in the Stone Age and has been worshiped in some of the greatest empires by priesthoods, becoming an entity only by making forbidden pacts with his Witches.

He, like the Goddess, has emerged to take his rightful place in the world once again. The God of witchcraft is the protector and guide to the Mysteries. His gift is one of raw power and liberation, of wild abandoning and secret pleasures. Ever foreboding and fearless, he bestows ecstasy, knowledge, and initiation upon those who would receive them.

---

[68] "Hymn to Pan," *Hermetic Library*, accessed June 22, 2019, https://hermetic.com/crowley/book-4/hymn.

Chapter 8

Magical Weapons

Throughout our history, mythic weapons have been wielded by gods, heroes, and magicians, filling our imaginations. We all recognize sacred tools like Thor's Hammer, Mjolnir, to King Arthur's Sword, Excalibur, the Holy Grail of the Last Supper to the Golden Fleece that the Witch Medea helped Jason obtain. Likewise, magical priesthoods have their own artifacts of power. In Egypt, the magician carved circles of protection with a knife, and the Pharaoh held the Crook and Flail as magical implements of sovereignty and fertility. In Greece, we find pictorials of naked witches drawing down the moon with wand and sword in hand.[1] Even Julius Caesar had a sword called *Crocea Mors*, or yellow death, said to hold supernatural powers.[2] It was also the Romans who recorded the white-robed Druids collecting the sacred mistletoe with a golden sickle.

When people step upon the magical path or become interested in Witchcraft, they will discover an array of books suggesting magical tools.

---

[1] Doreen Valiente, *An ABC of Witchcraft Past and Present* (New York, NY: St. Martin's Press, 1973), 43.

[2] Homer Nearing Jr., "The Legend of Julius Caesar's British Conquest," *PMLA Vol. 64, No. 4*, September, 1949, accessed June 14, 2019, https://www.jstor.org/stable/459639.

These might be a Witch's tools or a magician's. There is a distinction. Although they may both have a common thread in old grimoires like the *Key of Solomon*.

Initiatory Witchcraft has a specific magical training system, and within this system, there are magical weapons employed within our rites, and we have various methods in using them to both raise and direct power. These tools are not just symbolic gateways into different occult workings. Unless you are initiated into this system, these tools are unnecessary and, in fact, meaningless.

In ceremonial magic, you will find that they often use elemental tools. Some orders like the Golden Dawn have many tools that are specific to their training systems.

The elemental tools tend to be used by all, and these are the tools presented in most non-Initiatory Witchcraft books. It is natural that you will begin to collect your own symbols and tools to work the rites of the occult, and, indeed, if you are on the path of Initiation, these tools will come to you, change, and transform as your work progresses.

History of Occult Tools

In the occult, there is a myriad of implements and a plethora of blades, wands, pentacles, and other artifacts. As mentioned earlier, magicians and other occultists utilize the most basic, and perhaps the oldest of these: the Elemental Tools. These are generally the Dagger (Air), Wand (Fire), Cup (Water), and Pentacle (Earth). There is a frequent debate as to which is proper with Air and Fire, with some ascribing the Dagger to Fire and Wand to Air. I will be employing the most commonly used correspondences, as it is the preference among most occultists. The *Book of Shadows* does not actually have elemental tools. Our weapons are from a completely different system of magic. Alexandrians do have an elemental correspondence for our tools, because Alex Sanders was also a magician, and we do have strong occult leanings. The Alexandrian elemental system is more alchemical, although, in my experience, this is philosophical in nature, as we use the tools in a Witchcraft sense and not as magicians.

I keep separate tools for my occult workings, and we will explore some of these in the Grimoire. Possibly the oldest example for the elemental tools can be found in the myths of the Tuatha Dé Danann. Legend states that these gods brought four magic treasures to Ireland from four sacred islands. From the island of Findias, a sword wielded by their first king, Nuada, whose name means cloud maker. From the island of Gorias, a terrible spear that blazed with fire, belonging to the second king, Lugh. From Murias, the cauldron bestowed to the final king, the Dagda, and lastly, from Falias, the Lia Fail, the Stone of Destiny.[3] I think it is clear these are elemental tools from islands representing the astral realms of Air, Fire, Water, and Earth. We find another example of the elemental tools in Arthurian myths, hidden behind a veil of Christianity. The tale of Sir Gawain and the quest for the Holy Grail give different accounts of the manifestation or procession of four sacred artifacts, called the Grail Hollows: the Holy Grail and dish from the Last Supper, the bleeding lance that pierced the side of Jesus, and the sword that was used to execute John the Baptist.[4]

To an occultist, the Cup, Plate, Lance, and Sword also represent the elemental weapons. The Arthurian myths have, at least in part, Celtic origins woven within the tapestry of Christianity and poetic romance. It is not difficult to relate the Hallows to the Treasures of the Irish Gods. In my opinion, these elemental weapons and the Grail Hallows have another incarnation. At some point, they made their way onto playing cards that would eventually become essential to several occult systems, the Tarot. The Tarot cards' origins are obscure and slowly made the transition from recreation to divination, at least as far as the written record is concerned.

---

[3] D.J. Conway, *Celtic Magic* (St. Paul, MN: Llewellyn Publications, 1990), 91.

[4] Ulrich Müller, "The Grail Procession. the Legend, the Artifacts, and the Possible Sources of the Story," *Arthuriana* 16, no. 2 (2006).

The Tarot has complicated beginnings hailing from the Renaissance period in Southern Europe and much has been written about the history of these cards, mingling together ideas of the Roma ("Gypsies"), mystical occult histories, and secret meanings hidden in the symbols of the cards. The earliest full Tarot decks come from Italy, commissioned by the elite and created by popular artists of the time.[5] The earliest decks, such as the Visconti decks and those commissioned by the court of Ferrara contained four suits: a cup, a coin, a baton (a wand, or perhaps a lance or spear), and a sword.[6] Exactly when and how these cards became associated with the occult, we cannot really say, but the earliest source can be found in the 1700s, when a Frenchman named Antoine Court de Gebelin associated the Tarot with Egyptian and Hermetic concepts in his work *Le Monde primitif*.[7] Later, Jean-Baptiste Alliette (better known by his pseudonym Eteilla), began expounding the Tarot into a full divinatory system and created his own deck with Egyptian themes and correspondences.[8] Eliphas Levi would go on to link Tarot, using the Marseilles deck, to Qabalah,[9] something that would become quintessential in later occult uses of Tarot, particularly in occult orders such as the Golden Dawn. Mr. Alliette claimed he learned his system in Italy. However, its origins cannot entirely be ascertained. The elemental tools and the Tarot were fully solidified when Golden Dawn Initiate A. E. Waite created the Rider-Waite deck in 1909.[10] This deck has become the standard of Tarot today (at least in the English-speaking world), with Swords as Air, Wands as Fire, Cups as Water, and Pentacles as Earth.

---

[5] Paul Huson, *Mystical Origins of the Tarot, From Ancient Roots to Modern Usage* (Rochester, VT: Destiny Books, 2004), 11.

[6] Ibid, 11.

[7] Rachel Pollack, *Tarot Wisdom, Spiritual Teachings and Deeper Meanings* (Woodbury, MN: Llewelyn, 2015), xvi-xvii.

[8] Paul Huson, *Mystical Origins of the Tarot, From Ancient Roots to Modern Usage* (Rochester, VT: Destiny Books, 2004), 54-55.

[9] Ibid, 60-61.

[10] Rachel Pollack, *Tarot Wisdom, Spiritual Teachings and Deeper Meanings* (Woodbury, MN: Llewelyn, 2015), xx.

The four elemental tools can also be considered solar, for they are connected to the four seasons: spring, summer, fall, and winter, through the elemental correspondence. This is why Witches use a different method. We are, after all, children of the Moon. There is a curious example with a possible lunar origin, the 13 Treasures of Britain. These mythical treasure were a Sword, Baskets of Plenty, Horn, Chariot, Horse Halter, Knife, Cauldron, Wet Stone, Red Garment, a Pan, a Platter, a Chessboard, and the Mantel.[11] It is possible that each of these magic items has a deeper meaning related to the lunar calendar.

Witchcraft Tools

In Witchcraft, we have a distinct system of magic, and our tools are a manifestation of its practice. These tools have been published *ad nauseam* but, like the *Book of Shadows*, the oral lore and hidden methods remain a close-guarded secret. As stated already, if you are not initiated into Alexandrian or Gardnerian Witchcraft, they serve little purpose. For those who are going to pursue our path, they will become essential after Initiation. My advice is: if you desire tools as a non-initiate, use the elemental system or adopt some of the magic folk tools that I provide in the following pages.

With this piece of advice, why do I include mention of the tools at all? I think it is essential to make the distinction for seekers to understand that our Craft is a system unto itself and that it cannot be developed from public works. I also wish to highlight the possible origins and historical use of our magical implements. It has been said that any Witches worth their grain of salt do not require tools, and I think this is true. Our tools, however, do become powerful with continued use. They also possess an egregore of their own. As symbols, they contain the oral lore which is not in the *Book of Shadows*. Long before the written word, and when it has been dangerous to put things into writing, symbols have been used

---

[11] "The Thirteen Legendary Treasures of Britain," *Ancient Origins*, accessed June 14, 2019, https://www.ancient-origins.net/artifacts-other-artifacts/thirteen-legendary-treasures-britain-002898.

to tell stories. In this way, they become the keys to memories and are used to pass on secret teachings.

Magical Blades

The blade is both a useful tool and a weapon. It can be used for collecting herbs or harvesting wheat. It can be used for cooking, cutting, or carving beautiful works of art—and, yes, it can be used to harm or even kill. It is the primal tool, having its beginning as a sharp stone. In Witchcraft, we have three blades, each having its own use and meaning.

The Athame

It is no secret that the word, "Athame," comes from Gerald Gardner's *Book of Shadows*. It is a magical ritual tool within the Alexandrian and Gardnerian system of magic. In order to create an Athame, one must follow the exact methods and specifications held secret by Initiates. A magic knife is not the same tool. In fact, even Initiates have more than one magic knife and those of us who practice other systems often have several. We do have a few possible sources or links to the magical weapon. *The Clavicle of Solomon* (1572), from the British Museum, has a magic knife labeled an *Arthana*.[12] The French word attame means to cut, pierce, or to attack, and there is the quill knife with the Latin name, *artavus*. In Arabic, we have *al-thame*, or *adh-dhame*, which means arrow.

Regardless of where the name might originate, its only proper source remains the *Book of Shadows*. Today, like the title *"Book of Shadows"*, it has been co-opted by eclectics and solitary practitioners. I am not trying to turn back the tide but wish to point out that a label often has different usage and does not make something the same. The knife of the Initiate is a bit like the lightsaber of a Jedi, carefully constructed and wielded through years of training. In some lineages, even First-Degree Initiates are not permitted to have one.

---

[12] Doreen Valiente, *An ABC of Witchcraft Past and Present* (New York, NY: St. Martin's Press, 1973), 43.

The association of the knife with Witchcraft is nothing new. Folk magic is wrought with examples of a black-handled or black-hafted knife. In the Grimoire, there is an Irish spell from a 19th-century collection of folklore that features just such a blade. The Black-Handled Knife is a common theme in many old Grimoires, including the *Key of Solomon*. These ritual knives were used to make Spirits obedient as well as to carve circles of protection. Some Greek texts say that the Black-Handled Knife should be made from the horn of a he-goat. This practice of making goat horn daggers can still be found in the island of Crete today. The Witch's Athame is a purely magical ritual tool and is never used to cut anything. It has often been called the true Witch's weapon, and it represents the Witch's personal power. Rarely do Witches even let other Witches handle their Athames.

The White-Handled Knife
Another magic blade employed by Witches is the White-Handled Knife. It is a magical tool but has a more practical use such as carving, cutting, and marking. Like the Druid's Golden Sickle, used to harvest the sacred mistletoe, some knives are meant to be used for actual cutting in ritual. The use of the Black and White Knife as a pair can be found in the *Key of Solomon*, and also Gardner's grimoire, *Ye Bok of Ye Art Magical*. In his 1949 novel, *High Magic's Aid*, the Witch Morven digs up her mother's Black- and White-Handled Knives. The pictures in *High Magic's Aid* are straight from the Key of Solomon.[13]

Some may claim that the White- and Black-Handled Knives, or even the Athame, date only to the grimoire tradition and were taken up by the Modern Witchcraft Revival solely from these Renaissance and Early Modern occult sources. We do find, however, examples of these sacred and magical tools in antiquity, long before either the grimoires of Europe or the work of the British Witchcraft elders. Greek and Roman priests had special knives used for magic, ritual, and sacrifice. In Crete we find black-handled knives used to create magical circles, protect against ne-

---

[13] Gerald B. Gardner, *High Magic's Aid*, 2010 ed. (Aurinia Books, 2010), 125.

farious entities, and to work magic.[14] In Rome, priestesses could wield the *secespita*, which was a special sacrificial knife of iron with a white handle made of ivory.[15]

The Black- and White-Handled Knives are essentially twin blades, polarized in the Hermetic principle, "As Above, So Below," with one being used for the magical side of things—purely spiritual—and the other for practical needs.

The Sword

No other weapon has been as important to mankind as the Sword: a symbol of chivalry, nobility, sovereignty, and the primary weapons of gentlemen, knights, ancient warriors, and kings. A sword is one of the Four Treasures of the Tuatha Dé Danann, a symbol of Arthur Pendragon, and a necessary implement in today's knighting ceremonies and even coronations. In magic, the Sword is of equal importance. It is used in rituals by Masons, magicians, and, of course, Witches. In Witchcraft, the Sword is a symbol of authority and is generally only used by coven leaders. As the Athame represents the Witch's personal power, the Sword represents the coven's combined strength and, therefore, is mostly used within coven rituals.

The Black-Handled Knife, or Black Knife

This particular blade is a curious antiquity found within folklore. The Black-Handled Knife is a recurring theme in folk magic spells across Europe, and one of them from Ireland is in the Grimoire section of this book. There is no specification for the Black-Handled Knife as to whether or not it needs to be a dagger or one-edged blade, but clearly it was used for practical reasons, including cutting. This is a folk magic knife and, like the Athame, was the magician's companion. However, it was not used to direct energy like the Athame, at least not that we

---

[14] Nikos Vasilatos, *The Cretan Dagger* (Greece: Klassikes Ekdoseis, 1993).

[15] Meghan J. DiLuzio, *A Place at the Altar: Priestesses in Republican Rome* (Princeton, NJ: Princeton University Press, 2016), 27.

know of. It was used for working magic, so that would, therefore, imply some amount of energy was involved. It seems to me the folk magic knife is somewhere in between the White- and the Black-Handled Knife. It tends to be used more like the White-Handled Knife, yet it has the black handle. Whether this is the precursor of the Witch's blades or there is a connection at all is unknown. Regardless, I think this is an excellent alternative for non-Initiates or people who want to practice folk magic. This knife is used for cutting herbs, carving candles and making other etchings or carvings. It is not a ritual tool, although it has been used to cut circles in the earth by some.

The Black-Handled Knife is also often associated with harmful workings, so it may be something that arose out of folklore in general, and the assumption that any knife used for diabolical purposes would have to be black-handled. Raymond Buckland's book on Scottish Witchcraft gives an interesting tidbit concerning the Black-Handled Knife. In this system created by Mr. Buckland from older sources, the Scottish Dirk, which is a traditional Black-Handled Dagger that would be carried by folk magicians in Scotland and indeed used the very same way, is a constant companion for practical uses.[16] It is not used for casting spells, per se, but in preparation and conjunction with all the Arts in which the magician may be practicing.

Rods

Rods, like tools, come in many forms—wands, staves, brooms, spears, lances, crooks, and scepters. Like magical knives, they are used to direct energy, but may have particular meanings and purposes, depending on the work or ritual. In Ceremonial Magic, there are different wands for different forms of magic. If you choose to utilize magical rods in some way, once again make sure they are specific to a purpose. Research grimoires to receive proper information or ideas. How is your staff, wand or broom going to be used? And what does it symbolize? Rods have been

---

[16] Raymond Buckland, *Scottish Witchcraft: The History & Magic of the Picts* (St. Paul, MN: Llewellyn Publications, 1991), 50-51.

used in several forms, from the Bleeding Lance to the Spear of Lugh, the Scepter of Kings to the Crook of the Pharaoh.

Magic Wands

In Witchcraft and the occult, wands and magical staves are the most common. If you choose to use wands outside of a system, do your research and create one with specific intent. Keep in mind: personal tools will have to be replaced if you are initiated.

Wands have a rich, magical history. In Egypt, the gods are often depicted with the was-scepter, lotus wand or crook.[17] There is also a wand called the kohl-stick.[18] These Egyptian wands or staves may be the origin of the magical staff of Moses in the Bible. In the *Mabinogi*, Gwydion uses a magic wand to test Arianrhod's maidenhood, and as she steps over it, she instantly gives birth to the twins, Dylan and Lleu Llaw Gyffes. Wands were used by the Greeks and the Romans, as recorded by Strabo, Pliny, and Apuleius. The sorceress Circe used a magic wand, according to both Homer and Virgil. In modern occultism, the Wand derives from the grimoires, the various *Key of Solomon* manuscripts, and *The Magus*, being the most influential. These Wands have various markings and shapes and have been made of hazel, myrtle, elder and bay laurel. In the *Key of Solomon*, the wand is made from the virgin branch of a hazel tree cut at dawn with a single stroke on the day of Mercury.[19]

The length may vary, the *Abramelin* says the wand should be a finger's width, and its length should measure from your elbow to your fingertip. Franz Bardon said it should be 12-20 inches long and the *Key of Solomon*, Pierre Moras edition, 6 inches in length.[20] In most records, the wand or staff was used for invoking and praying, often employed when working with divinities. The grimoires appeared to retain this tradition, favoring the wand for both angelic and planetary magic. In Witchcraft, the Wand

---

[17] Eleanor Harris, *Ancient Egyptian Magic* (Newburyport, MA: Weiser Books, 1998), 45-50.
[18] Ibid, 43-44.
[19] "Magic Wands," *Twilit Grotto: Archives of Western Esoterica*, accessed June 18, 2019, http://esotericarchives.com/wands/.
[20] Ibid.

is a symbol of fertility and is used in specific rituals or workings. It is not a replacement of, nor is it interchangeable with, the Athame—as stated in so many books. The what-feels-right-to-you theory denotes a lack of both research and training.

If you're going to use a wand, make sure you are selecting a system and/or purpose for its use. Is it Air or Fire, or does that even matter? What kind of magic will you use it for? What size will it be and what will it be made of? Is it dedicated to a certain god or goddess? I have several wands for both Witchcraft and other occult systems. I have a beautiful lotus wand created by a member of the Hermetic Order of the Golden Dawn, and I dedicated this wand to the Goddess Isis, who is often depicted with one. When choosing a wood, you would be wise to consider its purpose. Fruit and flower trees are usually considered feminine, while nut trees are considered masculine. Below is a list of Celtic trees and their magical correspondences:

Birch: *purification, goddess, wishes.*
Rowan: *protection, divination.*
Ash: *astral travel, rune magic.*
Alder: *water magic, strength.*
Willow: *moon, enchantment.*
Hawthorn: *fairies, protection, wishes, sex.*
Oak: *fertility, strength, sovereignty, the sun and sky gods.*
Harley: *protection, banishing, leadership.*
Hazel: *inspiration, wisdom, magic, fertility.*
Apple: *love, glamour, wisdom.*
Vine: *ecstasy, freedom.*
Ivy: *binding, cursing, underworld.*
Reed: *music and nature spirits.*
Blackthorn: *cursing, protection.*
Elder: *goddess, renewal.*
Silver fir: *birth, rebirth.*
Firs: *balance and influence.*

Heather: *purification, blessing.*
Poplar: *success.*
Mistletoe: *healing.*
Yew: *death.* [21][22][23]

The Witch's Broom

Like the cauldron, the image of the broomstick reaches back to our earliest childhood memories of the Halloween Witch, and today it has become a symbol of the modern Craft movement. Most Witches have a magic broom of sorts, whether it is utilized in ritual magic or kept near the entrance to the home as a spell of protection, or simply to say that "a Witch lives here." Its connection to our Craft originates from the old woodcuts, trial records and folklore surrounding Witches flying upon various objects—rods, stangs, goats, and the broom. In Scotland, any staff or pole that a Witch rode upon was called a bune wand. Another term for the Witch's broom is the besom, which is also said to be the nickname for a shameless or immoral woman. In Witchcraft legend, it is often believed that the broom was a disguise for a phallic rod. And Witches used them in old fertility rites, straddling them like a hobby horse and running through the fields, jumping higher and higher in an effort to perform sympathetic magic to make the crops grow.

We do not actually have any proof that the Witch's broom was created to cloak some hidden phallic symbol, but it is, without a doubt, a symbol of female and male union, and maybe the oral lore is true! Perhaps it was once a way to disguise the bune wand or the stang. Maypoles throughout England, particularly in Sussex, at one point in time, were crowned with birch brooms, making these maypoles, quite literally, a giant broomstick,

---

[21] Pauline Campanelli, *Wheel of the Year Living the Magical Life* (St. Paul, MN: Llewellyn Publications, 1989), 51.

[22] Murry Hope, *Practical Celtic Magic, A Working Guide to the Magical Heritage of the Celtic Races* (London: The Aquarian Press, 1987), 194.

[23] Pattalee Glass-Koentop, *Year of Moons, Season of Trees: Mysteries & Rites of Celtic Tree Magic* (t. Paul, MN: Llewellyn Publications, 1991), 195.

and we all know that the Maypole is symbolic of the male and female union. It is interesting to note that birch is a popular wood for the assembly of magic brooms. If the Witch's broom had a dual purpose, one must wonder if the branches of the birch, like the birch branches once used for scourging or purification, may not have had similar value. The most popular Witchcraft broom is an ash pole, with birch twigs, tied with willow. Another alternative that may be older is a hazel pole with oak sprigs used for the broom, tied with birch. Officially, the oldest household broomstick was actually the plant broom tied around a stick, which is where the word may have originated.

In folk magic, brooms have a long association with weddings, and indeed, from various cultures, people have jumped over the broom while holding hands as the final act symbolizing their marriage. This is still performed in some Witch handfastings today. The Witch's broom is also a symbol of protection, hung over doorways, entrances or windows to keep evil at bay. The ritual gesture of sweeping, both within the home and the magic working space, is also a way to dispel and remove harmful or unwanted energies.

Some covens still utilize the Witch's broom as a fertility symbol, used in certain rites or when dancing. In spellwork, the broom is also used for weather manipulation or like the stang, astral travel. After all, there is a reason we fly on brooms. It has been suggested, if it was a phallic bune wand at one point in time, it may have actually been shaped like a phallus, and various herbs, the hallucinogenic property placed upon it, the Witch dancing upon it naked, would absorb these properties, and indeed, begin to have a visionary state. Of course, like with most myths, we have no such evidence.

Regardless of the reasons, the broom is a symbol of fertility, purification, and female power. Whether you use them in your rituals or merely prop them in a corner, just remember: always bristles up![24]

---

[24] Doreen Valiente, *An ABC of Witchcraft Past and Present* (New York, NY: St. Martin's Press, 1973), 68-70.

The Stang

Perhaps no tool associated with Witchcraft has had more recent attention among today's non-Initiates than the stang. The stang is a wand or staff that is forked. The inspiration for it can be found in old Witchcraft woodcuts where the Witches would ride or fly on forked branches alongside other Witches flying on brooms or goats. Most likely, this was a simple two-pronged pitchfork used for baling hay. A common agricultural tool, just like the broom, the stang would have been an everyday domestic object allegedly re-purposed by Witches for their nefarious purposes. Some may try to link the stang to historical wands used by English cunning men or other magical practitioners in folklore and historical records. Interestingly enough, in Wales and other rural places in England, there are ordinary walking sticks still sold today with a forked top, perhaps owing their origins to an older, forgotten past.

The stang, or at least the word "stang," has been attributed to the work of Robert Cochrane, who perhaps coined the name.[25] The word "stang" may have its origins in the Old Norse "*stong*," which means staff or pole.[26] There is no description of the stong having a forked branch, but that does not exclude the possibility.

Robert Cochrane did not have a *Book of Shadows* or a lineage. However, one of his associates was the Gardnerian High Priestess and Initiate, Doreen Valiente, who went on to speak about the stang and use it within her works for years to come, and perhaps it is because of her that we have the knowledge of it today.[27] Other Initiates did write about the stang. Patricia Crowther links the stang to the mythology of flying ointments as well as describing its use as a representation of the God of Witchcraft.[28] Something to note, Robert Cochrane and the Initiates

---

[25] Ronald Hutton, *The Triumph of the Moon: A History of Modern Pagan Witchcraft* (Oxford: Oxford University Press, 1999), 314-315.

[26] Ross. G. Arthur, *English-Old Norse Dictionary* (Cambridge, Ontario: In Parentheses Publications, 2002. 137.

[27] Philip Heselton, *Doreen Valiente, Witch* (Woodbury, MN: Llewelyn 2016), 130-134.

[28] Patricia Crowther, *Covensense, A Handbook for Witches* (London: Frederick Muller Limited, 1981), 102.

used the stang as a symbology of the horned gods, and it was used as an erect altar decorated for various holidays with different garlands, and stationed at different places within the circle—or, in Cochrane's case, working site, and not as a tool for directing energy.[29][30]

Today, the stang is used by different magical practitioners in different ways. It is a tool of energy used to project and direct energy by some, and it is symbolic of the Horned God and the seasons by others. The old woodcuts have had their inspiration as well, whereas some practitioners like to use the tool to help them in their astral journeys, or in other workings on the inner planes.

We have a stang in the New Orleans coven, and I have had others in my personal magical collection over the years as well. My stang is actually an old pitchfork that I found at a peculiar shop, so it's just a wooden pole with two very sharp prongs at the top, but we use it for certain symbolic rites. So, contrary to popular belief, the stang is not a "pre-Gardnerian" tool, as some critics of the Witch Cult would argue, any more than the broomstick is. We Initiates have always been aware of the regional folk magic of the British Isles and continental Europe. I have heard that it was an old custom to erect a stang in a garden or field with offerings of fruit, flowers, and other symbols of the harvest. This was not done by Witches but by country folk carrying on some half-forgotten ritual, no doubt.

The stang could be an agricultural symbol used as a form of sympathetic magic, a crude icon for the Old God or a resemblance of the ancient staff of the Druid. Regardless of if or how you choose to use it, it is a symbol of Witchcraft today.

Vessels

Bowls, cups, cauldrons, and censers are all used in various occult systems. These objects have been used to nourish ourselves through cooking, feasting, and celebration. They have been used as vessels to explore intoxication, and for their usefulness when making medicine. They are also

---

[29] Ibid, 102.
[30] Philip Heselton, *Doreen Valiente, Witch* (Woodbury, MN: Llewelyn 2016), 131.

symbols of sacrifice and used to make offerings to the Gods. Many kinds of vessels are seen as Goddess symbols, and they are also associated with Water, the censer being the exception due to its obvious connection to Fire. Magic vessels feature prominently in nearly all systems of religion and magic, and Witchcraft is no exception. Vessels in magic are often receptacles of transformation—and transformation is their most essential use. Wine—transformed into the Blood of Christ—potions, healing brews, holy water, smoldering incense, and sweet oils are all intimately attached to such implements.

The Censer

The Censer is a favorite tool in Alexandrian Craft, and its use originates in the cradle of civilization. Various forms of this tool were used by the Mesopotamians, Egyptians, Greeks, Romans, and other civilized peoples. The favored incense of their temples was frankincense or myrrh, which later would be adopted by the Church. Incense has been used as both an offering and as a beacon for the Gods and other spirits. Frankincense is sacred to both sun gods and moon goddesses and was also used in Rites of Demeter. As an incense, it is used for protection, purification, and general magic work.[31] Myrrh was a funerary herb in Egypt and is sacred to Hera, Saturn, Cybele, and Hecate. It can be used in power raising or for awareness.[32] The alternative to the Censer and its origin was the Sacred Fire, into which various herbs and woods were cast. Vervain was offered unto the fires by the Druids and also by devotees of the Goddess Diana. As an incense, it is used for power, consecration, purification, inspiration, and sometimes romance.[33] Bay laurel was burned at Delphi for visionary work and is sacred to Apollo, known as a plant of love.[34] Mastic, cinnamon, mint, honey, wine, sweet flag,

---

[31] Paul Beryl, *The Master Book of Herbalism* (Custer, WA: Phoenix Publishing, 1984), 220-221.
[32] Ibid, 236-237.
[33] Ibid, 252-253.
[34] Ibid, 202-203.

cypress, and raisins are all popular ingredients of Temple Incense but always mixed with frankincense.

The Cauldron

The Cauldron first emerges in our early childhood—a symbol associated with the Halloween Witch, filled with candy, or used in the game of bobbing for apples. But what is the origin of this enigmatic symbol? We do know that it is a sacred vessel generally associated with the Great Goddess. Most practitioners of Witchcraft view it as the original Holy Grail. In fact, many gods and goddesses have been linked to the Cauldron: Badb, the Dagda, and Ceridwen, to name just a few. The Cauldron is the most powerful of vessels in many ways, for, when actually used for its intended purpose, one must utilize all of the Elements. And there is no doubt that the Witches of old used their Cauldrons to make potions and work with herbs. Combine Fire and Water to a roiling bubble, then add a few magic plants and other ingredients, to create both aroma and steam. Few Witches heat Cauldrons in such a way today, but it is entirely possible and makes for a fantastic focal point in the center of your working area. You have the Womb of the Goddess with all the Elements actively involved. One imagines Witches partaking of its hallucinogenic contents at some old-time Sabbat and flying upward into the stars.

Today, there are other practical ways in which you can use the Cauldron. You can use it on your stove if you have a cauldron that is appropriate for such use, and use it to make your potions, your philters, and herbal brews. In this way, you are working with all of the elements magically—and it is quite powerful. This would be the old-style way to work with the Cauldron. In modern ritual, the Cauldron is often placed in the center of the working site. As for using it indoors, it is not practical to boil a Cauldron in most rooms outside of the kitchen. However, if you're working in your kitchen, how appropriate. If for whatever reason you cannot use the Cauldron in this way, it can still be used symbolically, filled with water, candles lit inside, or even used as a censer. We generally use the Cauldron at certain Sabbat rites or to symbolically represent the

Goddess. However, I do use the Cauldron when brewing certain herbal mixtures, and I have used it for all the reasons listed above at various times.

Traditionally, the Cauldron should be cast-iron, and it should have three legs. The symbology here is not lost on those in the Craft. Iron is extremely vital because it neutralizes all baneful energies. This is where we get the mythology that Fairies or spirits, sometimes even vampires, are afraid of iron, and iron is used for protection due to its neutralizing energy. Iron is actually essential for life as we know it, and it exists within our own body's, plants, animals, the Earth, and other planets in our solar system.

Iron was essential to the Celtic peoples, as they were an Iron Age culture. And it's believed that the pre-Celtic peoples whom they conquered, supplanted, and absorbed were the tribes of peoples that the Celts called the Sidhe—what we now call Fairies. These peoples were part of the Bronze Age culture. So the Iron Age culture, destroying the Bronze Age culture, or absorbing it—may be where the stories of the fairies' fear of iron originate. Iron, of course, is also sacred to Mars: the metal is masculine and adds an element of balance to this tool.

Pentacles

In Gardnerian and Alexandrian Craft, we have the Pentacle, a magical disc adorned with symbols explicitly created for our rituals. The inscriptions are for our Gods and ways of working magic. Pentacles originate from ceremonial magic. In fact, the *Key of Solomon* is one of the most significant sources used in their creation. Each pentacle is a plate of a specific metal, with particular symbols on it, and is not necessarily associated with a pentagram, which may or may not have symbols inscribed on it. Pentacles are used to consecrate and to command or invoke certain spirits. So, each pentacle is made for the specific spirits or gods that are going to be worked with. For instance, the First Pentacle of the Sun is created for sun spirits, angels, gods, names of gods, all associated with the Sun. Likewise, in Alexandrian and Gardnerian Witchcraft, those pentacles used within our systems are specially crafted for our Gods:

the Moon Goddess, the Horned One, the Gods of Witchcraft, and our Quarter Lords.

I created the Pentacle of Alexandria for use in the rituals in this book. You can purchase one of these from my shop, Hex Old World Witchery, or you can make your own, based on the inscriptions within these pages. However, if you're not going to work with Serapis and Isis, and you chose to work with Diana and Pan instead, create your own pentacle to those specific gods. The inscriptions for Serapis and Isis are not necessarily going to be the same as those that you might use for Diana and Pan, although my Pentacle is meant to be universal. As we have already discussed in our exploration of the Cults of Isis and Diana, those goddesses could be seen a one and the same; in the end, it is entirely your preference. The Pentacle of Alexandria should be made of silver, gold, or copper—or you might have more than one to use in particular rituals and workings. These are, of course, the metals of the Moon, the Sun, and Venus. In Alexandria, these metals would have been sacred to Serapis and Isis.

Pentacle of Alexandria

Other tools

In Witchcraft and magic, there are other tools employed by the Witch or magician that do not fall under any elemental scheme. The Scourge, the stang, the Cords, magic mirrors, and, of course, the Witch's Besom more commonly known as the broom, are just a few of the more common implements, but many other items could be used in the magical workings of the Witch

The Scourge

One of the earliest examples of the Scourge is the Egyptian flail. This was the symbol of the Pharaoh or the Gods' power. It is believed it was originally a weapon used to defend sheep, or an agricultural tool used to thresh grain; personally, I think threshing grain makes more sense, or perhaps herding sheep with a whip. The flail represents the severity of power. One might have also considered that the crook was the shepherd and symbolized animal husbandry, while the flail signified agriculture. Flagellation is a religious practice dating back to antiquity. It was used in the cults of Isis, Cybele, Dionysus, and by the Spartans in the worship of their Moon Goddess, Orthia Athena.[35] Flagellation was utilized by the early Church and is still practiced by some Shiite Muslims. The Scourge is a favorite tool of occultists and is used in many magical orders. In Europe, flagellation was often done with birch branches. This practice of whipping yourself with birch branches in steam rooms can still be found throughout Europe today, particularly in Germanic countries.

Another curious Germanic practice involving the birch is that of Krampus festivals. You can still find these today on YouTube with excellent documentation. Men dress to represent Krampus, the demonic spirit of winter who was probably once an old horned god associated with Witchcraft, and who always carries bundles of birch twigs to beat people with. This most likely originates from ancient purification rituals. It is interesting to note that birch branches have become the singular

---

[35] Raymond Buckland, *The Witch Book, The Encylopedia of Witchcraft, Wicca, and Neo-Paganism* (Canton, MI: Visible Ink Press, 2002), 175-176.

most popular wood used in Witches' brooms today and are a tool also associated with purification. Scourging, or whipping, is not new in the mythology of Witchcraft and does not have its origins with the Witchcraft revival. Witch trials in the Middle Ages recorded accounts of coven leaders, or the Devil, beating or scourging Witches as a form of punishment, or whipping of the dancers.[36]

In Witchcraft, the Scourge remains important to Initiates and is not generally used in other systems of magic. It is a symbol of domination used for purification, sacrifice, raising power, and trance work. Gerald Gardner was said to be very fond of this tool and has often been accused of its overuse. Witches do, however, use what works, so I see no reason to criticize.

One of the key differences often cited between Gardnerian and Alexandrian Witches is the use of this tool, and what importance is placed upon its use. Alexandrians do not purify or sacrifice with the Scourge. It is generally used symbolically. This being said, once again, every coven is different, and we approach ritual expecting results.

Cords

Cords and knot magic have a longstanding history in magic and Witchcraft. Perhaps this has something to do with the art of spinning thread and sewing, which, at one time, must have seemed magical indeed, as early people would have first witnessed this power in spiders or silkworms. The spinning threads would become mythological, like the Three Fates weaving the threads, or Arachne, This gift, then, of course, fell into the field of creation and sorcery. I think this must also come from the role of the midwife, with the Thread of Life symbolically being the umbilical cord. We are all born with that cord attached to our mother and, depending on one's fortune, it can even be deadly. Cords thereby become symbols of fate, and the making of knots was a way of shaping it. One such example of the magical importance of knots can be found in the art of Celtic knot-work. In its beautiful tapestry of carefully placed

---

[36] Ibid, 176.

symbols can be found heroes, animals, and even gods woven together by the threads of forgotten stories and imagery.

Legend states that Medieval Witches sold knotted ropes to sailors. They were said to have conjured winds into the knots, and all the sailor had to do was untie a knot to release a much-needed wind during one of his voyages.[37] Another curious example of knotted cords found in Witchcraft is in the Witch's Ladder. Relics of Witch's Ladders have been found inside of homes in Somerset and other areas of West Country, England. These are believed to have been curses and consisted of three strands braided together with feathers woven in and knots. Sometimes these were placed in victims' beds or in their house walls; sometimes, a stone was tied to them, and they were said to be thrown into the water. Curiously enough, there's a similar custom in Italy with an object called the Witch's Garland.[38]

When I was traveling in Wales, I made a curious discovery myself. We were in a little port town, and within a restaurant, they had a framed picture and inside it were sailor knots. These were artistically, beautifully crafted knots unlike anything I'd ever seen. I can only imagine that there are very few people alive today, if anyone, who knows the art of crafting these, and it looked extremely magical to me. You could imagine and see each one being a potent talisman for some particular purpose or reason, and not simply for practical uses. Many were far too complex-looking to me, and some even resembled animals or other objects.

Today, Cords are used within Initiatory Craft. Doreen Valiente said the Cords could be made of any color, though if one could obtain red, that was the preferred color used by the early Gardnerian Witches. Today, the traditions have their own colors used for their own particular reasons. These are magical tools that are used for magical work. In Alexandrian Craft, we never wear them as belts, but it has become customary in some lines and non-initiatory traditions to use the Cord as merely an

---

[37] Ibid, 503.
[38] Doreen Valiente, *An ABC of Witchcraft Past and Present* (New York, NY: St. Martin's Press, 1973), 398-399.

ornamental belt. A modern variation of the Witch's Ladder can be used very much like a Rosary, whereas the knots are used to keep count of your incantations or prayers. So, for instance, if you had a cord with 13 knots tied into it and you want to say the spell 13 times, you simply keep pulling the cord to the knot, and that way you can focus on repeating the spell without having to think about what number you are on. Invariably, if you practice Witchcraft or any form of folk magic at some point in time, you will utilize some method of cord magic.

The Magic Mirror
A perhaps often-forgotten implement used in magic is the mirror. It can be a standard mirror or a black mirror. Sometimes other colored mirrors are used for conjuring spirits, as in a red mirror for Mars or a green mirror for Venus. For many, our first introductions to the Magic Mirror probably came from the Walt Disney movie "Snow White," where the Wicked Queen invokes her magic mirror every day, asking, "Magic mirror, on the wall, who is the fairest one of all?" [39]

Magic mirrors are indeed potent portals used for invocation, scrying, protection and the casting of spells. Mirrors are associated with light, which gives them an obvious relationship with energy. Witches use them much in the same way one might use a crystal or a crystal ball. A curious Craft ritual exists whereby some Witches use the Mirror to reflect the light of the Moon into the Chalice as another way of blessing its contents. This brings to mind a place I have mentioned previously: Lake Nemi. The Lake is in a wooded valley and is perfectly round in June, near the Summer Solstice, the Full Moon is directly overhead, and its light radiates off the lake, which is sacred to Diana and Isis. This lake is called the Mirror of Diana. Appropriate indeed.

Reflections of light have often been associated with Witchcraft and magic. And, indeed, a mirror not only receives light and reflects it, capturing the imagery around it, but it can also contain images mostly

---

[39] Walt Disney, et al, *Snow White and the Seven Dwarfs* (Burbank, Calif: Walt Disney Enterprises, 1937).

seen only on the psychic level, even perceptions of yourself on the inner planes. I prefer a black mirror for scrying. Raymond Buckland, in his book *Scottish Witchcraft*, describes a tool called the Keek-Stane, which is a box. [40] Inside is a black mirror used for this very purpose. You can use any mirror—some prefer an average ordinary mirror, usually round; personally, I like a variety and prefer black. In most cases, however, a regular mirror is best, in my opinion, for some inner plane work and protection. When using the Magic Mirror, work in darkness, flanking it with candles and incense. This not only creates the correct atmosphere but aids in making the Mirror a focal point. When working with spirits, magicians often gaze at the channeler through a mirror flanked with candles for such a reason. The reflection begins to become the embodiment of the spirit therein invoked.

Another critical use for the Witch's Magic Mirror is protection. This can be used to reflect back any baneful energy working against you. It can be used to repel those things that you do not wish to have in your life. The Magic Mirror, just as it was for the Wicked Queen in "Snow White," can become a powerful companion for the Witch, for you can also use this Mirror to hold a spirit familiar or a thoughtform of your intent. In this way, the Magic Mirror becomes both housing for actual entities and a link to your magical workings. I had a very dear Witch friend of mine who once said, "Have you ever looked into your own eyes in a mirror, and something else was looking back at you?" I think we've all had this strange experience. Like all forms of magic, you might have to experiment to discover what is most effective.

Mystical objects and tools are universally used in every religion or magical system. In Witchcraft these weapons are more than just religious implements, badges of office, collector's items. They are not, as some try to argue, mere focal points but are themselves imbued with the magic of those who wield them and thus become extensions of the Witch's

---

[40] Raymond Buckland, *Scottish Witchcraft: The History & Magic of the Picts* (St. Paul, MN: Llewellyn Publications, 1991), 66-67.

power. They are physical manifestations of the Initiate's true will. They allow us to interact with the inner planes, enabling us to direct our intentions into the world and to reach states of consciousness by which we can commune with the old Gods. They are keys to the many paths of magic that are both overgrown and hidden. Each magical tool holds our oral traditions within its symbolisms waiting to be rediscovered. ny implement used in magic should be valued and have deep meaning to the wielder. Like the Arts Magical itself, they should be used wisely.

CHAPTER 9

The Grimoire Occultatum

AN OCCULT COLLECTION OF RITUALS, RECIPES, SPELLS, EXERCISES, AND WITCHCRAFT LORE

A grimoire is a book of magic. This one can be used by any occultist or practitioner of Witchcraft. It does not represent a tradition, nor does it contain any of the secret materials used by Initiates. Some of the rituals have been inspired by the magical practices of Alexandria, Egypt, and call upon the ancient gods Serapis and Isis. However, you could work with any sacred God and Goddess that suits you; or, simply call on them as God and Goddess. This collection is inspired by Golden Dawn rituals, the *Key of Solomon*, the *Egyptian Book of the Dead*, and Greek magical papyri. It also contains folk magic and lore from various sources and spells of my own design. I use these rites within the Temple at Hex New Orleans, and they are intended for public practice. I hope the exercises and rituals within will help you to open up your consciousness on the inner planes and, if it is your desire, lead you toward the path of Initiation.

Psychic Powers

What exactly is a psychic? A psychic is a person who is sensitive to non-physical or supernatural forces and influences, which are often defined through clairvoyance, telepathy, mediumship, and other forms of paranormal phenomena. Psychics are traditionally sought out by individuals seeking answers to life questions and can be found in occult shops, on street corners in New Orleans, and on telephone lines and computers across the world. They can be fortune tellers, animal empaths, and clairvoyants to the stars. They have been used by police, the military, intelligence agencies, and sitting presidents. Oracles were sought out in the ancient world, and the practice is alive and well today. Psychic abilities come in a wide-ranging variety of skills, or gifts, as they are often called. Visions, feelings, thoughts, and even voices. Most people think of a psychic as a rare individual. And, like any skill set, some people are just naturally gifted at it, while others have studied for years to attain their skill—developing their psychic muscle to gain far more proficiency than the average person. However, in truth, all human beings, and even animals, have this ability.

It has been coined the sixth sense. We've all had our hair stand up. We've all known something before we were supposed to. We've all received a message, whether through a thought, a dream, or a vision. And, in fact, anyone can train and become proficient in psychic powers. But what is the difference between a psychic and Witch? Or rather a psychic Witch. Psychics receive knowledge and wisdom via senses beyond the known five. They act as a sort of radio, collecting information. However, the Witch learns to not only obtain this information but to project it. Projecting your psychic power has long been a secret technique used throughout the occult traditions.

Telepathy and hypnosis have been used in the arts of healing and manipulation for centuries—the Witch is no stranger to such practices. Not all practitioners of Witchcraft profess to be psychic, nor do they necessarily all like the word. But in truth, they are developing their own psychic powers as they work magic. Initiates call this "the sight." And one must have it in order to be proficient in the Arts Magical. Teaching the Arts to someone without this skill would be like taking a blind person to a shooting range and handing him a gun. You need to be able to see what you're doing when wielding such weapon of force.

Initiates have various methods for employing or gaining "the sight," some more effective than others—but through the use of ritual and discipline of the mind, it is achieved. Your psychic powers are a tool of your mind, which is the vehicle for formulating thoughts, receiving information, the creative process, and the active imagination valued in the arts. When the Witch fertilizes this and projects it, the power moves and hits its mark.

Now how does one begin? If you are receiving formal training, the route may be decided for you, but I see no reason to object to non-Initiates exploring something that belongs inherently to all of us. How do you develop your psychic skills without formal training? Meditation, visualization, and other mental exercises are absolutely essential. I also highly recommend that everyone read one book, *The Silva Mind Control Method* by Jose Silva, which gives one the techniques and exercises necessary to achieve the psychic level of mind.

People generally think of meditation as silencing the mind and becoming tranquil, learning to listen and relax. These disciplines are very beneficial but not always the most effective avenue for every individual.

If you have a strong and active imagination, I recommend guided meditations featuring techniques of visualization. This is something we all naturally use as children, but for many adults it begins to fade away in the face of concrete reality. This is why it has been said children make the best magicians. The words magic and imagination have the same roots in words such as *magus* and *magi*, which mean wisdom. This same active imagination is used in ritual, for when performing ritual, you must bring the inner and the outer planes of reality into the same space.

Practicing occult exercises and rituals daily is a potent way to raise consciousness and develop your powers. When you are performing rituals, you must also visualize it playing out on your inner planes. Many kinetic people find ritual extremely important because of the combination of physical reality and the unseen. Persistence is key. When working with the mind, you're working with consciousness. And different levels of consciousness. The goal is to recognize these levels or planes of reality and learn how to shift into them at will.

THE VISIONARY STATE

In my husband, Christian Day's book, *The Witches Book of the Dead,* he presents a technique that he calls the Visionary State. Christian studied under Salem Witch Laurie Cabot, who taught him methods to lower the mind into an alpha brain wave state where it is easier to absorb psychic information. [1] Countdown-style methods are also used frequently in hypnosis; by counting backward to yourself, you can bring yourself into deeper levels of mind. It can be as simple as reciting "ten, nine, eight, seven, six, five, four, three, two, one." Witches often incorporate visualization with the countdown by including objects, numbers, or colors of the rainbow—or colors that have a substantial effect on the mind like white, red, black, or gray. Regardless of the method, the training is meant to help you shift your consciousness into the correct state for the work you are doing. With my husband's permission, I have adapted his own exercise to enter the Visionary State as a means to achieve psychic awareness.

---

[1] Laurie Cabot, *Power Of The Witch* (New York, Delta, 1990), 183-187.

Exercise: Entering the Visionary State

STEP ONE

Find a comfortable chair where you can relax and connect to the spiritual forces around you.

STEP TWO

When you are comfortably seated, close your eyes and focus on your breathing. Allow your breath to become slow, deep, and deliberate. In your mind's eye, see your breath as a living force of energy, inhaling the powers of the tides of magic and exhaling your own thoughts and visions that your intent becomes one with the universe. Realize that the air you exhale becomes part of the universal mind as it absorbs your essence through your breath. With each inhale, the universe aligns with your life force. Your breath should continue this way over the course of the visionary state.

STEP THREE

Feel the flesh of your body tingle as the forces of magic begin to flow through you. Notice the changes that take place: your breathing may become shallow, your limbs may become numb or tingly, and your heart rate may drop. Trust the process—it is like falling into a deep, dreamlike sleep, yet one in which you are still aware. Let your spirit release itself from the heaviness of your physical body. Breath after breath, slower, heavier, and deeper, descend into the depths of the inner places. To define the state, you will now count to yourself from ten to one. When you reach one, say in your mind,

> *"I am now in a visionary state. I am at one with the universe. It flows through me as I flow through it."*

Swim in the tides of magic, feeling those currents within your very blood. You are now able to interact on the inner planes at the core of your body and soul, able to share in their memories and experiences.

When you are ready to come back, count from one to ten and open your eyes. It is important to count back up whenever you can so that you do not have the feeling of suddenly being jarred awake. Do this exercise daily or whenever possible and you will have the key to reaching the Visionary State whenever you desire. [2]

DIVINATI⊕N

One of the best methods to work that psychic muscle is to use it, and perhaps the most direct route is the art of divination. This method is about jumping in and just doing it! After all, some of the best training is on-the-job training. Reading Tarot cards regularly will not only tap you into Western occult symbology but help you awaken your abilities. This is true of experienced Witches—if we turn it on often enough, it stays on!

Although I recommend the Tarot, all forms of divination can and will do this on some level. If you're drawn to runes, playing cards, or some other method, that is perfectly acceptable and okay. It's whatever shifts your consciousness and enables you to work. These tools are steeped in potent archetypes and images, and if you start using them on a daily basis, you will begin to develop your own psychic powers. At first, you may rely heavily on the cards, but in time, working with these images, you are working with archetypes on your subconscious level. That will begin to perform a ritual on your inner planes and within your mind, and you will start receiving information.

If you are reading for yourself, you might have to experiment on some level, because it's somewhat challenging to read for yourself in the beginning. You know, none of us wants to receive bad news, and it's easy to read into good news. It's sort of like giving yourself advice about your love life. We can't usually see what's right in front of our faces when it

---

[2] Christian Day, *The Witches' Book of the Dead* (New Orleans, Warlock Press, 2019).

comes to the matters of the heart. One of the things I do, when reading for myself, is I will do my spread and I will look at it. And I will leave it out. I won't try to get the answer right away. I'll look at it and contemplate, then I walk away.

Usually, I get psychic information within 24 hours because I've unlocked that subconscious. I've got no problem reading for other people, but this is the best way I've found to read for myself. I have to allow it to germinate.

When working magic, or the Arts Magical, it is essential to be able to able to see the bigger picture and the bird's-eye view. You do not want to work magic for someone unless you completely understand the situation. And that is equally essential for yourself. I recommend you do a reading on any magic beforehand. Doing this will ensure you do not make as many mistakes or act in a rash manner. It's always good to ask, what will occur if I cast this spell?

We are all psychic because we all have brilliantly designed minds. Perhaps this is a new word that sounds tacky to many individuals, but the prophetic powers of witches and magicians originate in antiquity, and they are alive and well today.

The Arts Magical

Magic is perhaps the most essential truth of the religion of Witchcraft, and this is often forgotten. Everything we do from the beginning to the end of any ritual is an act of magic. In his book, *Magick in Theory and Practice*, Aleister Crowley defines magic as "the science and art of causing change to occur in conformity with will."[3] This definition has been adopted by most members of the occult community as it is incredibly accurate regardless of your practice.

---

[3] Aleister Crowley, *Magick in Theory and Practice* (New York, NY: Dover Publications, 1976), 12.

It must be understood there are different systems of magic, and they are not all regarded as Witchcraft. Magic is without a doubt a key component of our Craft, but it is coupled with ecstatic experience, psychic power, and knowledge of the natural world, and it contains an emotional catalyst found through divine love. Witchcraft also has a magical system of its own taught to the Initiate.

Because we are a mystery tradition and a fertility cult, our way of approaching the art is very different. Because this is a religion, it's very different than other systems of magic. It is a system unto itself.

Witches work from the core of their own being, using their own psychic powers. We draw upon the forces of nature. We invoke the gods for power. This is why Witches do not pray. We generally do not petition for things. In our magic, we become an active part of the creative process. In essence, within our Circle, we are co-creators.

Aside from the unique methods outlined in the *Book of Shadows*, Witches, and particularly Alexandrians, do experiment with other systems of magic. However, we identify them as just that: other systems of magic. And we do not mix our drinks. For instance, magicians work very differently than Witches. Magicians invoke spirits, angels, genii, demons, and sometimes gods. But they petition them or command them, primarily relying on these entities to make it all happen. Witches invoke for power. This is why we do not invoke everything into the Magical Circle. We invoke the God and the Goddess and the elemental forces, and that's generally where it ends unless we are experimenting in some other system.

The Five Elements

Both magicians and Witches work with the five elements of nature. And, as we explored in the tools, these elements have ancient origins. They are not, of course, scientific elements, but the magical elements: earth, air, fire, water, and spirit. This is what the pentagram primarily represents—the five elements of nature and magic. And it is for this reason that the pentagram has become the predominant symbol of Witchcraft. The pentagram within a circle, sometimes called a pentacle (like the tool), symbolizes these powers alchemically united within a Magic Circle. To the Witch, these elements exist not only in the physical but the spiritual or astral realms. Each element represents a host of spirits and divine beings we call the Mighty Ones.

Life, at least on our planet, requires each of these forces to exist on this plane. Our body, like the planet, is mostly made of water and returns to dust. We require heat and oxygen, and all of this must be in a perfect balance. The spirit is, of course, the unexplained force that gives it life or a soul! In magic, each element has unique attributes. Air represents knowledge, intellect, inspiration, and new beginnings. Fire represents power, strength, passion, and ambition. Water is psychic power, emotional matters, otherworlds and transformation. Earth represents fertility, stability, abundance, and the foundation of all things.

The Witch seeks to harmonize, understand, and explore these powerful occult symbols, both within the mundane world and within the inner planes. In the magical system of Witchcraft, polarity is also essential and can even be found in the way we work with the elements. This is a way of creating balance, and it mirrors the inherent creative process found in nature. This balance is required to fertilize the magic.

In Western Alchemy, fire/water and air/earth work as polar opposites that, when combined, create the desired results. The barren earth, being stone, must be fertilized with water to create life, which can only be brought by the air. And without the perpetual fires, there would be no water but ice, and there would be no light to fertilize the sacred seeds. All of these things must come together for that spark of life to manifest, as stated in the Hermetic Principle, "As Above, So Below." This is also essential to the Art. The physical and spiritual realms are not separate but polarized.

The Witch's Pyramid

So now that I've defined what magic is, and I've spoken a little bit about Witchcraft in its relation to magic, what powers Witches draw upon and why, let us contemplate technique for a moment. I find it quite humorous and depressing that social media is filled with people bragging about all the spells they cast or posting pictures of their magical altar with some curse they've woven or their fridge-art talismans. Any astute occultist will immediately recognize that these individuals not only lack training, but also magical wisdom.

A magical philosophy that has been utilized by many practitioners is the Witches' Pyramid. Its origins are obscure, and it has also been called the "Four Secrets of the Sphinx." The Four Powers of the Magus is generally believed to come from Hermetic magic or the Magi. I first discovered it in Paul Huson's book, *Mastering Witchcraft*, which I suspect is responsible for its popular use in the Craft today.[4]

The Witches' Pyramid has four corners and a point. You could use the pentagram for the same symbology. Each corner of the Pyramid represents the foundation of magical work, with the tip representing manifestation and success.

They are: To Know, To Will, To Dare, and To Keep Silent. To Know implies that you must have the knowledge and you must know precisely what your goal is and what it is you wish to achieve. To Will is your psychic power and your willpower and confidence (magic is in conformity with the will.) To Dare is to have the courage to not only meddle with the universe but to take responsibility for the results. And To Keep Silent: When you talk about your magic, you ground it. Grounding it essentially means you strip it of its power, and you don't let it go into the inner planes where it can manifest. When a thing is complete, you should let it be. When you work your magic, you should let it go, and you should not talk about it. Only after it has manifested should it ever be discussed.

---

[4] Paul Huson, *Mastering Witchcraft*, 2006 ed. (Lincoln, NE: iUniverse, Inc., 2006), 22.

Do not discuss your work with anyone until you have achieved your desired results. Every person you tell becomes linked to that work—you are quite literally giving pieces of it away.

Another way of looking at it is if you're approaching magic through the vein of religious Witchcraft or some holy order, you are doing something sacred. And the old saying, "Do not throw pearls before swine," comes to mind if you do not want it to be profaned. Silent, secret, and sacred are words that have the same origins.

The Threefold Law

If you are going to muck about with the forces of the universe, it is wise to consider the possible consequences, something you should do with any decision you make—magic or otherwise. Karma, the Law of Return, rebound, and balance have all been taught as a universal truth within various branches of the occult. Now that I've discussed some philosophies on the art magical—which, of course, I'm only briefly covering—let us take a moment to approach the ethics and universal law. This is something people don't like to discuss today, or when they do, they want to ridicule it. The first thing I'm going to address is the oft-discussed Threefold Law. The Threefold Law has been published by countless authors who collectively invented a new concept based entirely on misinformation. This is often put out as one of the foundational beliefs in Witchcraft, and this is absolutely untrue.

They taught that whatever you do is going to come back to you threefold. In essence, it's karma with a strange mathematical equation. So if you do something good, it'll come back to you threefold. If you do something terrible, it'll come back to you threefold. There is a mystery that is taught in one of the initiations, that it relevant for Initiates, and I do believe this is where the public idea of the Threefold Law originates. The confusion arose when individuals began interpreting the Craft without having experienced it.

What we do believe in as Initiates is that we must take full responsibility for everything good and bad. We are in control of our choices, actions, and reactions. If you throw a pebble into a pond, it will ripple. The number three is very potent and often used in our magic, but we do not believe in a judgmental system—Witches know that we are writing the script, and as a species, we are all mere actors in a great play written by ourselves. Those who follow the public threefold law are giving themselves a check-and-balance, and I see no harm in that, nor do I ridicule them. It is simply not a concept I share with them.

The Witches' Rede

The second very popular (and unpopular) law to be brought up is the Rede that states, "An it harm none, do what ye will," and is more commonly known as the Wiccan Rede. You will find no lack of individuals who claim to be Witches spouting off about how the Rede is a Wiccan law or a Wiccan belief, and that real Witches curse, real Witches hex. It is said the Rede is impossible to follow, or unrealistic. Clearly, everyone harms. It cannot be avoided, so, therefore, is not logical.

In recent years, people increasingly desire Witchcraft to be darker, nonreligious, and free from ethics, something that reflects our current social climate, in my opinion. I also believe this has happened before many, many times. Authenticity has nothing to do with cruelty! Predominantly, the arts have been used benevolently throughout history. But when people become powerless, disenfranchised, or desperate, they become hostile regardless of the medium. A healer is a thousand times more powerful than an assassin, and Witches know this to be true.

Like the Threefold Law, there is some misunderstanding surrounding the Rede. The Rede is not a Ten Commandments-style law in Witchcraft. The word "rede" means advice or counsel. And the Witches' Rede, Witches' Creed, or Wiccan Rede became a useful tool for public education but over time lost its original purpose in the face of a cosmopolitan witchcraft world.

The Rede is good advice and wise counsel. Correctly interpreted it means that you should find and fulfill your true will. You should do as you will because you are a magical person. And magic is about conformity with your will.

And Initiates can fulfill their will without having the intent of causing harm. In other words, if you want to make a billion dollars and you're given the option of destroying an indigenous tribe in the rainforest, then the Rede is discouraging you from doing that—because your true will comes from your higher self, which is of the divine creative force. Your true will would never want to destroy, for desire that is false will poison the ego. There's no reason why you cannot achieve your will without causing harm. So the intent to harm should not be there.

The Rede is also just a good way to live unless you desire to be an unkind, corrupt individual. I think most people like to think of it as just applying to magic. It doesn't just apply to magic. It is a philosophy. I personally do not want to be friends with or know someone who wants to live in a different way. If you want to go around harming people, whether it's magically or with a gun, if you want to kill people, maim or abuse them, if your life is focused on revenge and destruction, you're not someone I want to know or would consider trusting. It is a huge burden to carry hate in your heart.

And on the subject of checks and balances, everything you do in your life is a record of you. And we all must ask ourselves, "What record do we want to have?" What do you want to contribute upon this divine stage?

The Rede can be found in many forms. The Golden Rule is "Do unto others as you would have them do unto you." In Buddhism, "Hurt not others in ways that you yourself would find hurtful," or from Egypt, the Goddess Maat proclaims "Do to the doer to make him do."

I have said before, and I will say again, that the only ethics in Witchcraft is intent. So, it is your intent followed by actions that are good or bad. Causing harm by chance or for survival lacks intent bent toward cruelty. The lion does not kill the zebra to be cruel but because he is hungry and does not have the option of becoming vegan. The death is not always kind, but the lion's aim is not malicious by nature any more than the average cheeseburger eater's aim.

If you end a relationship because you are not happy in it, it's not wrong that you harmed the other person emotionally. Most of us enter into relationships with good intentions.

The origins of the Rede are often attributed to *The Book of the Law* by Aleister Crowley, where it says, "Do what ye wilt shall be the whole of the law." Gerald Gardner clearly had some connection with the OTO and Aleister Crowley, so it is not unreasonable to make the connection. And, in fact, their meanings are quite similar. However, in his book, *Witchcraft Today*, Gardner gives us another source entirely. He says, "Witches are inclined to the morality of the legendary Good King Pausole: 'Do what you like as long as you harm no one.' But they believe a certain law to be important. You must not use magic for anything that will cause harm to anyone, and if to prevent a greater wrong being done, you must discommode someone, and you must do it only in a way that will abate the harm."[5]

Good King Pausole is a 1901 literary creation of French novelist Pierre Louÿs (1870 to 1925). And in his novel, the King has the statement, "Thou shalt not harm they neighbor, this being understood do as you wouldest."[6] We don't absolutely know for sure if this was the inspiration to the Rede or if it was Aleister Crowley, but there certainly are other sources. The Hippocratic Oath is a good example where we get the phrase, "Harm none." St. John said, "Love and do as ye will." In truth, regardless of its origins, I think we can all safely say this is a universal philosophy and has its roots in the occult and many, many religions. There is cause and effect in everything we do. Witches take on the mantle of co-creator, and in that role, we must reflect on what it is we

---

[5] Richard Jones, "Part One: King Pausole and the Wican Rede," *Hermetic Library*, accessed June 20, 2019, https://hermetic.com/jones/wican-ethics/part-one-king-pausole-and-the-wican-rede#note10.

[6] Ibid.

are contributing to the universe. We must also accept full responsibility for what we unleash in the reality of our own design. Witches know we create our own heaven or our own hell. In a world filled with disease, famine, greed, war, cruelty, and mass extinction, I think we could all use a little more "An it harm none, do what ye will."

The Seven Hermetic Principles

As a collection, these principles were first published in 1908 under the pseudonym of the Three Initiates in a work titled the *Kybalion*. This book attributed its teachings to the legendary figure Hermes Trismegistus. Many speculate the book was actually written by William Walker Atkinson, and is therefore fraudulent, but in truth we cannot be certain. It is also possible that it was created by occult Initiates at the time through channeling, and they chose to remain anonymous for social reasons. It must also be noted that much of the material is indeed older and can be traced to sources such as the Emerald Tablet attributed to the same Hermes Trismegistus mentioned above. Regardless of its origins, the book has at least as much credibility as the Rider Waite Tarot deck, which came out just two years later. In the end, it is an effective occult philosophy used by many today and has even become foundational for some groups such as the Builders of the Adytum. Effectiveness and knowledge are vastly more important than antiquity.

THE PRINCIPLE OF MENTALISM
"THE ALL is MIND; The Universe is Mental."

THE PRINCIPLE OF CORRESPONDENCE
"As above, so below; as below, so above."

THE PRINCIPLE OF VIBRATION
"Nothing rests; everything moves; everything vibrates."

THE PRINCIPLE OF POLARITY
"Everything is Dual; everything has poles; everything has its pair of opposites; like and unlike are the same; opposites are identical in nature, but different in degree; extremes meet; all truths are but half-truths; all paradoxes may be reconciled."

THE PRINCIPLE OF RHYTHM
"Everything flows, out and in; everything has its tides; all things rise and fall; the pendulum-swing manifests in everything; the measure of the swing to the right is the measure of the swing to the left; rhythm compensates."

THE PRINCIPLE OF CAUSE AND EFFECT
"Every Cause has its Effect; every Effect has its Cause; everything happens according to Law; Chance is but a name for Law not recognized; there are many planes of causation, but nothing escapes the Law."

THE PRINCIPLE OF GENDER
"Gender is in everything; everything has its Masculine and Feminine Principles; Gender manifests on all planes."[7]

A Dedication to the Gods

I have addressed Initiation as one of the single greatest acts of magic in the Craft. However, for many, finding a suitable teacher and coven in your desired tradition is difficult. You can work with our Gods without Initiation and certainly, for most of us, we did, and I believe my dedication to them was recognized as part of my long and winding path towards my own initiation. For many, a dedication to the Gods is their only option, at least until they can find a suitable teacher, and such a rite,

---

[7] William Walker Atkinson writing as Three Initiates, *The Kybalion: The Definitive Edition* (New York, NY: Penguin, 2011), 64-72.

while not the same as initiation, is a powerful way to step upon the path of Witchcraft. I performed a self-dedication rite myself, and I also did a spell in which I worked for the correct teachers and path, and I have included it here. You can use the rite below simply to dedicate yourself to the Witch gods or perform it in full and make known your desire to be initiated into the Witch Cult, asking for the proper aid and guidance.

DEDICATION RITE

To make your pact with the Witch Gods, you will need some sweet oil, frankincense, red wine, honey, bread, a cup or drinking horn, and a knife.

At midnight on a Full Moon or Witches' Sabbath, go to a place in nature, a grove of trees—perhaps near a stream or a secluded crossroads. An ancient working site is best if one resides in your area. Place all of your ritual items in the center of the space. If you can find an area with a stone in the center to use as an altar, all the better.

Next, using the knife, cutting a circle in the earth around the space you will be working in, face the four directions each in turn, starting in the east. Declare,

> "In the east, I serve the gods of Witchcraft."

Walking backward, you will then move to the west, saying,

> "In the west, I serve the Gods of Witchcraft."

Again, walking backward to the south:

> "In the south, I serve the Gods of Witchcraft."

And then,

> "In the west, I serve the Gods of Witchcraft."

Return to the center. Facing east, say,

> "I invoke the formless, bornless bitter sea, the primordial first fire that fell from the heavens and rose from the abyss, the first breath of life and the gasp of death, the fertile earth, and the barren stone."

Kneel, still facing the east, and continue:

> "Goddess of the Rounded Moon, Night Mother, First of Witches, Queen of the Waters and the Waiting Earth. Elphame, Diana, Artemis, Astarte, Morgan, Andred, Luna, Selena, Hecate, Ishtar, Isis. Many-named creatrix, mistress of magic!

> "Shadow cloaked in green leaves, Fairy King, Devil. Robin, Pan, Puck, Herne, Cernunnos, Dionysus, Lucifer, Serapis, Sabbat Lord, Hidden One, Prince of both Tempest and Flame.

> "Gods of Witchcraft, I declare this rite by your many names, known and unknown, remembered and forgotten."

Next, pour the wine and raise it up, saying:

> "I drink not wine, but the blood of my Gods. Even as it flows through me, it also courses through the vineyards, fields, and forests."

Drink the wine. Next, take the bread and say,

> "This is the body of my God." Dip it in the honey, saying, "Kissed by the Great Mother's love." Dip it in the wine, saying, "Whom I swear my life's blood to serve." Eat it, saying, "This is my body."

Next, anoint your brow, saying,

> *"With this sweet oil, I pledge everything below my crown to the Gods of Witchcraft. May they bless me in my service both within the realms of magic and in the mundane world."*

A SPELL TO SEEK INITIATION

If you choose to request Initiation, then conclude your Dedication Rite with the following spell. You will need virgin parchment paper, red ink, some red thread, a white candle, and a small pot or cauldron. Write on your paper. Request that at the correct time and place, your teacher will appear. Then sign it with your name. On the other side, inscribe the names of the Gods of Witchcraft—the ones used here, and in the ritual, are very suitable, but you may use whatever names you choose. Proceed with making your dedication pact with the Gods before performing the spell.

Burn some of the frankincense and then read your spell aloud. Then burn it in the pot with the white candle. Remain silent and watch it burn. Wait for as long as you desire. Observe nature for signs and omens. Close your eyes and feel the presence of power.

When you feel the ritual is complete, and you have been duly heard, gather your things, erase any sign of your presence, and leave the working site.

Occult Exercises

Occult power does not come by merely rubbing a genie's lamp, wishing on a star or blowing out a birthday candle. Yes, all humans are inherently connected to the force behind the worlds of form; however, tapping into this power and truly harnessing it requires intense study and discipline. Both Witches and magicians generally have ritualized daily practices or meditations that fall under this heading. Magic is a lot like music: the more you do it, the more natural it becomes.

RELAXATION RITUAL

The first occult practice I wish to teach you today is to simply quiet yourself and go into a meditative state. Put yourself into a relaxed position, whether that's on a chair sitting up against the wall, or lying down if that will not lull you to sleep. Personally, I recommend sitting comfortably on a floor with your back up against a wall. Close your eyes and begin to breathe naturally. This is not the practice of the guru or the yogi. This is Witchcraft, let it come naturally. Breathe in and breathe out. Let your heartbeat guide your natural rhythmic breath.

Now, begin to unwind by tightening up your feet, then releasing. Tighten your calves, release. Your knees, thighs, buttocks—tighten them up, then release. Tighten your stomach and chest, release. Don't forget to breathe in and out naturally; you are relaxing. Your shoulders, arms, hands, fingertips, each tightening, releasing, and relaxing. Your chest, your shoulders, your neck, and finally your face and the crown of your head, tighten, and release. You are in a reposed state.

Now, I wish you to remain in this state. Try not to think, but do not control your thoughts. Let them wander, as if in a daydream. Continue this practice to develop your mind, so that you can begin to shift in and out of consciousness at will. Do it daily, before any works that you wish to undertake to put yourself into that natural state of relaxation.

An alternative method is to count down. Simply tell yourself, "I am going into a relaxed state," and count down: ten, nine, eight, seven, six, five, four, three, two, one. You are in a perfect state of relaxation. Experiment with both of these methods and see which one works best for you. The goal is what is important. It is necessary to relax, to let go of your mundane concerns, so you can begin to work with other worlds, and in altered states of consciousness.

MIDDLE PILLAR RITUAL

The middle pillar ritual does come down to us from the Golden Dawn, and in its authentic form, you intone various god names in Hebrew. This is easy to find if you're interested in the original format. However, I like the mechanics of this ritual and prefer using names that I work with or simply focusing on the elements, which is what we will be doing here in this exercise.

To begin with, put yourself into a relaxed state. Then imagine a sphere of white light forming above your head. See this white light spin and pulsate with vital energy. This sphere represents the element of spirit. This is divinity.

Once you feel it's sufficiently charged and pulsating with the vital energy of spirit, you will allow it to descend into the core of your being, moving slowly down until it reaches your throat area. Feel the white sphere pulsating and spinning. Now you will draw into it the essence of the element of air. All the things that the element of air represents to you, pulsating within this sphere as it spins. Once you feel that this has occurred and it is filled with the vital energies of air, allow it to descend. Right below your chest, the ball begins to spin. And now, you will fill it with the element of fire. The orb spins and charges you with the element of fire, and all the things that the element of fire represents to you. Allow the sphere to descend to the genital area. Here it will spin, and ebb and flow with the element of water. This charges you with water and all the things that water means to you. The sphere descends a final time to your feet, spinning halfway between your feet and the earth. Spinning and spinning, and being filled with the vital energies of earth, and all the things that the elemental earth means to you.

Continue to breathe deeply in and out. As you breathe in, allow the energy at your feet to rise up your left side and descend down your right. As you breathe in, it goes up your left. As you breathe out, it goes down your right, circling in your entire energy sphere. Next, you will allow it to rise up your back and go down your front. As you breathe in, it rises up from your back. As you breathe out, it rises, descends from your front, circulating energy through your whole sphere.

Now, you will breathe in and allow the energy to rise up from the core, all the way from your feet to your head in the path of the spheres. As it comes out your head, it will shower down over your entire body, circulating energy inside of you and out. As you breathe in, it comes up. As you breathe out, it flows back down on the outside of you, circulating energy into your entire sphere.

This completes the middle pillar ritual and elemental balancing that you should incorporate as part of your daily exercises. This will tune you in with the five elements of Witchcraft—earth, air, fire, water, and spirit. It will balance your energies and raise your consciousness.

WITCH'S CIRCLE AND PSYCHIC SHIELD

The first thing that comes to mind when performing Witchcraft rituals is the Magic Circle. I am not going to teach you how to cast an Alexandrian or Gardnerian circle; you do not require that yet. If you do not get initiated, you do not need it at all.

The circle is an ancient symbol and has been used by practitioners of magic from the beginning of time. You can see it in stone circles, cave paintings. It has been used in magic rituals from their origins, from a simple ring of firelight to the Egyptians casting a circle around their beds with a knife for protection.

Ceremonial magicians create circles to protect them from the spirits that they invoke. The Witchcraft circle is a much more ancient and potent symbol—it is the place between the worlds. It does act as a boundary of protection, but it is also a portable temple. It is a place of worship, a place of creation.

I am going to teach you how to create your own magical space, your psychic shield that will prepare you to cast an occult circle that will be used later in the Rite of Alexandria. This technique can be used both in and outside of ritual for protection.

Exercise: The Psychic Shield

To begin, if you can be outside, all the better, but it is not necessary. Put your bare feet on the earth itself, and focus on your feet. Concentrate, close your eyes and go into a relaxed state. Breathe deeply, inhale, exhale, inhale and exhale, continue breathing in a relaxed state. I want you to focus on the earth beneath your feet. I want you to feel it as a living breathing force, feel it breathing and pulsating with power.

Breathe in, breathe out, inhale, exhale, until you are in a relaxed state, until you can feel the energy of the earth pulsating beneath you. Now I want you to visualize golden light coming up from the bottoms of your feet, rising up your legs, to your knees. It is invigorating, it is potent and powerful, it is the force of life, of nature, coming up. See it move up your thighs to your buttocks, your stomach, your chest, shoulders, arms, hands, neck, and head. Feel the potent life force coming up from nature, energizing you with its life-giving, healing, protective love and power.

Now breathe in, breathe out. See this light begin to extend around you into a protective sphere, perhaps one that matches the planet itself. For this is the life force of the planet earth; it flows through all nature. It is flowing through you. Let it extend around yourself.

You can do this exercise anytime you feel the need for protection, extra energy, strength or healing. Better still, perform this exercise at your altar before you begin any worship or any work with the Gods of Witchcraft.

The Rites of Alexandria

I have developed the following occult rites for daily use by those seeking the ways of magic. They are inspired by the practices of the occult lodges as well as the Hellenized gods of Alexandria Egypt.

THE TRIAD ⊕F ALEXANDRIA

The Triad of Alexandria is drawn from the Kabbalistic Cross but filtered through the lens of the gods of Alexandria. Essentially, it is the same occult practice, and you can use it as an invocation to draw power, to center yourself, or as a safety trigger. You are working with the gods. You are working with your own astral light, the light of the universe. To perform the Triad of Alexandria, you must be in a relaxed state. For this, you should be standing and, if possible, facing the east.

Put yourself into a relaxed state and begin to visualize yourself as becoming larger and larger, growing to be like a giant. And, as you continue to grow, the place that you are becomes smaller and smaller until you tower above your city, above your continent, eventually above the planet. As you grow so enormous, the size no longer matters, for you are infinitely among the stars. You are in the middle of the universe. You cannot perceive your size any longer, only the dazzling stars.

Take a deep breath in and exhale. You see the light of the universe. You know this is the Goddess Isis. Yet, she hides in the darkness, her starry veil before you. So, with two fingers, you're going to lower your hands from above your forehead, all the way down to your genitals. And, you will say,

"*Isis veiled.*"

In this act, you are drawing the light of the Goddess of the Universe through your body, from the crown of your head to the soles of your feet. You are in perfect balance: As Above, So Below. When you reach the genital area, you say,

"Isis Unveiled."

Next, using two fingers, you will position them over your right shoulder and, you will say,

"Harpocrates."

Move straight to your left, from south to north and say,

"Serapis."

A second light passes through, forming a beautiful white light—a cross centering in your chest area. This is essentially the same as the Kabbalistic Cross. You are drawing from the four quarters of the universe all light. The light of the Triad of Alexandria is the light of Isis veiled and unveiled, Harpocrates, who is the sun and the secret mystery, and Serapis, who is the Underworld, the Darkness, the Hidden God. Yet, he too is the light, Osiris Slain, and Osiris Risen.

These are the archetypes of nature, found in the ancient mysteries of Alexandria. And, you are drawing upon that power current to draw upon the Universal Light, bringing it within you, charging you. When you feel the power is at full height, you will cross your hands together in the sign of Osiris Risen and you will say,

"Amun."

This is the Triad of Alexandria. It can be done before and after every ritual; you can do it anytime. I want you to continue trying this exercise daily, following your universal relaxation to help center yourself and tune yourself in with these deities.

THE SALUTATION OF THE SUN

This ritual was developed to work as an opening rite and occult working space. It is a ritual of protection and is solar in nature. It can be used to banish unwanted forces or as a means to clear a space for occult workings or devotions.

The direction we work with in this rite is the east, for we are working with the rising and setting sun and its four stations.
To begin, you face the east and put yourself into a state of relaxation. Then perform the Triad of Alexandria:

"Isis Veiled, Isis Unveiled, Harpocrates, Serapis, Amun."

Facing the east, you say,

"Khepe Ra,"

… with vibration. This is followed by the chime of a bell. The Pentacle of Alexandria is also held up in the east. When working with others, you may employ assistants for these purposes. When working on your own, you will have to make it two phases of the operation, perhaps three. Next, you visualize a white light, and you project this white light from the east to the south.
In the south, you intone the name,

"Ra,"

… with vibration, the bell, and the Pentacle. You continue to visualize the white light, projected south to west.

In the west, you intone the name,

"*Ra Atum,*"

… with vibration, bell, and Pentacle employed. The white light continues to be projected west to north.

In the north is intoned the name,

"*Amun Ra,*"

with vibration, bell, and Pentacle. The white light continues to be projected north to east. This completes a ring of white light that surrounds the space in which you work.

Facing east again, arms are outstretched in the sign of the cross. This is Osiris Slain. You then say,

"Before me, the breath of life. Behind me, the waters of rebirth."

You move your right arm slightly up and your left leg slightly left, with your heel slightly lifted, and you say,

"In my right hand, fire from heaven. Under my left heel, the kingdoms of Earth forever."

You then resume the cross position, saying,

"I am encircled with the wings of Isis, and within me shines the light of Ra."

You should now repeat the Triad of Alexandria above.

It is most appropriate to follow with the Eternal Rose Rite, and then any devotions or work. For extra protection or attunement, you may also use the Banishing Pentagram of Earth at each station with the old Roman spell,

"Isis Victrix"

THE ETERNAL R✠SE RITE

For this ritual, you will be working at an altar. The altar should be placed in the east, facing east. Upon it you will put, from left to right, a bowl of water and a single red rose; in the middle, The Pentacle of Serapis-Isis; on the right, a large ankh or a symbol of an ankh; and on the far right, your incense. This ritual is performed at the altar, for its primary purpose is in consecrating, blessing, and charging the altar, and then tuning yourselves to the inner mysteries of the work. It also serves the purpose of balancing the elements with your ritual space. Used daily it is utilized as a simple devotional and requires no other rites.

First, you will hold up the red rose above the Pentacle, visualizing the sun bathing the rose and the altar in its golden light, saying,

"This pure rose came forth from the sunshine, which pleases the nostrils of the gods."

The rose is then dipped into the water and placed over the ankh, saying,

"With pure waters, may we guard its mysteries."

Then say,

"Amun,"

and make the sign of Osiris Risen.

Next, you place incense upon the censer, and as the smoke begins to billow, you say,

> "For thou who startles the heart, darling of air, far stretched across the sky, a blinding light, a flame before the wind, to the limits of the heaven, the ends of the Earth."

This can be used daily for balance and devotion or used in conjunction with other rituals.

THE RITE ⊕F SERAPIS AND ISIS

After the opening rite, a circling procession is made to the altar, upon which are the following items: a candle or lantern, a loaf of bread wrapped in white cloth or linen, a chalice filled with wine, a sistrum, bell, pitcher of water, feather, mirror, and symbols of the Gods that are meaningful to you. As the procession of these items is being made, a chant can be used.

> "Dua Aset, Dua Aset, Dua Aset, Nehes, Nehes, Nehes, Nehes em hotep, Nehes em neferu."
> (Awake, Awake, Awake! Awake in peace, flower in beauty!)

The chant continues until a man and a woman approach the altar. One invokes Serapis:

Serapis Invocation

> "Bullheaded, ram-horned serpent formed Serapis! A God you are such as you show us. The starry heavens your head, your trunk the sea, the earth your feet. The air your thoughts and the brilliant rays of the Sun your eyes. Thou who art Osiris and the Apis! Apollo and Dionysus, Hades, and Amun. Great Serapis, come to us quickly and without delay from whatever quarter and climate in the world where ye may be."

The woman then invokes Isis.

Isis Invocation

"Isis, veiled in heaven. On earth Persephone, Diana of the moon and Aradia of the ways, Morrigu of the mists and Brigit of the flames. Oh Anu of the fields, oh goddess hear thy names. Arianrhod of the Caer and Epona the mare, Nicnevin of the skies and Cailleach the wise. You who have been invoked, of old by men. Artemis and Ceridwen. Hecate in Hell, and Aphrodite of the sea. Isis Unveiled, goddess come to me."

The Witches' Mass

This is often performed after the Rite of Serapis and Isis or in conjunction with the Witches' Sabbath. The Chalice is held up before the altar, saying,

"God of Grape, God of the Vine, bless this chalice with thy wine."

The Chalice is then lowered, and the invoker turns to face the other participants, continuing,

"Before the cup was filled the first seed was planted. Receive now the love and will of Isis in the name of Serapis."

Each participant, in turn, comes forward to partake, after which the bread is held up to the altar, saying,

"Goddess of the Moon, Goddess of the Night, bless thy children with thy Light. Guide us to eat your boundless love, Queen of Magic, below and above. Receive now the love and will of Serapis in the name of Isis."

The bread is then unwrapped. A piece is torn off, and it is passed around with the participants tearing the bread apart and consuming it.

Sabbat Rites

Witches have eight festivals, or holy days, called Sabbats. The four great Sabbats are Halloween, Candlemas, May Eve, and Lammas. These can be found in the Catholic practice but actually derive from the Celtic peoples of Britain. The lesser Sabbats are the stations of the sun—the solstices and equinoxes found in every culture in the world. To witches, the Sabbats are not mere holidays but gateways filled with deep mysteries and power.

HALLOWEEN (OCTOBER 31)

Also called Hallowmas, Samhain, All Saints' Eve, the Festival of Pomona, and by many other names, this Great Sabbat is observed on the eve of November 1st. This is in the peak of the Water tide also called the tide of recession, and is the Witches' New Year. This great Sabbat is governed by the Horned God of the Witches, who is the Lord of Death and Resurrection, King of the Underworld, and the Great Magus. Because it is influenced by the tide of water, it is associated with the mighty dead, ancestors, and nature spirits. All gods and goddesses, angels, genii, elementals, and even demons. It is also strongly associated with astral travel, divination, and herbs.

Halloween Ritual

The altar is decorated with images and tributes to the dead, your ancestors, and other spirits of importance to you. Images of the deities of the dead or the Underworld can adorn the space: all horned gods, Hades, Pluto, Serapis, Arawn, Woden, Loki, Dis Pater, Saturn, Pamona, Persephone, Morrigu, Nicnevin, Diana, Hecate, Hel, Ceridwen, and the Cailleach. Fruits of the harvest, leaves and other plants gathered at this time can decorate the altar and circle. An offering feast in a dish or cauldron flanked with candles should be placed on or near the altar.

Perform the Rites of Alexandria above; however, in place of the Serapis Invocation, you will instead use the "Halloween Invocation of the Witches' God" below. You will still use the Isis Invocation above but preface it with the "Halloween Invocation of the Witches' Goddess" below.

A HALLOWEEN INVOCATION OF THE WITCHES' GOD

"As hallowed tide falls, we gather for thee,
oh Lord of the Shepherds, lover, in the lea.

When the midnight hour gathers its power, the moon glistens brightly and clear.
Shadows awake and spirits partake in the mystical rites of the year.

As in days past, the circle is cast, the quarters are called to be here.
The round is trod in the name our God, that ol' horny may appear.

We raise the sword and light the fire in the ancient names.
We lure him near and draw him in to join our Sabbat games.

Horned One, God of Hidden Might, oh Goat-Footed One, be here on this night.
Half man, half beast, assemble the shades for thy feast.

Guide the dead into our land through the hidden gates.
Hound of Hell with scales in hand, by threads of winding fate.

Lord of Death! Lord of Life! The magic spell I speak!
Come from every corner of Earth or rise from blackest deep!

With wings on wind made of fire, your gift of light we keep!
For we, your hidden children remain the blackest sheep!"

Light the candles flanking the offerings and say:

"Return to us Keeper of the Fates
Ruler of Winter, Guardian of the Gates.

Father of men, Father of beasts.
God of Witch's, God of Priests.

Open the way for the Spirits of old
Your Flying Hunt for all to behold.

Lord of the Sabbat, on you we call,
Lord of the Dead, master of all!

"Hermanubis, Dumas, Dianus, Arddhu, Janicot, Artisson, Cernunnos, Serapis, Amun, Atho, Herne, Sabaoth, Homme de Bouc, Harrahya!"

A HALLOWEEN INVOCATION OF THE WITCHES' GODDESS

"Shadowy One, Hooded One, Harvest Mother! Sea Hag, Bone Crone, Spectral Queen!

"Nut-Nyx-Nephthys. Lilith-Macha-Ishtar. Demeter-Hel-Tiamat"

(Follow with the Isis Invocation within the Rites of Alexandria)

After this, the Witch's Mass is performed. Divination then proceeds. It's most appropriate to select an individual to act as the oracle and with a pack of Tarot cards. This person can pull one card for each participant and give them a reading, for this is the time when the veil is truly thin and psychic phenomenon abounds. The Rite ends, and all may leave an offering for the dead, their ancestors, and the spirits of nature.

THE WINTER SOLSTICE (DEC. 20 - 23)

Also called Yule, Christmas, Feast of Mary, and Feast of Sol, this Sabbat is observed December 20-23. This Sabbat begins the tide of Earth (also called the tide of lustration) and ends that of water. On the surface, the Winter Solstice celebrates the birth of the Divine Sun God, and many gods of the sun are indeed associated with this season. To Witches, however, this is a Sabbat about the life-giving mother—after all, the God is a child and fully requires her love and care. Because this Sabbat is associated with Earth, its magic centers around fertility, new beginnings, and resurrection.

Winter Solstice Ritual

For this ritual, the altar is decorated with appropriate objects of the season. Evergreens, dried branches, a Yule Log, and garlands of mistletoe and holly. In this ritual, you can use a chair and turn it into a throne or obtain a small wooden chair that can fit on the altar to represent a throne. A candle is placed on it, in either a bowl or cauldron if necessary. At Hex New Orleans, I have a small Egyptian chair that can hold a votive. Images of mother goddesses and sun gods are also most appropriate: Isis, Demeter, Gaia, Freya, Fortuna, Don, Diana, Harpocrates, Horus, Apollo, Helios, Ra, Sol.

Perform the Rites of Alexandria then commence with the Sabbat.

Light the candle on the throne and say:

"Great Queen of the Stars, Mother of All Life, we receive your Light with great rejoicing. Bring forth your offering. Your Light is the Light of Life. Your Light is the Gift of Love. Your Light is the King of Kings. May the rays of his crown grow even brighter, giving us strength, peace, vitality, wisdom, abundance, and love."

The Witch's Mass follows. When the bread is passed, we add:

"Mother Goddess of the Divine Spiritual Sun, Goddess of the Moon, Goddess of the Night, bless thy children with thy Light. Give us to eat your boundless love, Queen of Magic, below and above. Receive now the love and will of Serapis in the name of Isis."

CANDLEMAS (FEBRUARY 1 OR 2)

Also called Imbolc, Imbolg, Oimelc, Saint Brigid's Day and Lupercalia. February 1 or 2. This is the peak of the Earth's tide, also called the Tide of Lustration. This Great Sabbat is governed by the young, fertile Horned God, the Resurrected One, who seeks spiritual purification. Because this Sabbat is linked to the peak tide of Earth, it is associated with purity, protection, and renewal. This is the time to recharge your inner powers through the Hermetic arts and inner disciplines.

Candlemas Ritual

The first of the three spring rituals occurs in the dead of winter. First flowers or new greenery in your local area would be most appropriate for the altar. You will also need a red rose for each participant, oil and ash, a gold water vessel, and a silver water vessel. Deities appropriate for the altar include: Pan, Faunus, Cupid, Eros, Harpocrates, Cernunnos, Brigid, Selene, Branwen, Aphrodite, Venus, and Vesta.

Perform the Rites of Alexandria then commence with the Sabbat.

The theme for this ritual is purification. After the opening rites, each person to undergo the blessing kneels between a man and a woman. He holds the gold vessel of water. She holds the silver vessel of water. A little water from each is poured over the head of the kneeling person at the same time. After standing, they are then censed with incense and anointed on the forehead with ash that has been moistened with the sweet oils. A single rose is given to him or her with the sign of silence. After everyone is finished, all face the altar, and the invocation is made.

> "Aphrodite, Isis, Eros, Harpocrates! Awaken within our hearts a resurrection. Before you, we are made clean and pure. As we receive thy love, we shall give it to others in silent adoration. May we go forth bearing thy light."

The Witches' Mass is then performed.

SPRING EQUINOX (MARCH 20 - 23)

Also called Ostara, Easter, Eostre's Day, Lady Day, and Bacchanalia, it takes place March 20-23. This is the second Spring Sabbat, and it begins the tide of air and ends that of earth. It is a Lesser Sabbat and is governed by sun gods and fertility goddesses. The Spring Equinox is a time of balance, day and night are in equal measure and represented by the sun and moon in a romantic chase and struggle for power. The Goddess is young, wild, and free, and flees the Sun as he pursues her. The Equinox is a time of fertility, inspiration, new beginnings, and natural balance.

Spring Equinox Ritual

The altar should be decorated with objects of the spring and fertility. Some appropriate deities you might also add include Aphrodite, Diana, Artemis, Selene, Eostre, Melusine, Ishtar, Isis, Athena, Minerva, Persephone, Nuada, Horus, Helios, Apollo, and Ra.

Perform the Rites of Alexandria then commence with the Sabbat.

A woman stands in the west with a basket of flowers. A man stands in the east with a lit taper in hand. Another participant proclaims:

> "Twins who suckled at Thea's breasts ride their chariots from east to west, drawn by light both day and night, the dance of moon and sun takes flight. But in the spring, Selene doth hide from the rays of her brother's pride."

All begin chanting:

> "Blessed be the moon. Blessed be the sun. Light puts flight to darkness. Helios has won."

The man and the woman begin moving clockwise. She sprinkles flowers while he seems to pursue her slowly. He slowly gains on her during the chant. When all her petals are gone, he catches her and kisses her, giving her the lighted candle.

After this, the Witch's Mass is performed. A seed of light meditation may be done with the participants, the seed representing something they wish to manifest in themselves that year.

MAY EVE (MAY 1)

Also called Mayday, Beltane, Bealtaine, Walpurgis Eve, Rudemas, Floralia, and the Crowning of Mary, on May 1. For the Celts, this was the beginning of summer, and it is the last of the three spring rites. This is the peak of the tide of air or the tide of activation. This great Sabbat is governed by the Goddess as Queen, and all gods of love, sex, and fertility. Because it is influenced by the tide of air, it is associated with personal manifestation, thought, creativity, and your innermost desires. The sovereignty of May is that which you attain at the end of desire. It is the power within, the true knowledge of the self.

May Eve Ritual

The altar should be decorated with beautiful flowers, and a cauldron should adorn it, also decorated with flowers. A simple candle is placed within it. Appropriate gods might be historic couples or gods of love and fertility. Some examples include Aphrodite, Isis, Diana, Blodeuwedd, Artemis, Damara, Venus, Cybele, Freya, Flora, Luna, Selena, Morrigu, Ariadne, and Hera. Sol, Bel, Cernunnos, Cupid, Eros, Frey, Pan, Osiris, the Green Man, Dagda, Apollo, Dionysus, Ares, Lleu, Vulcan, Zeus, and Serapis.

Perform the Rites of Alexandria then commence with the Sabbat.

A candle is lit, saying:

> *"As the light warms the earth, the moon blends with the sun.*
> *As rain falls on the fields, the sacred pair are one.*
> *And with a kiss, they greet, as sky and land do meet,*
> *like lovers in the lea, the sacred pair are one.*
> *When lightning strikes the sea and foam flecks on the shore,*
> *the waves are turning high and doves of love do soar, the sacred pair are one.*
> *Sunset in the west, sickle unto shaft.*
> *Without the love of darkness, the hearth flame will not last."*

The candle is extinguished, continuing:

> *"Sacred pair crossed by time and space, land and mist, darkness and light, life, and death.*
>
> *"Luna, Sol*
> *Selena, Pan*
> *Morrigu, Dagda*
> *Diana, Apollo*

Ariadne, Dionysus
Blodeuwedd, Lleu
Venus, Vulcan.
Hera, Zues
Isis, Serapis.

"The moon cannot shine without the sun. With love, the flame is rekindled. The sacred pair are one."

The candle is then re-lit.

The Witches' Mass follows. Participants should be given colored ribbons that they may go leave on a tree as an offering. The ribbon should represent what they wish to manifest in the coming year.

SUMMER SOLSTICE (JUNE 20 - 23)

Also called Midsummer, Litha, Vestalia and St. John's Eve, June 20-23. This is a Lesser Sabbat and begins the tide of fire and ends that of air. It is governed by sun gods, kings and queens, fathers and mothers and goddesses of nature. The Summer Solstice is a magical time to focus on mundane needs, health, vitality, strength, leadership, and abundance. This is the solar equivalent to a full moon but with a masculine, fiery nature.

Summer Solstice Ritual

The altar should be decorated with summer flowers, oak leaves, and symbols of the sun. Appropriate deities include Olwen, Athena, Bona Dea, Damona, Erce, Hathor, Isis, Freya, Juno, Sekhmet, Dagda, Llew, Helios, Apollo, Ra, Baal, Lugh, Balder, Sol, Serapis.

Perform the Rites of Alexandria above; however, in place of the Serapis Invocation therein, you will use the version for the Summer Solstice below.

SERAPIS INVOCATION FOR THE SUMMER SOLSTICE

"Thou art Osiris Slain and the Apis Risen.
The hidden god of the starry realms, king of the elements.
The god of power, Pan, the vine, the wine, the ecstasy sublime of Dionysus.
The Eye of Ra, Helios the Sun, the God who is many, the God who is one.
Apollo the Healer and Hades in Hell, the lover of Isis who yields to her spell.
Fertile erect seed of light, given the throne by the mother of life!
Dread god of darkness, bringer of death. Spoken of with bated breath
Serpent of Knowledge, Goat of Mendes. Bless all your cult, and always defend us.
Hear now our call, oh master of all.
Dua-Ausir, Banebdjedet, Khnum, Dhul Karnayn, Serapis Amun."

After this follows the Witches' Mass.

LAMMAS (AUGUST 1)

Also called August Eve, Lughnasa, Lughnasadh, Cerealia and the Assumption of Mary, August 1. This is the first harvest festival and the peak of the Tide of Fire—also called the Tide of Consolidation. One of the Witch's Great Sabbats. This is the time of the grain goddesses, earth mothers, and the dark side of nature. The God represents the slain king myths like Tammuz and Ishtar, or Isis and Osiris. Lammas is a time of gratitude and service. The magical sacrifice is kept in mind as a desire for continued blessings, true love, kinship, and community.

Witches use this time as a reminder to serve humanity and focus on its abundance, protection, guidance, and health.

Lammas Ritual

The altar should be decorated with grains, corn dollies, and other symbols of the harvest. A large glass bowl filled with water adorns the altar, scattered with sweet flowers and oils. A small image of a bull, or a flower-decorated horn, is placed in the south. It should be small enough to fit inside the bowl. Divine images appropriate for this time include Ceres, Demeter, Habondia, Aine, Isis, Ceridwen, Ishtar, Don, Llew, Lugh, Bran, and Odin.

Perform the Rites of Alexandria then commence with the Sabbat.

A procession is done around the circle, chanting while carrying the bowl:

> "Isis, Isis, bless this land,
> seed and grain, soil and sand.
> Isis, Isis, bless this land,
> let the waters rise again."

This can be repeated or turned into a round. At the end, the symbol is placed within the bowl and adorned with oils, flowers, and sprinkled water.

The Witches' mass is then performed.

FALL EQUINOX (SEPTEMBER 20 - 23)

Also called Michaelmas, Autumn Equinox, Mabon, Festival of Dionysus, and Cornucopia, September 20-23. This is a Lesser Sabbat and begins the tide of water, also called the Tide of Recession, and ends that of fire. This is the second harvest festival, and, like its spring counterpart, is a time of balance when the light will begin to yield and fade in power. It is a celebration of life in the face of death, a time to remember that, alth ough the harvest is reaped, the seeds have been planted. It is a time to enjoy the first fruits and wine. The Fall Equinox is a great time to focus on the emotional world, dreams, and astral journeys.

Fall Equinox Ritual

The altar is decorated with first fruits and other fall symbols. Two chalices or horns filled with wine should be featured prominently, and you will need a pine cone. Divine statues might include Ceridwen, Epona, Pamona, Modron, Morgan, Dionysus, Bacchus, Mabon, and Taliesin.

Perform the Rites of Alexandria above; however, in place of the Serapis Invocation therein, you will instead use the Invocation to Dionysus below.

AN INVOCATION TO DIONYSUS

"I call upon loud, roaring and reveling Dionysus. Primeval, two-natured, thrice born, Bacchic lord. Savage, ineffable, two-horned and two-shaped. Ivy covered, full-faced, war-like, howling, pure. You take raw flesh, you have triennial feasts wrapped in foliage, decked with grape clusters. Immortal Son of Zeus, come to us like sweet wine and perfect kindness."

The first chalice is then used by inserting the pine cone into the cup, saying,

"We offer a portion of the harvest to the ancestors and the spirits of the land. As we take, we must give. Dionysus has given forth his abundance and even now, dwells as the secret seed"

The Witches' Mass has been performed and the first chalice is given as an offering.

Folk Magic from Antiquity

I've assembled the following collection of spells and magical folklore from various sources, as both a curiosity and historical point of reference for those interested in Medieval or classical folklore and magic. I did not write the spells and lore in this section, though I add comments in *italics* where I wish to point something out. These spells are not necessarily part of the Craft, nor am I promoting the idea of using any of these formulas without responsibly considering the moral or ethical implications involved. I do believe the Art is a holy gift and meant to be used in need, and it should never be used to abuse, control, or cause harm unnecessarily.

However, research into myth, folklore, and the historic records does give us insight into the older beliefs about Witchcraft, and perhaps some of the practices that lie therein. I do think you can look at some of these spells and use them as inspiration to create your own. Some of them are also, of course, quite beneficial and harmless.

CORNISH LORE ON CHARMS

The words of charms must be muttered (they lose their efficacy if recited aloud), and the charmer must never communicate them to one of the same sex, for that transfers the power of charming to the other person.[8]

Brian's Commentary: As mentioned elsewhere in the book, it is part of the Craft that initiation and magic be done between members of the opposite sex. This bit of lore shows that this idea is not a new one.

CORNISH WITCH LORE

In every small Cornish village in olden times (and the race is not yet extinct) lived a charmer or "white witch." Their powers were not quite as great as those of a pellar, but they were thoroughly believed in, and consulted on every occasion for every complaint. They were not only

---

[8] M.A. Courtney, *Cornish Feasts and Folk-Lore* (Penzance, Beare and Son, 1890), 156.

able to cure diseases, but they could, when offended, "overlook" and ill-wish the offender, bringing ill-luck on him, and also on his family and farm-stock. The seventh son of the seventh son, or seventh daughter of the seventh daughter, were born with this gift of charming, and made the most noted pellars; but anyone might become a witch who touched a Logan rock nine times at midnight. These Logan rocks are mentioned elsewhere as being in Cornwall their favourite resorts, and to them they went, it is said, riding on ragwort stems, instead of the traditional broomsticks.[9]

LOVE SPELLS

An English Spell to Bring Back a Lover

A knife thrust violently into the post at the foot of the bed accompanied with the following rhymes—

> *"It's not this post alone I stick,*
> *But (lover' name) heart I wish to prick;*
> *Whether he be asleep or awake,*
> *I'd have him back to me and speak."*

—is supposed to bring the sulkiest of lovers back to his mistress.[10]

An Irish Love Charm

Keep a sprig of mint in your hand till the herb grows moist and warm, then take hold of the hand of the woman you love, and she will follow you as long as the two hands close over the herb. No invocation is necessary; but silence must be kept between the two parties for ten minutes, to give the charm time to work with due efficacy.[11]

---

[9] M.A. Courtney, *Cornish Feasts and Folk-Lore* (Penzance, Beare and Son, 1890), 145.

[10] *County Folklore Printed Extracts No. 1*, Ed. Edwin Sidney Hartland (Gloucester, Davies & Son, 1892), 100.

[11] Lady Jane Wilde, *Ancient Legends, Mystic Charms, and Superstitions of Ireland* (London: Ward and Downey, 1888), 186.

A Moorish Love Charm

A woman who wishes to gain the love of a man should procure the following materials from neighbors with whom she has never eaten : coriander, caraway, gum of terebinth, lime, cummin, verdegris, myrrh, some blood of an animal whose throat has been cut, and a piece of a broom hailing from a cemetery. On a dark night she is to go into the country with a lighted brazier and throw these different articles one after another into the fire speaking these words:

> *"O coriander, bring him mad!*
> *O caraway, bring him wandering without success!*
> *O mastic, raise in his heart anguish and tears!*
> *O white lime, make his heart wakeful in disquietude!*
> *O cummin, bring him possessed!*
> *O verdegris, kindle the fire of his heart!*
> *O myrrh, make him spend a frightful night!*
> *O blood of the victim, lead him panting!*
> *O cemetery broom, bring him to my side."* [12]
> *An Egyptian Love Amulet*

Take a band of linen of sixteen threads, four of white, four of green, four of blue, four of red, and make them into one band and stain them with the blood of a hoopoe, and you bind it with a scarab in its attitude of the sun-god, drowned, being wrapped in byssus, and you bind it to the body of the boy who has the vessel and it will work magic quickly. [13]

An English Love Spell

Females who desire to pry into futurity, should cross their hands on the appearance of the new moon, and exclaim—

---

[12] James A. Montgomery, *Publications of the Babylonian Section Vol. III* (Philadelphia, Univ. of PA Museum, 1913), 215.

[13] *The Demotic Magical Papyrus of London and Leiden*, ed. F.L. Griffith and H. Thompson (London, H. Grevel, 1904), 39.

"All hail! new Moon; all hail to thee!
I pray thee, good Moon, declare to me
This night who my true love shall be."[14]

A Hindu Love Spell from the Atharva Veda

"The Philter, burning with the pangs of yearning love,
which Gods have poured within the bosom of the floods,
That spell for thee I heat by Varuna's decree.

"The charm which, burning with the pangs of love,
the General Gods have poured within the bosom of the floods,
That spell for thee I heat by Varuna's decree.

"The Philter, burning with the pangs of longing,
which Indrani hath effused within the waters' depth,
That spell for thee I heat by Varuna's decree,

"The charm, aglow with longing, which Indra and
Agni have effused within the bosom of the floods,
That spell for thee I heat by Varuna's decree.

"The charm aglow with longing which Mitra and
Varuna have poured within the bosom of the floods,
That spell /or thee I beat by Varuna's decree."[15]

A Malaysian Love Spell

Take a cane (of rattan or rotan sega), in length as long as your body, fumigate it with incense and recite a charm over it seven times, striking your own shadow with the cane once after each recital. Repeat this at

---

[14] *Lancashire Folk-Lore*, Ed. John Harland and T. T. Wilkinson (London, Frederick Warne and Co., 1867), 70.

[15] *The Hymns of the Atharva-Veda Vol. I*, ed. Ralph T. H. Griffith (Benares, E.J. Lazarus, 1895), 319.

sundown, mid night, and early morning, and sleep under a coverlet made of five cubits of white cloth, and the soul you wish for will assuredly come to you. The following is the charm—

> "Ho ! Irupi, Shadowy One,
> Let the Queen come to me.
> Do you, if Somebody is awake,
> Stir her and shake her, and make her rise,
> And take her breath and her soul and bring them here,
> And deposit them in my left side.
> But if she sleep,
> Do you take hold of the great toe of her right foot
> Until you can make her get up,
> And use your utmost endeavours to bring them to me.
> If you do not, you shall be a rebel to God!"[16]
> Protection and Exorcism Spells

An English Protection Spell against Witches

... a horse-shoe nailed on a cottage threshold as a preservative against a witch—the idea being that she could not step over cold iron.[17]

Brian's Commentary: Witches might use this spell as a protection against baneful magic.

A Scottish Spell against Malediction

> "Bis, Bis, Byo!
> Bulva reeka tyo
> Tak laigen,
> Slogan veggin ;

---

[16] Charles Otto Blagden, *Malay Magic* (New York, MacMillan, 1900), 575.

[17] *County Folklore Printed Extracts No. 1*, Ed. Edwin Sidney Hartland (Gloucester, Davies & Son, 1892), 185.

Bulva reeka tyo." [18]

Old English Blessing

"Thrice I smites with Holy Crock, With the mell (hammer) I thrice do knock, One for god, One for Wod, And One for Lok."[19]

A Scottish Spell to Protect Against Temptation

The following verse it is said would preserve young people from being led by evil spirits into the way of sinners:

"Clapa, clapa süda
Boochs ina schöl ina Bjöda
Bauta deeraa kjota schin
Swala clovena vjenta in
Roompan poman söda." [20]

An Irish Charm for Safety

Pluck ten blades of yarrow, keep nine, and cast the tenth away for tithe to the spirits. Put the nine in your stocking, under the heel of the right foot, when going a journey, and the Evil One will have no power over you. [21]

Welsh Magic for Protecting the Home

In Wales it is considered highly lucky for the peasantry to have the roofs of their houses covered with the house-leek, as it is supposed to preserve and protect them from disease, and to insure prosperity. [22]

---

[18] *County Folklore Vol. III Printed Extracts No. 5*, Ed. G.F. Black and Northcote W. Thomas (London, David Nutt, 1903), 157.

[19] *Transactions of the Cumberland & Westmorland Antiquarian & Archaeological Society*, vol. III, new series, ed. W.G. Collingwood (London: T. Wilson, 1903), 388.

[20] *County Folklore Vol. III Printed Extracts No. 5*, Ed. G.F. Black and Northcote W. Thomas (London, David Nutt, 1903), 157.

[21] Lady Jane Wilde, *Ancient Legends, Mystic Charms, and Superstitions of Ireland* (London: Ward and Downey, 1888), 208.

[22] T.F. Thiselton Dyer, *English Folk-Lore* (London, Hardwicke & Bogue, 1878), 12.

Old-World Protection against Baneful Magic

To spit on cut hair before throwing it away is thought in some parts of Europe sufficient to prevent its being used by witches.[23]

A Medieval Spell to Banish Spirits from a Home

Hang in everie of the foure corners of your house this sentence written upon virgine parchment;

> "Omnis spiritus laudet Dominum:
> Mosen habent & prophetas:
> Exurgat Deus et dissipentur inimici ejus."[24]

A Babylonian Spell to Expel a Demon

> "The man of Ea am I !
> The man of Damkina am I !
> The messenger of Marduk am I !
> To revive the (   ) sick man,
> The great lord Ea hath sent me ;
> He hath added his pure spell to mine,
> He hath added his pure voice to mine,
> He hath added his pure spittle to mine,
> He hath added his pure prayer to mine.
> "O Ea, King of the Deep, to see...
>
> I, the magician, am thy slave.
> March thou on my right hand,
> Be present on my left;
> Add thy pure spell unto mine,
> Add thy pure voice unto mine,

---

[23] Frederick Thomas Elworthy, *The Evil Eye* (London, John Murray, 1895), 416.

[24] Reginald Scot, *The Discoverie of Witchcraft*, ed. Ernest Rhys (London: Elliot Stock, 1886), 199.

Vouchsafe (to me) pure words,
Make fortunate the utterances of my mouth,
Ordain that my decisions be happy,
Let me be blessed where'er I tread,
Let the man whom I (now) touch be blessed.
Before me may lucky thoughts be spoken,
After me may a lucky finger be pointed.
Oh that thou wert my guardian Genius,
And my guardian Spirit!"[25]

LUCK AND PROSPERITY SPELLS

A Medieval Charm for Prosperity

An old woman that healed all diseases of cattle for the which she never took any reward but a penny and a loaf. Being seriously examined by what words she brought these things to pass confessed that after she had touched the sick creature she always departed immediately saying,

"My loafe in my lap,
my penie in my pursse;
Thou are never the better,
and I am never the wursse."[26]

A Cornish Spell for Good Luck

Another potent spell is the rude draft of the planetary signs for the Sun, Jupiter, and Venus, followed by a cross, pentagram, and a figure formed by a perpendicular line and a divergent one at each side of it united at the bottom. Under them is written,

---

[25] *The Devils and Evil Spirits of Babylonia*, trans. R. Campbell Thompson (London: Luzac and Co., 1904), XXV - XXVI.

[26] Reginald Scot, *The Discoverie of Witchcraft*, ed. Ernest Rhys (London: Elliot Stock, 1886), 198.

"Whosoever beareth these tokens will be fortunate, and need fear no evil."

The charms are folded in a paper on which is usually written,

"By the help of the Lord these will do thee good,"

... and inclosed in a little bag to be worn on the breast. [27]

A Cornish Good Luck Charm

In some parts of Cornwall one may frequently hear the following charm made use of for invoking good luck:

"Even ash, I thee do pluck,
Hoping thus to meet good luck.
If no luck I get from thee,
I shall wish thee on the tree." [28]

GLAMOUR AND DECEPTION SPELLS

A Scottish Spell to Assume the Likeness of a Cat

If a witch wishes to go in the shape of a cat, she says thrice:

"I sall goe in till ane catt, I
With sorrow, and sych, and a blak shot 1
And I sall goe in THE DIVELLIs nam,
Ay quhill I com hom again

[translation]
"I shall go into one cat,
With sorrow and such and a black shot!

---

[27] M.A. Courtney, *Cornish Feasts and Folk-Lore* (Penzance, Beare and Son, 1890), 144.
[28] T.F. Thiselton Dyer, *English Folk-Lore* (London, Hardwicke & Bogue, 1878), 12.

*And I shall go in the devils' name,
Ay, until I come home again."*

To get out of a cat's shape, she will say:

*"Catt, catt, God ſend thé a blak ſhott
I wes a catt juſt now,
Bot I ſalbe in a woman's liknes evin now."*

*[translation]
"Cat, cat, God send thee a black shot,
I was a cat just now,
But I shall be in womans' likeness even now."*
[29] (original), [30] (translation and instruction)

HEALING SPELLS

An Irish Spell for Hip Disease

Take three green stones, gathered from a running brook, between midnight and morning, while no word is said. In silence it must be done. Then uncover the limb and rub each stone several times closely downwards from the hip to the toe, saying—

*"Wear away, wear away,
There you shall not stay,
Cruel pain—away, away."*[31]

---

[29] Robert Pitcairn, *Criminal Trials in Scotland Volume III* (Edinburgh: William Tait, 1833), 607-608.

[30] *Encyclopedia of Superstitions, Folklore, and the Occult Sciences of the World Vol. III*, ed. Cora Linn Daniels, and C.M. Stevans (Milwaukee, J.H. Yewdale & Sons Co., 1908), 1462.

[31] Lady Jane Wilde, *Ancient Legends, Mystic Charms, and Superstitions of Ireland* (London: Ward and Downey, 1888), 199.

A Medieval Spell against the Falling Evil

Take the sicke man by the hand, and whisper these wordes softlie in his eare,

> *"I conjure thee by the sunne and moone,*
> *and by the gospell of this daie*
> *delivered by God to Hubert, Giles, Cornelius, and John,*
> *that thou rise and fall no more."* [32]

A Scottish Spell for the Forespoken

In Orkney and Shetland, praise ... receives the name "Forespoken." If one says to a child "He is a bonnie bairn;" or "Thoo are looking well the day," it is regarded as coming from an "ill-tongue," unless the expression "God save the bairn," or some such blessing is also used. When one was "Forespoken," the cure in Orkney was "Forespoken Water"—that is water into which something has been dropped, supposed to possess magical powers, and over which an Incantation has been pronounced,—probably a reminiscence of Holy Water. The articles dropped in the water were, as a rule, three pebbles of different colours gathered from the sea shore. The charm was considered most potent when one stone was jet black, another white, and the remaining red, blue, or greenish.

An incantation was then muttered over the water, the reciter commencing by saying the word " Sain," and at the same time making the sign of the cross on the surface of the water. The incantation was as follows:

> *"In the name of Him that can cure or kill,*
> *This water shall cure all earthy ill,*
> *Shall cure the blood and flesh and bone,*
> *For ilka ane there is a stone ;*
> *May she fleg all trouble, sickness, pain,*
> *Cure without and cure within,*

---

[32] Reginald Scot, *The Discoverie of Witchcraft*, ed. Ernest Rhys (London: Elliot Stock, 1886), 195 - 196.

Cure the heart, and horn, and skin."

The patient for whom the "Forespoken Water" was prepared had to drink a part of it; the remainder was sprinkled on his person. [33]

A Medieval Charm for Witches to use while Gathering their Medicinal Herbs

*"Haile be thou holie hearbe
growing on the ground
All in the mount Calvarie
first wert thou found,
Thou art good for manie a sore,
And healest manie a wound,
In the name of sweete Jesus
I take thee from the ground."* [34]

A German Lunar Cure for Goiter or Warts

For increasing goitre or warts, fix your eyes on the waxing moon, and say three times,

"May what I see increase, may what I suffer cease." [35]

A Cornish Lunar Cure for Warts

wash the hands in the moon's rays focussed in a dry metal basin, saying,

*"I wash my hands in this thy dish,
Oh man in the moon, do grant my wish,*

---

[33] *County Folklore Vol. III Printed Extracts No. 5*, Ed. G.F. Black and Northcote W. Thomas (London, David Nutt, 1903), 141-142.

[34] Reginald Scot, *The Discoverie of Witchcraft*, ed. Ernest Rhys (London: Elliot Stock, 1886), 198.

[35] Jacob Grimm, *Teutonic Mythology Volume 4*, trans. James Stallybrass (London, George Bell & Sons, 1888), 1796.

And come and take away this."[36]

Cornish Kinning Stones

Of amulets mention must be made of certain small crystal balls called 'kinning stones,' held in high esteem for cure of ailments of the eye. I examined one of these 'kinning stones' recently, which had been lent to a person with a bad eye, who on recovering from his ailment had returned it to the owner. It proved to be a translucent, blueish-white globular crystal, about one-and-a-quarter inch in diameter; in texture, horny rather than vitreous; apparently not made of glass, but perhaps of rock crystal; pierced by a hole containing a boot lace for suspension; having striae running through the substance of the crystal perpendicular to the hole. It had been for many generations in possession of the family of the owner, who valued it very highly, "but was willing to lend it to anyone to do good." This kind of amulet is worn around the neck, the bad eye being struck with the crystal every morning. There are other 'kinning stones' within reach, but examples are not common; their virtues are familiar to the people, and instances are to be met with among the country folk, whose recovery from a 'kinning' in the eye ('kennel,' West Cornwall) is attributed solely to the use of these charms.[37]

CURSES, HEXES, AND JINXES

An English Curse to Hurt an Enemy

A wise woman at Aldershot [... advised one to ...] to take a piece of red cloth, stick pins in it, and then burn it in a clear fire.[38]

---

[36] M.A. Courtney, *Cornish Feasts and Folk-Lore* (Penzance, Beare and Son, 1890), 148.

[37] M.A. Courtney, *Cornish Feasts and Folk-Lore* (Penzance, Beare and Son, 1890), 144-145.

[38] *County Folklore Printed Extracts No. 1*, Ed. Edwin Sidney Hartland (Gloucester, Davies & Son, 1892), 188.

An Old World Curse of Nails

... nails were consecrated to evil by spells and invocations, then nailed cross wise above the imprint of the feet of the one who is destined for torment. [39]

A Old World Curse of Wax

The last and most favoured method was by the use of waxen images. Into the wax was mixed baptismal oil and ash of consecrated hosts, and out of this was fashioned a figure resembling the one to be bewitched. It was then baptised, receiving the persons name in full; received the Sacraments, and next subjected to curses, torture by knives or fire; then finally stabbed to the heart. It was also possible to bewitch a person by insufflation, breathing upon them, and so causing a heaviness of their will and corresponding compliance to the sorcerer. [40]

Scottish Lore on Witches Wrecking Ships

[Stories of the Shetland Islands speak of...] Witches on the shore, who, by means of wooden cups, wreck boats at sea. The cups are put into a Storm-Raising tub of water; each cup means a boat; and the witch names them. Then she violently agitates the water, and the number of upset cups corresponds to the number of wrecked boats. [41]

The Roman Invocation by the Sorceress Medea:

> "O Night, most faithful to these my mysteries, and ye golden Stars, who, with the Moon, succeed the fires of the day, and thou, three-faced Hecate, who comest conscious of my design, and ye charms and arts of the enchanters, and thou, too, Earth, that dost furnish the enchanters with powerful herbs; ye breezes, too, and winds, mountains, rivers,

---

[39] Lewis Spence, *An Encyclopædia of Occultism* (New York, Dodd, Mead & Co., 1920), 70.
[40] Lewis Spence, *An Encyclopædia of Occultism* (New York, Dodd, Mead & Co., 1920), 70.
[41] *County Folklore Vol. III Printed Extracts No. 5*, Ed. G.F. Black and Northcote W. Thomas (London, David Nutt, 1903), 154-155.

and lakes, and all ye Deities of the groves, and all ye Gods of night, attend here; through whose aid, whenever I will, the rivers run back from their astonished banks to their sources, and by my charms I calm the troubled sea, and rouse it when calm; I disperse the clouds, and I bring clouds upon the Earth; I both allay the winds, and I raise them; and I break the jaws of serpents with my words and my spells; I move, too, the solid rocks, and the oaks torn up with their own native earth, and the forests as well. I command the mountains, too, to quake, and the Earth to groan, and the ghosts to come forth from their tombs. Thee, too, O Moon, do I draw down, although the Temesæan brass relieves thy pangs. By my spells, also, the chariot of my grandsire is rendered pale; Aurora, too, is pale through my enchantments. For me did ye blunt the flames of the bulls, and with the curving plough you pressed the necks that never before bore the yoke. You raised a cruel warfare for those born of the dragon among themselves, and you lulled to sleep the keeper of the golden fleece, that had never known sleep; and thus, deceiving the guardian, you sent the treasure into the Grecian cities. Now there is need of juices, by means of which, old age, being renewed, may return to the bloom of life, and may receive back again its early years; and this ye will give me; for not in vain did the stars just now sparkle; nor yet in vain is the chariot come, drawn by the necks of winged dragons."[42]

FLIGHT AND TRANSPORTATION SPELLS

A Medieval Spell of Flight

The witches leave behind them, in bed, a besom or three-legged stool, which assumes their shape till their return, a feature exactly corresponding with the Mora trials. When proceeding to the spot where their work is to be performed, they either adopt the shape of cats, hares, etc., or else, mounting upon corn or bean straws, and pronouncing the following charm,

---

[42] Ovid, *Metamorphoses*, trans. Henry T. Riley (London: George Bell and Sons, 1898), 231.

"Horſe and hattok, horſe and goe,
Horſe and pellattis, ho ho!"

[translation]
"Horse and hattock, horse and go,
Horse and pellattis, ho! ho!"

...they are borne through the air to the place of their destination. [43]
(original), [44] (description)

Brian's Commentary: The phrase, "Horse and Hattock" is an old Scottish term that the fairies were said to utter before magically transporting through the air from one place to another. [45]

WEATHER WITCHING SPELLS

A Scottish Spell to Raise a Tempestuous Wind

Take a rag of cloth, wet it in water, and then take a beetle (with which washerwomen beat their linen) and knock it on the stone, repeating thrice—

"I knock this rag upon this stane,
To raise the wind in the devil's name!
It shall not lie until I please again!"

To appease the wind, they dried the rag, and said—

"We lay the wind in the devil's name,

---

[43] Robert Pitcairn, *Criminal Trials in Scotland* Volume III, (Edinburgh: William Tait, 1833), 608.

[44] *Magic and Witchcraft*, Issues 1-10, ed. George Moir (London, Chapman and Hall, 1852) 83.

[45] *Folk-lore and Legends: Scotland* (London:W.W. Gibbings, 1889), 151-152.

It shall not rise till I like to raise it again!"[46]

A Scottish Charm of Storm-Laying

Placing himself on the "brigstane" with his face towards the east, and taking his staff in his left hand, [the man] raised his right arm, and pronounced the following incantation, sawing the wind with his arm as he spoke:

*"Robbin cam ower da vaana wi' a shü nü;
Twabbie, Toobie, Keeliken, Kollickin, Palktrick alanks da robin.
Güid sober da wind."*[47]

A Scottish Rain Charm

When a peat fire is nearly consumed, some of the brands often remain standing in an upright in the light white ashes by which they are surrounded. And it was the fancied resemblance which those brands bore to persons, animals, ships, &c., which furnished the fire-reader with the means of foretelling events. One solitary upright brand, resembling a man or woman, was always called a "guest," i.e. a stranger or visitor from a distance. If it could be guessed who the person might be, and if welcome, the brand was lifted in the tongs and placed in the centre of the fire, and other brands heaped around it; but if the person was looked upon as an intruder, the brand was dipped in a tub of water, so that the individual represented might get a drenching of rain if he or she attempted the journey.[48]

---

[46] Thomas Wright, *Narratives of Sorcery and Magic, from the Most Authentic Sources* (New York, Redfield, 1852), 358.

[47] *County Folklore Vol. III Printed Extracts No. 5*, Ed. G.F. Black and Northcote W. Thomas (London, David Nutt, 1903), 155-156.

[48] *County Folklore Vol. III Printed Extracts No. 5*, Ed. G.F. Black and Northcote W. Thomas (London, David Nutt, 1903), 156.

DIVINATION SPELLS

A Cornish Hallowe'en Apple Love Divination

On the nearest Saturday to Hallowe'en, October 31st, the fruiter ers of Penzance display in their windows very large apples, known locally as "Allan" apples. These were formerly bought by the inhabitants and all the country people from the neighbourhood (for whom Penzance is the market-town), and one was given to each member of the family to be eaten for luck. The elder girls put theirs, before they ate them, under their pillows, to dream of their sweethearts. A few of the apples are still sold; but the custom, which, I have lately been told, was also observed at St. Ives, is practically dying out. On "Allantide," at Newlyn West, two strips of wood are joined crosswise by a nail in the centre; at each of the four ends a lighted candle is stuck, with apples hung between them. This is fastened to a beam, or the ceiling of the kitchen, and made to revolve rapidly. The players, who try to catch the apples in their mouths, often get instead a taste of the candle. [49]

A Cornish Hallowe'en Water Divination for Love

Rolling three names, each written on a separate piece of paper, tightly in the centre of three balls of earth. These were afterwards put into a deep basin of water, and anxiously watched until one of them opened, as the name on the first slip which came to the surface would be that of the person you were to marry. [50]

A Cornish Hallowe'en Keyhole Divination for Love

In Cornwall, as in other parts of England, many charms were tried on Hallowe'en to discover with whom you were to spend your future life, or if you were to remain unmarried, such as pouring melted lead through

---

[49] M.A. Courtney, *Cornish Feasts and Folk-Lore* (Penzance, Beare and Son, 1890), 2-3.
[50] M.A. Courtney, *Cornish Feasts and Folk-Lore* (Penzance, Beare and Son, 1890), 3.

the handle of the front door key. The fantastic shapes it assumed foretold your husband's profession or trade. [51]

Sifting your Siller: A Scottish Love Divination

Take a sieve, keys, a pair of scissors, a comb and a bit of silver. Open two or three doors, and all the better if there are four, and if they are opposite each other. The person who wants to see his or her future husband or wife looks out the outer door, and then turns the sieve three times with the sun, and then three times against the sun, repeating the following each time they turn it:

"I sift, I tift; I sift, I tift,
I sift dis night for dee,
And he (or she) it is to be my true love,
Let them appear presently."[52]

A Cornish Hair Divination for Love

To see if a friend loves her, a Cornish girl pulls out a hair from her friend's head, and then tries to suspend it by the root from the palm of her own hand. If this can be done the test is successful. [53]

A Spell from Brittany to Divine One's Enemies

Divination is common in Brittany. It is accomplished by means of needles. Five and twenty new needles are put into a plate, water is poured over them and as many needles as cross each other, so many are the diviners' enemies. [54]

---

[51] M.A. Courtney, *Cornish Feasts and Folk-Lore* (Penzance, Beare and Son, 1890), 3.
[52] *County Folklore Vol. III Printed Extracts No. 5*, Ed. G.F. Black and Northcote W. Thomas (London, David Nutt, 1903), 160.
[53] M.A. Courtney, *Cornish Feasts and Folk-Lore* (Penzance, Beare and Son, 1890), 164-165.
[54] *Encyclopedia of Superstitions, Folklore, and the Occult Sciences of the World Vol. III*, ed. Cora Linn Daniels, and C.M. Stevans (Milwaukee, J.H. Yewdale & Sons Co., 1908), 1226.

A Cornish Fern Divination for Love

Draw a bracken fern, cut it at the bottom of the stalk; there you will find your lover's initials. [55]

An Irish Spell to Dream of Your Future Lover

The girl who wishes to see her future husband must go out and gather certain herbs in the light of the full moon of the new year, repeating this charm—

> *"Moon, moon, tell unto me*
> *When my true love I shall see?*
> *What fine clothes am I to wear?*
> *How many children shall I bear?*
> *For if my love comes not to me*
> *Dark and dismal my life will be."*

Then the girl, cutting three pieces of clay from the sod with a black-hafted knife, carries them home, ties them up in the left stocking with the right garter, places the parcel under her pillow, and dreams a true dream of the man she is to marry and of all her future fate. [56]

A Cornish Apple Love Divination

Take an apple-pip between the forefinger and the thumb, flip it into the air, saying,

> *"North, south, east, west,*
> *tell me where my love doth rest,"*

and watch the direction in which it falls. [57]

---

[55] M.A. Courtney, *Cornish Feasts and Folk-Lore* (Penzance, Beare and Son, 1890), 165.
[56] Lady Jane Wilde, *Ancient Legends, Mystic Charms, and Superstitions of Ireland* (London: Ward and Downey, 1888), 185.
[57] M.A. Courtney, *Cornish Feasts and Folk-Lore* (Penzance, Beare and Son, 1890), 165.

An English Love Divination for St. Mark's Eve (April 24)

There is another Vigil kept by young women on St. Mark's Eve, for the purpose of ascertaining their future husbands. Precisely at midnight the husband-seeker must go alone into the garden, taking with her some hemp-seed, which she is to sow, repeating at the same time the following lines:

"Hemp-seed I sow;
Hemp-seed, grow;
He that is my true love
Come after me and mow."

It is believed that if this be done with full faith in the efficacy of the charm, the figure of the future husband will appear, with a scythe, and in the act of mowing. [58]

A Cornish Yarrow Love Divination

Go into the fields at the time of the new moon and pluck a piece of herb yarrow; put it when going to bed under your pillow, saying—

"Good night, fair yarrow,
Thrice good night to thee;
I hope before to-morrow's dawn
My true love I shall see."

If you are to be married your sweetheart will appear to you in your dreams. [59]

---

[58] *County Folklore Printed Extracts No. 1*, Ed. Edwin Sidney Hartland (Gloucester, Davies & Son, 1892), 96.
[59] M.A. Courtney, *Cornish Feasts and Folk-Lore* (Penzance, Beare and Son, 1890), 165.

SPELLS FROM MY MEMORY

These are spells I've learned over the years. Some come from training, some from experimentation, and others from lore and the experiences I have had in my journey as a Witch. All Witches develop their own methods and as I have said in this book, Witchcraft is a scavenger religion. We take what we need and what works and we weave it into the warp and weft of our Craft."

The Witch Bottle

Procure a bottle, and within it place sharp objects until it is half-full: broken glass, nails, iron shavings, thorns, or bones. Fill the bottle with your own urine and seal it. Recite the following incantation: "To bane, to bane, be gone from whence you came." Now bury the bottle somewhere where no one will find it.

Crossroads Work

The crossroads is a magical place. We have already spoken of Hecate, a goddess heavily associated with Witchcraft, and her place at the crossroads. Many magical systems and folk traditions place significant importance on the crossroads. It is, after all, a place where worlds and meanderings come together and nothing could represent Witchcraft better because we, as Witches, walk between the worlds as well. Magic done at the crossroads is a potent reminder that all magic lies at the meeting place that exists between worlds, that special place between the Inner Planes and the mundane existence we inhabit.

— To banish someone from doing you harm, collect 13 stones and boil them in a pot until the water completely evaporates. At midnight, take the stones and scatter them at the crossroads.

— For prosperity, bury a coin at the crossroads.

— For love, leave a red rose with your petition at the crossroads, knowing and believing that your desire will be fulfilled. If it is fertility you seek, and not just love, an egg may be left.

— For protection, an iron nail can be used during your work at the crossroads. Iron has always been associated with protection work and is a powerful symbol for this kind of magic.

Fairy Offering

The Fae are a rich part of Witchcraft lore. Contracts, deals, and mysterious meetings with the inhabitants of the Otherworld are integral parts of Celtic legend and the Fairy Faith is alive and well even today. Fairy trees and Fairy mounds exist aplenty in the British Isles and the magic of place is palpable in these sites. The Fae can conjure images of the most helpful and eager sprites to the most malefic and baneful spirits that act as harbingers of death, battle, and mystery. Working with the Fae is a complex and tricky path but I can offer one bit of lore and spellwork.

— To trick a fairy into being obedient unto you, put an offering of mead in an eggshell. Any fairy who takes the offering will be under your power.

For Protection

Protection work is something all Witches engage in. We have already discussed the psychic shield, but physical protection work is also used in Witchcraft. Our home and hearth are sacred places, and the home itself was always considered holy by the ancients. Hestia and Vesta watched over the hearths of Greece and Rome and Brigid tended the fires of Celtic lands. Ancient peoples had household gods and household spirits that were served and cared for such as the Lares in Rome and even modern peoples often have ancestor or spiritual shrines in their homes and places of business for protection. This can be seen from Confucian ancestral shrines in East Asia to the images and statues of folk saints in the homes of Catholics across the world. We do not engage in protection work because of some paranoia that other magical people are out to get us (this is a slippery slope) but instead because we wish to imbue our Light into the spaces we live in and feel at home in our own microcosm.

— To protect your home, hang a horseshoe above your front entrance or place iron in the four corners of the house. You may also display a mirror facing out to repel the Evil Eye.

To Exorcize a Home

Exorcism may conjure up images of horror movie demon possession, but the term goes far beyond expelling demons with Latin incantations on campy movie sets. To exorcize is to expunge something. It is to cast something out. It is to remove a negative energy or force within a space or person. Exorcisms in magical work can vary from the extremely complex to the very simple. They can involve detailed rituals torn from the pages of Renaissance grimoires, complete with the invoking of angels and the drawing of arcane sigils. Or, they can involve the humblest acts of magic (often the most powerful) that only need simple tools and a clear intent.

A simple house exorcism: take a head of garlic. Break up the bulb and place the cloves around your house. Wait three days, collect the garlic and then cast it out!

Magical Systems

As I have stated, Witchcraft has a system of magic until itself as recorded in our *Book of Shadows* and in the oral teachings handed down to us. However, the occult world has much to offer, and any occultist is generally knowledgeable about the most well-known systems deriving from the old grimoires and early occult lodges. These include Kabbalah, astrological rites, alchemy, and Hermetic Tarot. I am providing a brief outlook and introduction to some of the more practical inclusions in this grimoire, but I encourage you to explore them further.

PLANETARY MAGIC

Planetary Magic is used by both Witches and magicians. Its origins are obscure, being said to have originated in the cradle of civilization, among the Sumerians, Babylonians, Egyptians, and later adopted by the Greeks and the Romans. This system is based on what the ancients called the Seven Planets. These were the first heavenly bodies studied and visible to the human eye. In truth, they are more appropriately called luminaries, as the moon and the sun are not planets. These luminaries were associated with the Gods and continue to be today. They are also associated with a host of other entities, angels, spirits, and demons.

In Western occult tradition, this system was popularized through the various texts in the *Key of Solomon* and other Grimoires. Planetary Magic can be very simple or extremely complex depending on the work. It is used for evocation, pentacles, candle magic and sometimes general spell work. All one needs is an understanding of the system and proper preparation. Using the planetary correspondences (or, today, the right app on your smartphone) determines which day and hour you will be working. For prosperity, you might select the day of Jupiter and the hour of Mercury to enhance communication regarding your pursuit of success. For your relationship, you might work on the day of Mercury and the hour of Venus; it is situational. If you are interested in making pentacles, I recommend *The Key of Solomon* by Mathers. *The Abramelin* and *The Magus* by Francis Barrett also have alternative talismans. The Magus also has an excellent angelic planetary correspondence. The Goetia has become increasingly popular for its planetary demons. I personally do not recommend this route—not out of some Christian-based fear but out of logic. These entities are from an egregore of unknown origins and, in my opinion, attempt to feed on their would-be masters. I have also noted a lack of positive long-term results for those who go down this path of magic. The first step is to learn each planet's magical associations:

Sun: *healing, physical, success, renown, music, poetry, confidence, hope, vitality.*

Moon: *divination, psychic power, female fertility, childbirth, transformation, family, secrets, nature, spiritual healing, medicine, herbs, Witchcraft.*

Mars: *conflict, victory, potency, surgery, ambition, courage, strength, protection, male potency.*

Mercury: *wisdom, knowledge, communication, travel, astral magic, truth, ritual, occult power.*

Jupiter: *influence, wealth, leadership, justice, control, sovereignty.*

Venus: *love, fertility, peace, friendship, passion, lust, fidelity, youth, beauty, compassion, emotional healing.*

Saturn: *curses, death transitions, exorcism, purification, binding, banishing, buildings, meditation, spirits, familiars.*

COLOR MAGIC

Color magic is something that glares at all of us in the face in the modern magic traditions. We use it for stones, candles, and magical bags. Some people even incorporate it into their clothing or visualizations. However, the many, many books written about magic have obscured this system beyond recognition. They will have color associations without any context or background beyond their imaginations. There are in fact actual systems. The one we use in the New Orleans Coven is from the *Key of Solomon* and is planetary in origin. For example, red is Mars. Many individuals associate red with love, because, quite frankly, they're mentally connecting it to red roses and Valentine's Day. However, there is really no magical system that supports this.

The color of love would be the color of Venus, which is green. And many people want to associate green with prosperity. Why? Because money is green, not because it's supported by any sort of magical system. Green is the color of Venus, and she is the Goddess of love. This is not to say Mars never has a use in matters of passion, but that is situational.

As you can guess, I suggest using this system for colors because it not only has a history, but it is fluid with other established occult workings. Color magic is really working with light and perception, and it is used by all of us. My advice is pick one system, and make sure it is a system. Most of us are first exposed to color magic by working with candles, so in this spirit I have provided you with a planetary candle spell.

PLANETARY CANDLE SPELL

Using the correspondences in the back of the book, select which planet you will be working with for your purpose.

Once you have chosen which planet you will be working with, select a candle of the appropriate color, then plan to work on the day and or hour of your chosen planet or planets. For instance, if you are looking to seek gainful employment, you might choose Jupiter and work on the day and hour of Jupiter, which is Thursday. The color for the candle of Jupiter would be blue. When it is time to work, you will make your magical space ready. Working at your altar, you will anoint the candle of Jupiter with appropriate oils. If you do not have oil of Jupiter or incense of Jupiter, you may use something as simple as olive oil. Any oil will do. The correspondence chart in the back also gives fumigations for the planets. You can use this for making both incense or oils. Anoint the candle with your oil, and sprinkle it with appropriate herbs. Ask that the God and Goddess charge the candle and fill it with your vital energies. Focus on the purpose of your work, and instill it in the candle with your active imagination.

State the reason you are doing the work and what you wish to achieve. Light the candle and focus on it for a length of time, instilling it with your vital energies. Repeat this process every day for the next six days until you have completed a seven-day cycle—seven being sacred to the seven luminaries of planetary magic. In some shops, you may be able to obtain seven-day candles, which could also be used for this purpose. But any candle is appropriate.

Chant:

"(Planet name) by the essence of your light,
By this candle burning bright,
Empower now this magic rite."

MOON MAGIC

Moon magic is essential in Witchcraft, and many authors have written about it. Simply put, it is about working with the tides of the moon and is exceptionally potent when actually put to use. From the new moon to the full moon, the moon waxes, becoming larger and larger. The magic to be done in this circumstance is one of increase. From the full moon to the new moon, the moon wanes. You use this to decrease. This is preferred by most Witches over planetary magic, but it is one of those "planets" with which the systems can be combined when appropriate. Another factor in working with the lunar tides is their 28-day cycle. Always give yourself this cycle between works.

I am going to provide a moon talisman ritual for you that may be useful in understanding the nature of this old form of magic.

New Moon Talisman

The new moon talisman is created for an increase. On the new moon, you will create the talisman using white paper and silver ink, inscribing the talisman on one side and writing the name of your chosen moon goddess and your request on the other. Then sign your name, and conceal the talisman in a hidden place until the moon is full. On the full moon, place the talisman on your altar and consecrate it with incense and holy water, then invoke the moon goddess, stating your purpose and desires, instilling the talisman with your vital energies. Once again, conceal the talisman in a hidden place and tell no one. Keep the talisman for 28 days, then burn it after the next new moon.

On the back side of the sigil, write the names:
Goddess, Isis, Selene
Write your request and sign your name.

Full Moon Talisman

This talisman will be created on the full moon. You will create the talisman using black paper and silver ink. Inscribe the talisman on one side, and on the other write the name of your chosen moon goddess, your request and then sign your name. Conceal the talisman in a hidden place until the new moon. On the new moon, place the talisman on your altar and consecrate it with incense and holy water, then invoke the moon goddess, stating your purpose and desires, instilling the talisman with your vital energies. Once again, conceal the talisman in a hidden place and tell no one. Keep the talisman for 28 days, and then burn it on the next full moon.

On the back side of the sigil, write the names:
Goddess, Diana, Luna
Write your request and sign your name.

HERMETIC TAROT

Hermetic Tarot really originates with the Golden Dawn and the publication of the Rider-Waite deck. However, it has become a prolific system of magic in Western occultism, and almost every magician and Witch utilizes it in some way. Whereas we do not incorporate in the rituals what some Hermetic practitioners use the Tarot for, Witches do use it for divination and to understand the archetypes as they relate to the Craft. I will not be exploring the entire system of Hermetic Tarot, as that would be a book unto itself. However, I am going to provide you with a Tarot spell and suggest that this is a system you should look into. The Golden Dawn developed a unique correspondence, linking the Tarot, the Kabbalah, and other systems of magic that are found throughout Western occultism. Today, every occultist should have some understanding of these practices, whether they incorporate them or not. I am providing a correspondence based on this from my own personal point of view.

Tarot Divination Spell

Considering your purpose, select a Tarot deck that you are very familiar with, or the one with which you work the most. On your altar, you will do a three-card spread, left to right, representing your past, present, and future. If the outcome is favorable to your desire, leave it out and do not work with the deck for 28 days. Once 28 days have passed, wait until the full moon and then put it away. If the reading is not in your favor, select a card that is, and replace it with the future card. Contemplate the reading and the present card until you have gained insight, then replace the present card with one that would help you reach your desired outcome. Once again, leave it out and do not work with the deck for 28 days. Once 28 days have passed, wait until the full moon and then put it away.

Recipes

HOLY MOON WATER

Used for consecrations, protection, and exorcism.
Add to water from the sea:

A pinch of Hyssop
A pinch of Vervain
A pinch of Mint

Under the full moon, recite: "Goddess who rules the tides and the seasons, may this water be blessed by your holy and sacred names." Leave the water in a place to catch the moon's rays until the next full moon.

HERBS THE DRUIDS OFFERED IN FIRES

These were used in open fires outside.

Vervain: *for magic spells*

Saint John's Wort: *for protection*

Juniper: *for gods*

Agrimony: *for goddesses*

Fern: *to make it rain*

ISIS OIL OR INCENSE

This recipe be used when working rituals for the Goddess.

1 Part Pink Lotus
1 Part Storax

1 Part Rose
1 Part Honey (for incense) or 1 Part Beeswax Absolute (for oil)
3 Parts Frankincense

SERAPIS INCENSE
Can be used when working rituals for the god,

3 parts Frankincense
1 part Myrrh
Few drops Wine
1 part Raisin
1 part Cinnamon
1 part Pine resin
1 part Mastic

KYPHI INCENSE - PAPYRUS EBERS
Used in any rituals favored by Egyptian, Greek, and Roman Gods.

Honey
Frankincense
Mastic
Genen
Pine Kernels
Cypress Grass
Camel Grass
Inektun
Cinnamon

KYPHI INCENSE - PAPYRUS HARRIS

Raisins
Wine
Honey

Mastic
Pine resin
Camel grass
Mint
Sweet flag
Cinnamon

Poems, Invocations, and Chants

Most of the rituals and poetry in this book were written by me, with the only exceptions being quotes or the folklore spells I included above for historical reasons. Here are some my more personal works that I have created over the years.

A WITCH'S PRAYER

Magic Circle oh so bright,
fill the darkness with my light.
Ertha, Fier, Waeter, Eir.

Ancient winds I now invite,
gather at my sacred site.
Ertha, Fier, Waeter, Eir.

Spoken spell I do recite,
to the moon goddess white.
Ertha, Fier, Waeter, Eir.

Horned hunter God of might,
hearken ye unto my rite.
Ertha, Fier, Waeter, Eir.

Heed the witch's prayer this night,
Gods of old now hear my plight.
Ertha, Fier, Waeter, Eir.

Grant me fertile power tonight,
may the magic now ignite.
Ertha, Fier, Waeter, Eir.

Cone of power now take flight,
sent by will and second sight.
Ertha, Fier, Waeter, Eir.

CHARGE ⊕F THE SUN

High Priestess:

Maiden, Mother, Crone these are seen in me. Yet I am one. So it is with the Twin Gods.

They are spokes on the same wheel, each a horn on the same head. And yet there is a third horn made of fire and it will burn forever.

High Priest:

I am the god of the sun.
I am the faun of spring
I am the Greenman of summer.
I am the barley king of autumn.
I am the stag of winter.
I am the twin faced god of the dance;
I am the spear and I am the lance.
I am the spokes on the great wheel.
I can cause harm and I can heal.
I am a consort.

I am a King.
I travel by hoof and I travel by wing.
I am the Hunted I am the Hunter...
I am your Lover, Father and Brother.
I am he who dies in the corn....
I am the third Fiery Horn.... and through the mother I am reborn.

CIRCLE CASTING

I carve this circle, out of time, out of space, out of land, out of mist, out of what is hidden and what is known. Circle of the sun. Circle of the moon. Circle of waters and earth. Goddess of birth and rebirth. Circle of wind and flame, I forge thee in the Horned One's name.

THE CIRCLE

Call the winds, chant the rite, dance the fires, reclaim the night. Asperge the circle, draw it round, salt of earth with water bound. Bring the censer, bless the grail, raise your voice, the Goddess hail. Light the candles, carve the runes, reach the stars, draw down the moon. Wind Father, Lord of Sun, move your power, become as one. Earth Mother, Lady Sea, share your magic, blessed be.

THE ONE

In a circle, I sit, awaiting the one, the laughing lord of the glade. With flower and leaf, I wait for the chief of the time-worn way.

In a circle, I stand, awaiting the one, he who dies in the corn; he who falls at the hands of the mother that all may be reborn.

In a circle, I dance, awaiting the one; he who hunts with the hounds; he who hears all noise; he who knows all sounds; the one that laughs in the dark; the one who knows no bounds.

In a circle, I chant, awaiting the one who is enthroned in the dark of the year; he who is king; he who is master; he who is lord of all fear.

In a circle, I sing, awaiting the one, heaven's horned master, the bright lord, God of the Sun.

DRAWING DOWN THE MOON

Go to a hidden stream, a quiet and alone place. When the moon in all her glory beams, behold the night wonder and choose a space of fog and mist and dew. You are not solid nor vapor nor liquid nor fire. On bank or stream, limb or rock, on any of these sentinels, stand not but float in the in between. Menstruating muse, cup of life, shadow of wisdom.

Goddess, moon above our heads, earth beneath our feet, passion within our souls, primordial foam of the sea. Descend, and make fertile all nature. Guardian of the wells. Keeper of the flame. Mistress of the cave, and voice of the wind. Embrace your hidden children and pour fourth your love.

Boil over your cauldron, let us taste from the high cup and be bathed in your light.

I AM MY ANCESTORS

I search for high ground.
I stand in a ring of stones.
I carry a torch in procession from hill to hill.

I make holy ground in sacred land by ocean foam, the wind in my hair, and a fire within in my head. At still midnight in the stark blast of winter,
I stand upon a high place on hard rock, crowned with a blue flame.
I witnessed the sun at the birth of creation.
In the rays of summer light,
I dance in the glory, and when that light fades,
I do not mourn, for
I have tasted the secrets that flow from the cauldron of life.
I cry in echo with my ancestors.
I am a servant of sovereignty.
I am a creator of unwoven space and un-spiraled time.
I am one with the ebb and flow of the elemental tides.
I divide truth from falsehood.
I pierce the shadows of the unknown.
I pass through the honeyed plane of bliss. In the northern court of the sidhe, my lawful chair is set.
I wield the sharpest sword.
I cast the swiftest spear.
I drink from the brew of the most high.
I am the red berry of the yew and the white berry of the mistletoe.
I am the golden wheat at harvest and the wisdom of the black hen.
In total darkness, I know the way.
I am the furze and the Gorse.
I am the dove and the hawk that pursues it.
I am with the first, primordial wind that filled the lungs of the living.
I am the sweet heather.
I am the oak tree's brother.
I am the hare and the hound.
I am the aspen and white poplar.
I am a salmon, filled with knowledge and an otter that craves it.
I am the ninth wave washed ashore.

I am a sacred tree, reaching high to the heavens and rooted deep within the underworld.

I am one with all things, source of life, fountain of mead, place in which and from which all directions meet and flow.

I stand centered in middle earth and join the tides of the moon, the waves of the sea, and bounty of the earth.

I am sovereign by the nine-fold muse my throne is preeminent.

I am the guardian of the sacred grove.

I am the blossom of the untouched meadow.

I am a virgin that holds the brightest pearl.

I offer acorn, milk, and dew from a cup of gold.

I am a sacred branch bearing fruit.

I bring light out of darkness.

I am the storyteller.

I give wisdom to those who seek.

I sing the dying to sleep.

I stand in vigil before the holy flame.

I bathe in a sacred stream.

I move with the wind and change with the season.

I am the reason the lance bleeds, and I am the one the grail serves Who but I knows the wisdom of the sacrifice?

THE FAIRY ARROW

In the gloom of the winter's chill, there is no fruit and little harvest wheat, only the catch of the hunter's feast. And at the sacred shrine of Kildare, nine priestesses chant before the sacred flame an invocation of the lady's name.

Brid has come. Brid is welcome.
Brid has come. Brid is welcome.
Brid has come. Brid is welcome.

And at the edge of a mystic stream, a lone druid holds up a chalice of the most high. Then, he partakes of the milk that flows from the triple muse. And at that moment, when all ritual's complete, from the brilliance of God's own eye comes forth the fairy arrow of the sky.

She reaches out and takes his hand, saying, "My people have kept vigil, and I will bless their land." She passed by the forest, village, and glen, stroking her harp, commanding winter to end. And with her promise of the coming spring, she faded away like she had never been. But with the vision that the lady will return, torches are lit and the butter is churned. And in a procession up the raft mound, the bonfire is lit and inspiration found.

GREENWOOD WEDDING

The May Queen comes to claim her crown on the eve of May.
She comes to dance about the pole on Beltane Day.

Fire burns on the hills on the eve of May.
The lady brings the smoldering flame on Beltane Day.

The lady comes to wash her face in the dew of May.
The lady comes to bless the earth on Beltane Day.

The flower maiden releases her dove on the eve of May.
Robin Goodfellow courts her love on Beltane Day.

The piper notes begin to play on the eve of May.
The green man makes his greenwood bed on Beltane Day.

The lord and the lady make their marriage on the eve of May.
The lord and the lady join as one on Beltane Day.

The lady returns from the underworld on the eve of May.
The lady returns to us all on Beltane Day.

MORRIGAN'S DECREE

Anu, Fea, Nemon, Badb, and Macha, I have been! Morrigu, Morgana, Margawse, Modron and Morgan Le Fay I am. To many tribes I have had many names and in 10,000 battles have they been called. Yet I am one, born before time and shaped by the myths of men. When the Gods arrived, I watched them from a high cliff weaving my mists around them.

I have been called War Goddess, I the great queen. Yet I am the shape shifter, black, white, and grey are my shades. Eel, heifer, and wolf am I. If you invoke my name in conflict, I will be your shield. I will sharpen your swords and put your spears in order. On swift wings I will make your blood to boil and bury the brave. But in the end victory shall be mine to claim, for I am the trickster. Know this I am of the oldest of gods. Most ancient of spirits, ancestress of the of the earth. I am the carrion crow, the raven, goddess of war, fate and death.

You who think to summon me be warned, it is my will that shall be done. I am the patroness of the hidden path, mistress of spells, enchantress of the barge. I am the rays of the moon that casts shadows upon the spectral realms and invoke mystery in magic. I am a decrepit hag, yet I seduce and give live to gods. I am the perfumed essence of sacrifice covering the night and demanding justice. I am the dark mother. In the land of apples my throne is placed and the laws of old enshrined. My decree shall echo to the four winds. My children shall be covered in my feathered cloak. My banner shall again be taken up. My enemies shall be destroyed. My realms will be restored.

DIANA'S HUNT

Oh, stag of seven tines hear my call, in winter, spring, summer, and fall.
Lord of the Chase reveal thy face, as the heartbeat quickens to a steady pace.
The virgin huntress is hot on thy heels, it is your life she wishes to steal.
And as the arrow begins to fly, you raise your chest, ready to die.
For you are the Stag King, the lord of us all! In winter, spring, summer and fall.

EARTH MOTHER CHANT

Erce, Erce mother earth,
Erce, Erce father son,
Erce, Erce mother moon,
Erce, Erce horned one.

Tables of Correspondences

Witches and occultists use tables of correspondences to cross-reference magical properties, associations, and intents, as well as astrological, planetary, and deity rulerships to help their magic achieve its greatest potency. I have created the following tables from years of research into ancient grimoires, occult classics, past teachings, and trial and error.

a Table of Roman, Saxon, and Celtic Gods Worshipped in Britain with their Planetary Associations

	Sol · Sunday	Luna · Monday	Mars · Tuesday	Mercur · Wendsday	Jupiter · Thursday	Venus · Friday	Saturne · Saturday
	☉ The Sun	☾ The Moon	♂ Mars	☿ Mercury	♃ Jupiter	♀ Venus	♄ Saturn
Roman	Apollo/Sol	Diana/Isis	Mars	Mercury	Jove/Serapis	Astarte/Isis	Saturn/Serapis
Briton	Maponos	Andred	Camulos	Nodens	Cocidius	Damara	Hern/Cern
Welsh	Beli Mawr	Don	Bran	Gwydion	Lludd	Branwen	Gwyn Ap-Nudd
Anglo-Saxon	Sunne	Mona	Tiw	Woden	Thunor	Frige	Lok

The Table of Planetary Correspondences

	Magical Intent	Color	Metal	Fumes
☉ Sun	healing ✤ physical health success ✤ renown ✤ music poetry ✤ vitality ✤ inspiration happiness ✤ confidence ✤ hope	Yellow	Gold	All gums & resins
☽ Moon	divination ✤ psychic powers transformation ✤ female fertility secrets ✤ medicine ✤ nature childbirth ✤ family ✤ herbs spiritual healing ✤ witchcraft	White	Silver	All edible leaves & herbs
♂ Mars	conflict ✤ victory ✤ surgery protection ✤ courage ✤ strength ambition ✤ conquest ✤ war male potency ✤ domination	Red	Iron	All odorous woods
☿ Mercury	wisdom ✤ knowledge ✤ truth communication ✤ astral magic ritual ✤ occult power ✤ sigils writing ✤ hermetics ✤ ritual	Mixed Colors	Mixed Metals	All pairing of woods or fruits
♃ Jupiter	influence ✤ wealth ✤ leadership justice ✤ politics ✤ control sovereignty ✤ prestige manipulation ✤ political power	Blue	Tin	All odorous fruits
♀ Venus	love ✤ fertility ✤ compassion passion ✤ lust ✤ friendship youth ✤ beauty ✤ fidelity emotional healing ✤ peace	Green	Copper	All Flowers
♄ Saturn	curses ✤ death ✤ transitions exorcism ✤ building ✤ spirits purification ✤ meditation binding ✤ familiars ✤ banishing	Black	Lead	All odorous roots

The Table of the Planetary Hours

Divide the Minutes from Sunrise to Sunrise for 24 Planetary Hours

☉ The Sun	☽ The Moon	♂ Mars	☿ Mercury	♃ Jupiter	♀ Venus	♄ Saturn
☉ 1	☽ 1	♂ 1	☿ 1	♃ 1	♀ 1	♄ 1
♀ 2	♄ 2	☉ 2	☽ 2	♂ 2	☿ 2	♃ 2
☿ 3	♃ 3	♀ 3	♄ 3	☉ 3	☽ 3	♂ 3
☽ 4	♂ 4	☿ 4	♃ 4	♀ 4	♄ 4	☉ 4
♄ 5	☉ 5	☽ 5	♂ 5	☿ 5	♃ 5	♀ 5
♃ 6	♀ 6	♄ 6	☉ 6	☽ 6	♂ 6	☿ 6
♂ 7	☿ 7	♃ 7	♀ 7	♄ 7	☉ 7	☽ 7
☉ 8	☽ 8	♂ 8	☿ 8	♃ 8	♀ 8	♄ 8
♀ 9	♄ 9	☉ 9	☽ 9	♂ 9	☿ 9	♃ 9
☿ 10	♃ 10	♀ 10	♄ 10	☉ 10	☽ 10	♂ 10
☽ 11	♂ 11	☿ 11	♃ 11	♀ 11	♄ 11	☉ 11
♄ 12	☉ 12	☽ 12	♂ 12	☿ 12	♃ 12	♀ 12
♃ 13	♀ 13	♄ 13	☉ 13	☽ 13	♂ 13	☿ 13
♂ 14	☿ 14	♃ 14	♀ 14	♄ 14	☉ 14	☽ 14
☉ 15	☽ 15	♂ 15	☿ 15	♃ 15	♀ 15	♄ 15
♀ 16	♄ 16	☉ 16	☽ 16	♂ 16	☿ 16	♃ 16
☿ 17	♃ 17	♀ 17	♄ 17	☉ 17	☽ 17	♂ 17
☽ 18	♂ 18	☿ 18	♃ 18	♀ 18	♄ 18	☉ 18
♄ 19	☉ 19	☽ 19	♂ 19	☿ 19	♃ 19	♀ 19
♃ 20	♀ 20	♄ 20	☉ 20	☽ 20	♂ 20	☿ 20
♂ 21	☿ 21	♃ 21	♀ 21	♄ 21	☉ 21	☽ 21
☉ 22	☽ 22	♂ 22	☿ 22	♃ 22	♀ 22	♄ 22
♀ 23	♄ 23	☉ 23	☽ 23	♂ 23	☿ 23	♃ 23
☿ 24	♃ 24	♀ 24	♄ 24	☉ 24	☽ 24	♂ 24

Occult Tarot Correspondences

Card	Occult Name	Ruler	Meaning
The Fool	Spirit of Aether	🜁 Air	Initiation + beginnings + Leap of faith
The Magician	Magus of Power	☿ Mercury	High Priest + Balance Skill + Adept Occultist + Trickster
The High Priestess	Priestess of the Silver Star	☾ The Moon	High Priestess + Moon Goddess + Silence Intuition + the Muse + Female Magician
The Empress	Daughter of the Mighty Ones	♀ Venus	Earth + Mother + Queen + Fertility Health + Hearth and home
The Emperor	Sun of the Morning Chief among the Mighty	♈ Aries	Father + Provider + Benefactor King + Leadership
The Hierophant	Magus of the Eternal	♉ Taurus	Initiator + Guide on the Inner Planes Wisdom + Ritual power + Tradition
The Lovers	Children of the Voice and Oracle of the Mighty Gods	♊ Gemini	Recognition of Higher Self + Beauty Love + union + Desire + Self-Reflection
The Chariot	Child of the Powers of the Waters + Lord of the Triumph of Light	♋ Cancer	As Above, so Below + Triumph + Courage Abundance + Balance of Matter and Spirit
Strength	Daughter of the Flaming Sword	♌ Leo	Knowing One's Will + confidence Self-Discipline + Action + Overcoming
The Hermit	Prophet of the Eternal Magus of the Voice of Power	♍ Virgo	Higher Self + Magical Teacher Caution + Prudence + Awareness
The Wheel of Fortune	Lord of the Forces of Life	♃ Jupiter	A Choice of Destiny + Seeking Initiation Luck + Success + Great Change + Control
Justice	Daughter of the Lords of Truth + Ruler of the Balance	♎ Libra	Balance + equality + righting wrongs forgiveness & severity + karmic forces
The Hanged Man	Spirit of the Mighty Waters	▽ Water	Higher Initiations + Self-Sacrifice + Purification Dedication + Inner Knowledge + Prophesy.
Death	Child of the Great Transformers + Lord of the Gate of Death	♏ Scorpio	Guardian of Hidden Knowledge + End Transformation + Mortality + the Abyss
Temperance	Daughter of the Reconcilers + Bringer Forth of Life	♐ Sagittarius	Guardian of Hidden Knowledge + End Transformation + Mortality + the Abyss
The Devil	Lord of the Gates of Matter + Child of the Forces of Time	♑ Capricorn	The Horned God + Power + Earthly Desires Sex + Grounding + Blessings from Adversity
The Tower	Lord of the Hosts of the Mighty	♂ Mars	Conflict + Catastrophe + Loss + Letting Go Destruction of the Temple in order to Rebuild
The Star	Daughter of the Firmament + Dweller between the Waters	♒ Aquarius	Manifestation + Hope + Expectations Promises + Personal Power
The Moon	Ruler of Flux and Reflux + Child of the Sons of the Mighty	♓ Pisces	Isis Veiled + Occult Forces + Illusion Intuition + Facing One's Negative Aspects
The Sun	Lord of the Fire of the World	☉ The Sun	Divine Child + Happiness + Joy Rebirth + Health + Prosperity.
Judgment	Spirit of the Primal Fire	△ Fire	Reincarnation + Family + Coven Bonds Ancestors + Renewal + Results.
The World	The Universe + The Great One of the Night of Time	♄ Saturn	The Material Plane + Time + Glory + Prestige Dominance + Crossing the Abyss + Isis Unveiled

Magic Words

Athame: A magical knife deriving from the Gardnerian *Book of Shadows* having specific criteria and consecrations. The primary working weapon of an Initiate.

Astral: A nonphysical world that mirrors all reality as pure energy.

Amulet: An amulet is a talisman used for protection. Sometimes referring to a natural object.

Book of Shadows: The Grimoire compiled by Gerald Gardner and the Bricket Wood coven passed down to Initiates of witchcraft.

Boline: A knife used for cutting and gathering herbs, sometimes compared to the white knife.

Charm: An object carried for luck or an incantation.

Coven: A group of three to thirteen Witches.

Covenstead: Location of the coven meetings.

Covendom: A three-mile radius around a covenstead.

Cowan: A non-Initiate or a non-Initiated intruder.

Esbat: Full moon gatherings.

Familiar: An entity or spirit companion of a Witch.

Deosil: Pronounced *jeshel*, going with the sun, clockwise.

Fith-Fath: A doll or poppet used to constrain or bind someone.

Evocation: Summoning an entity into a confined location like magician's triangle. Summoning an entity for a specific task or purpose with no personal connection or relationship. A non-religious method of working with Gods or other spirits.

Garter: In Witchcraft, a mark of a high priestess or Witch queen.

Hiving: When Witches leave one coven to form a new one.

Invocation: Summoning an entity into a circle or temple in which you directly are involved for the purpose of communication, worship, channeling, petitioning. A religious rite by nature.

Incantation: Words used to put on a spell.

Magic: The science and art of causing change to occur in conformity with will. An unseen force that manipulates events.

Magician: A non-religious magical practitioner. One who practices ritual magic, an occultist.

Magus: A magician or sometimes a title used for a Witchcraft high priest who leads a coven in which two other covens have hived. Being responsible, in lineage, for the creation of three covens.

Occult: Hidden or concealed. Matters regarded as involving the action or influence of supernatural or supernormal powers or some secret knowledge of them.

Occultist: One who studies or practices the occult.

Pentagram: The geometric five-pointed star that represents the five elements, five aspects of creation, five alphas, and the human body.

Pentacle: A pentagram with a circle around it or any plate inscribed with magical inscriptions.

Sabbat: The eight Witchcraft festivals.

Warlock: A male Witch, one who binds an Initiate.

Wicca: Pronounced witcha, an old English word for a male Witch.

Wicce: Pronounced witche, an old English word for a female Witch.

Wiccian: Pronounced witchan, an old English word for Witchcraft.

Witch: An English word for a male or female adherent of the religion of Witchcraft. An Initiate of Witchcraft.

Witchcraft: A fertility cult, modern mystery tradition, and religio-magical system rooted in Western Occultism and the mystery cults of antiquity.

Talisman: Talisman is an item used for some specific magical purpose usually manmade.

Appendix A

Suggested Reading List

General European Witchcraft

Aradia, or the Gospel of the Witches by Charles Leland

Between the Living & the Dead: A Perspective on Witches & Seers in the Early Modern Age by Eva Pocs

Drawing Down the Moon by Margot Adler (North-American in focus, but tying in to a lot of European traditions)

Ecstasies: Deciphering the Witches' Sabbat and *The Night Battles: Witchcraft and Agrarian Cults in the Sixteenth and Seventeenth Centuries* by Carlo Ginzburg

Mastering Witchcraft by Paul Huson

Popular Magic: Cunning-folk in English History by Owen Davies

Power of the Witch, *The Witch in Every Woman*, *Celebrate the Earth,* and *Laurie Cabot's Book of Shadows* by Laurie Cabot

The Trial of Tempel Anneke: Records of a Witchcraft Trial in Brunswick, Germany, 1663 by Peter A. Morton

Triumph of the Moon by Ronald Hutton

The Visions of Isobel Gowdie: Magic, Witchcraft and Dark Shamanism in Seventeenth-Century Scotland and *Cunning-Folk and Familiar Spirits:*

Shamanistic Visionary Traditions in Early Modern British Witchcraft and Magic by Emma Wilby

The Witch-Cult in Western Europe and *The God of the Witches* by Margaret Murray

The Witch-Hunt in Early Modern Europe, *The Witchcraft* Sourcebook, and *Witch-Hunting in Scotland: Law, Politics, and Religion* by Brian P. Levack

Witchcraft and Magic in Europe: The Period of the Witch Trials (Part of the Witchcraft in Europe Series) by Bengt Ankarloo and Stuart Clark (editors) (The entire Witchcraft and Magic in Europe series edited by Ankarloo is worth a look)

Witchcraft in Europe: 400-1700 by Alan Charles Kors and Edward Peters (editors)

The *Witchcraft Reader* (Routledge Readers in History) edited by Darren Oldridge

Witchcraft: A History by P.G. Maxwell-Stuart

Witches, Werewolves, and Faeries: Shapeshifters, Astral Doubles in the Middle Ages and *The Tradition of Household Spirits: Ancestral Lore and Practices* by Claude Lecouteaux

The Witches: Salem, 1692 by Stacy Schiff (obviously in North America but rooted in Europe)

Western Occult Classics

The Book of Abramelin the Mage (many translation are available. Mathers' translation was the most used by our Craft elders but has its flaws. Newer editions are available).

T*he Book of Ceremonial Magic* and *The Book of Black Magic* by Arthur Edward Waite

The *Book of Magic: From Antiquity to the Enlightenment* by Brian Copenhaver and Coraline Bickford-Smith

The Collected Works of Aleister Crowley (Particularly *The Book of the Law* and *777*)

Collected Works of Eliphas Levi (Particularly: *Dogma and Ritual of High Magic* and *The History of Magic*)

APPENDIX A: SUGGESTED READING LIST | 295

The collected works of Rudolph Steiner (Particularly: *How to Know Higher Worlds*)

An Encyclopædia of Occultism by Lewis Spence

The *Fairy-Faith in Celtic Countries* by W.Y. Evan Wentz

Forbidden Rites: A Necromancer's Manual of the Fifteenth Century and Magic in the Middle Ages by Richard Kieckhefer

The *Golden Bough* by Sr. James George Frazer

Grimoires such as *The Sworn Book of Honorius, Grimorium Verum, The Black Pullet, The Red Dragon,* The Sixth and Seventh Books of Moses, *The Book of Raziel the Archangel*, etc. There are many. Researching into them leads down a lot of rabbit-holes.

The Hermetic and Alchemical Writings of Paracelsus (two volumes) edited by Arthur Edward Waite

T*he Hieroglyphic Monad* by John Dee

Initiation into Hermetics by Franz Bardon

Isis Unveiled (and her other works, particularly T*he Secret Doctrine)* by Madame Blavatsky

John Dee's Five Books of Mystery: Original Sourcebook of Enochian Magic by Joseph Peterson (translator)

T*he Kybalion: Th*e Definitive Edition by William Walker Atkinson writing as Three Initiates

T*he Lesser Key of Solomon* (multiple versions/translation are available, the most impactful has been the work by Crowley using Mathers' translation)

Magic: An Occult Primer by David Conway

The Magus: A Complete System of Occult Philosophy by Francis Barrett

T*he novels* and nonfiction works of Dion Fortune (*Sea Priestess, The Goat Food God, Moon Magic, The Winged Bull, Mystical Qabalah, The Cosmic Doctrine, Psychic Self-Defense, The Training & Work of an Initiate*, etc.)

T*he Occult* by Colin Wilson

Perdurabo: The Life of Aleister Crowley by Richard Kaczynski

T*he Picatrix* (multiple versions)

The Queen's Conjurer: The Science and Magic of Dr. John Dee, Advisor to Queen Elizabeth I, by Benjamin Wooley

The Rosicrucian Enlightenment, Giordano Bruno and the Hermetic Tradition and *The Occult Philosophy in the Elizabethan Age* by Frances Yates

The Rosicrucian Manifestos (17th Century), there are three: *Fama Fraternitatas, Confessio Fraternitatis, The Chemical Wedding of Christian Rosenkreutz* (multiple versions available)

The Secret Teachings of All Ages by Manly P. Hall

Techniques of Solomonic Magic, The Goetia of Dr. Rudd, The Key of Solomon, The Magician's Tables by Stephen Skinner

Three Books of Occult Philosophy by Cornelius Agrippa

The Tree of Life, The Middle Pillar, A Garden of Pomegranates, and *The Complete Golden Dawn System of Magic* by Israel Regardie

*Western Esoter*icism: A Concise History by Antoine Faivre

The White Goddess by Robert Graves

Gardnerian & Alexandrian Initiates

A Coin for the Ferryman and *All the King's Children* by Jimahl Di Fiosa

Buckland's Complete Book of Witchcraft by Raymond Buckland

Fifty Years of Wicca by Frederic Lamond

Firechild by Maxine Sanders

Gerald Gardner and the Cauldron of Inspiration, Witchfather (Two Volumes), and *Doreen Valiente: Witch* by Philip Heselton

High Priestess, Covensense, Lid off the Cauldron, Witchcraft in Yorkshire, and *The Zodiac Experience* by Patricia Crowther

King of the Witches by June Johns collaborated with Alex Sanders

The Alex Sanders Lectures by Alex Sanders

The Enchanted Candle by Lady Rhea

The Witch's Book of the Dead by Christian day

Transformative Witchcraft: The Greater Mysteries, The Witchs Book of Shadows, and *The Witch's Athame: The Craft, Lore & Magick of Ritual Blades* by Jason Mankey

Traditional Wicca: a Seekers Guide by Thorn Mooney

What Witches Do, Eight Sabbats for Witches, (also combined as *The Witches Bible*). *The Witches' God*, and *The Witches' Goddess* by Janet and Stewart Farrar

Witch Amongst Us: The Autobiography of a Witch, Conversations with a Witch, and *Dancing with Witches* by Lois Bourne

Witchcraft for Tomorrow, The Rebirth of Witchcraft, Collected Poetry, Where Witchcraft Lives, and *An ABC of Witchcraft Past and Present* by Doreen Valiente

Witchcraft Today, The Meaning of Witchcraft, A Goddess Arrives, High Magic's Aid by Gerald Gardner

Witch Crafting: A Spiritual Guide to Making Magic by Phyllis Curott.

APPENDIX B

Resources

Witchcraft, Magic, & Occult Shops

Here are some of my favorite shops for Witchcraft and magic, including the shops I co-own with my husband Christian Day, Hex and Omen in Salem, Massachusetts and Hex in Netw Orleans, Louisiana:

SALEM, MASSACHUSETTS

Hex: Old World Witchery
246 Essex Street, Salem, MA 01970
(978) 666-0765 | *www.HexWitch.com*

Omen: Psychic Parlor and Witchcraft Emporium
184 Essex Street, Salem, MA 01970
(978) 666-0763 | *www.OmenSalem.com*

Bewitched in Salem
180 Essex St, Salem, MA 01970
(978) 744-9904

Crow Haven Corner: Salem's Oldest Witch Shop
125 Essex Street, Salem, MA 01970
(978) 745-8763 | www.CrowHavenCorner.com

Enchanted: A Magical Shop
98 Wharf Street, Pickering Wharf, Salem, MA 01970
(978) 745-2856 | www.EnchantedOfSalem.com

Nu Aeon: A Magical Shop
88 Wharf Street, Pickering Wharf, Salem, MA 01970
(978) 745-8668 | www.NuAeon.com

New Orleans, Louisiana

Hex: Old World Witchery
1219 Decatur Street, New Orleans, LA 70116
(504) 613-0558 | www.HexWitch.com

Conjure New Orleans
506 Dumaine Street, New Orleans, LA 70116
(504) 522-6866 | www.ConjureNewOrleans.com

Crescent City Conjure
2402 Royal Street, New Orleans, LA 70117
(504) 421-3189 | www.CrescentCityConjure.us

The Voodoo Spiritual Temple
1428 North Rampart Street, New Orleans, LA 70116
(504) 943-9795 | www.VoodooSpiritualTemple.org

Island of Salvation Botanica
2372 Saint Claude Avenue, New Orleans, LA 70117
(504) 948-9961 | *www.IslandOfSalvationBotanica.com*

London, United Kingdom

The Atlantis Bookshop
49A Museum Street, Holborn, London WC1A 1LY, UK
+44 20 7405 2120 | *www.TheAtlantisBookShop.com*

Watkins Books
19-21 Cecil Ct, Covent Garden, London WC2N 4EZ, UK
+44 20 7836 2182 | *www.WatkinBooks.com*

Glastonbury, United Kingdom

The Cat & Cauldron
7 Market Place, Glastonbury, Somerset BA6 9HW, UK
enquiries@witchcraftshop.co.uk | *www.WitchCraftShop.co.uk*

Magical Events

Christian and I host an annual festival in both Salem and New Orleans:

Festival of the Dead
Festival of the Dead explores death's mysteries through events that investigate the favored and forbidden ways in which people have honored, celebrated, and secretly delved into life's inevitable destination *www.FestivalOfTheDead.com*

HexFest: A Weekend of Witchery in Old New Orleans
Join us each August in Old New Orleans with a Riverboat Ritual dinner and two days of workshops with Witches and conjurers from across the magical community!
www.HexFest.comv

Facebook Groups
I host two Facebook groups of interest to those seeking information on British Traditional Witchcraft:

British Traditional Witchcraft
This group was created to promote and celebrate the work of the British Craft Elders and their down lines which primarily consist of the Alexandrian and Gardnerian traditions of Witchcraft.
www.facebook.com/groups/britishtraditionalwitchcraft

The New Orleans Coven
The New Orleans Coven is of the Alexandrian Tradition of Witchcraft. We have a lineage with strong ties to our magical roots in the United Kingdom. We follow the teachings of Alex and Maxine Sanders and are dedicated fully to the Alexandrian movement and its magical training. The New Orleans Coven is open to those who seek Initiation and a true connection to the Craft of the wise.
www.facebook.com/groups/NewOrleansCoven/

Bibliography

"About Puck/Important Information." Puck Fair. Accessed June 21, 2019. https://puckfair.ie/information.

Alleau, Rene. *History of Occult Sciences.* London: Leisure Arts, 1967.

"Apis." Encyclopedia Britannica. Accessed June 20, 2019. https://www.britannica.com/topic/Apis-Egyptian-deity.

Arthur, Ross. G. *English-Old Norse Dictionary*. Cambridge, Ontario: In Parentheses Publications, 2002.

Atkinson, William Walker, writing as Three Initiates. *The Kybalion: The Definitive Edition*. New York, NY: Penguin, 2011.

Bøgh, Birgitte. "The Graeco-Roman Cult of Isis." in *The Handbook of Religions in Ancient Europe*. ed. Lisbeth Bredholt Christensen, Olav Hammer, and David Warburton. New York: Routledge, 2014.

Baghdjian, Alice. "Half of European men share King Tut's DNA." *Reuters*. August 1, 2011. Accessed June 13, 2019. https://uk.reuters.com/article/oukoe-uk-britain-tutankhamun-dna/half-of-european-men-share-king-tuts-dna-idUKTRE7704OR20110801.

"Bath—Aquae Sulis." Cornwall School of Mystery and Magic. Accessed June 11, 2019. http://cornwallschoolmysteryandmagick.uk/bath-aquae-sulis.

Beryl, Paul. *The Master Book of Herbalism*. Custer, WA: Phoenix Publishing, 1984.

Blagden, Charles Otto. *Malay Magic*. New York, MacMillan, 1900.

"Brigit." Druidry. Accessed June 3, 2019. https://www.druidry.org/library/gods-goddesses/brigit.

Buckland, Raymond. *Scottish Witchcraft: The History & Magic of the Picts*. St. Paul, MN: Llewellyn Publications, 1991.

Buckland, Raymond. *The Witch Book, The Encylopedia of Witchcraft, Wicca, and Neo-Paganism*. Canton, MI: Visible Ink Press, 2002.

Cabot, Laurie. *Power Of The Witch*. New York, Delta, 1990.

Caesar, Julius. *"De Bello Gallico" and Other Commentaries of Caius Julius Caesar*. ed. Ernest Rhys, trans. W. A. Macdevitt. New York: J. M. Dent, 1915.

Campanelli, Pauline. *Wheel of the Year Living the Magical Life*. St. Paul, MN: Llewellyn Publications, 1989.

Cartwright, Mark. "Dionysos." *Ancient History Encyclopedia*. September 16, 2012. Accessed February 27, 2019. https://www.ancient.eu/Dionysos.

Cartwright, Mark. "Eleusis." *Ancient History Encyclopedia*. January 14, 2015. Accessed February 27, 2019. https://www.ancient.eu/Eleusis.

"Celts." Ancient History Encyclopedia. Accessed June 17, 2019. https://www.ancient.eu/celt/.

"Cernunnos." Encyclopedia Brittanica. Accessed June 21, 2019. https://www.britannica.com/topic/Cernunnos.

Chulev, Basil. "The Gods of Macedon." *Ancient Macedonia*. 2016. Accessed June 15, 2019. https://www.academia.edu/21627850/Ancient_Macedonia_-_The_Gods_of_Macedon.

Conway, D.J. *Celtic Magic*. St. Paul, MN: Llewellyn Publications, 1990.

County Folklore Printed Extracts No. 1. Ed. Edwin Sidney Hartland. Gloucester, Davies & Son, 1892.

County Folklore Vol. III Printed Extracts No. 5. Ed. G.F. Black and Northcote W. Thomas . London, David Nutt, 1903.

Courtney, M.A. *Cornish Feasts and Folk-Lore*. Penzance, Beare and Son, 1890.

"Coventina's Well." PastScape. Accessed June 4, 2019. https://www.pastscape.org.uk/hob.aspx?hob_id=1013364.

Crowley, Aleister. *Magick in Theory and Practice*. New York, NY: Dover Publications, 1976.

Crowther, Patricia. *Covensense, A Handbook for Witches*. London: Frederick Muller Limited, 1981.

Day, Christian. *The Witches' Book of the Dead*. New Orleans, Warlock Press, 2019.

Day, John. *Yahweh and the Gods and Goddesses of Canaan*. London and New York: Sheffield Academic Press Ltd, 2ooo.

"Devil." Online Etymology Dictionary. Accessed June, 22, 2019. https://www.etymonline.com/search?q=Devil.

Di Fiosa, Jimahl. *A Coin for the Ferryman, The Death and Life of Alex Sanders*. Boston: Logios, 2010.

Dickie, Matthew W. *Magic and Magicians in the Greco-Roman World*. London: Routledge, 2001.

Dijkstra, Henk. *History of the Ancient and Medieval World*. vol. 2. New York: Marshall Cavendish, 1996.

DiLuzio, Meghan J. *A Place at the Altar: Priestesses in Republican Rome*. Princeton, NJ: Princeton University Press, 2016.

"Dionysos Loves." Theoi Greek Mythology. Accessed June 17, 2019. https://www.theoi.com/Olympios/DionysosLoves.html.

"Dionysos Titles." Theoi Greek Mythology. Accessed June 18, 2019. https://www.theoi.com/Cult/DionysosTitles.html.

Disney, Walt et al. *Snow White and the Seven Dwarfs*. Burbank, Calif: Walt Disney Enterprises, 1937.

Duir, Alexa. "Who is Cernunnos?". *Association of Polytheistic Traditions*. 2005. Accessed June 21, 2019. http://www.manygods.org.uk/articles/essays/Cernunnos.shtml.

Dyer, T.F. Thiselton. *English Folk-Lore*. London, Hardwicke & Bogue, 1878.

Elworthy, Frederick Thomas. *The Evil Eye*. London, John Murray, 1895.

Encyclopedia of Superstitions, Folklore, and the Occult Sciences of the World Vol. III. ed. Cora Linn Daniels, and C.M. Stevans. Milwaukee, J.H. Yewdale & Sons Co., 1908.

Fairbanks, Arthur. *The Mythology of Greece and Rome*. New York: D. Appleton, 1907.

Farrar, Janet and Stewart. *The Witches' God*. Custer, WA: Phoenix Publishing, 1989.

Farrar, Janet and Stewart. *The Witches' Goddess*. Custer, WA: Phoenix Publishing, 1987.

Foley, Keelan. "The History Of Puck Fair | Killorglin 1613-2013." YouTube video, 02:55, Posted July 2, 2013. Accessed June 23, 2019. https://www.youtube.com/watch?v=-8slTCWkG0A.

Folk-lore and Legends: Scotland. London:W.W. Gibbings, 1889.

Ford, Patrick K., ed. *The Mabinogi and Other Medieval Welsh Tales*. trans. Patrick K. Ford. Berkeley and Los Angeles, California: University of California Press, 1977.

Frazer, James George. *The Golden Bough: A Study in Magic and Religion*. Abridged ed.. New York: Macmillan, 1963.

"Freemasonry and Initiation." Pietre-Stone's Review of Freemasonry. Accessed June 4, 2019. http://www.freemasons-freemasonry.com/Freemasonry_and_Initiation.html.

Gardner, Gerald B. *High Magic's Aid*. 2010 ed.. Aurinia Books, 2010.

Ginzburg, Carlo. *Ecstasies: Deciphering The Witches' Sabbath*. trans. Raymond Rosenthal. New York: Pantheon Books, 1991.

Glass-Koentop, Pattalee. *Year of Moons, Season of Trees: Mysteries & Rites of Celtic Tree Magic*. t. Paul, MN: Llewellyn Publications, 1991.

Green, Miranda. *Animals in Celtic Life and Myth*. London and New York: Routledge, 1992.

Green, Miranda. *Symbol and Image in Celtic Religious Art*. London: Routledge, 1992.

Gregory, Bishop of Tours. *History of the Franks*. 591. Book VIII, 195. https://archive.org/stream/historyoffranks00greguoft/historyoffranks00greguoft_djvu.txt.

Grimm, Jacob. *Teutonic Mythology Volume 4*. trans. James Stallybrass. London, George Bell & Sons, 1888.

Harris, Eleanor. *Ancient Egyptian Magic*. Newburyport, MA: Weiser Books, 1998.

Harrison, Michael. *The Roots of Witchcraft*. Secaucus, N.J.: Citadel Press, 1973.

"Hekate." Theoi Greek Mythology. Accessed June 14, 2019. https://www.theoi.com/Khthonios/Hekate.html.

Henderson, William. *Notes on the Folk-Lore of the Northern Counties of England and the Borders*. London: W. Satchell, Peyton and Co., 1879.

Heselton, Philip. *Doreen Valiente, Witch*. Woodbury, MN: Llewelyn 2016.

Heselton, Philip. *Witchfather: A Life of Gerald Gardner, Volume 1– Into the Witch Cult*. Loughborough: Thoth Publications, 2012.

Heselton, Philip. *Witchfather: A Life of Gerald Gardner, Volume 2 – From Witch Cult to Wicca*. Loughborough: Thoth Publications, 2012.

"History and Origins of Puck Fair." Puck Fair. Accessed June 21, 2019. https://puckfair.ie/history.

"History of Freemasonry." Masonic Service Association of North America. Accessed June 4, 2019. http://www.msana.com/historyfm.asp.

Hope, Murry. *Practical Celtic Magic, A Working Guide to the Magical Heritage of the Celtic Races*. London: The Aquarian Press, 1987.

Huson, Paul. *Mastering Witchcraft*. 2006 ed.. Lincoln, NE: iUniverse, Inc., 2006.

Huson, Paul. *Mystical Origins of the Tarot, From Ancient Roots to Modern Usage*. Rochester, VT: Destiny Books, 2004.

Hutton, Ronald. *The Triumph of the Moon: A History of Modern Pagan Witchcraft*. Oxford: Oxford University Press, 1999.

Hutton, Ronald. *The Witch, A History of Fear, from Ancient Times to the Present*. 2017 E-book edition. New Haven and London: Yale University Press, 2017.

"Hymn to Pan." Hermetic Library. Accessed June 22, 2019. https://hermetic.com/crowley/book-4/hymn.

Indo-European Language Dictionary. entry: HORN. Accessed June 21, 2019. https://indo-european.info/dictionary-translator/translate/English/Indo-European/?q=Horn.

Indo-European Language Dictionary. entry: OINOS. Accessed June 21, 2019. https://indo-european.info/dictionary-translator/translate/Indo-European/English/?q=Oinos.

"Initiation." Oxford Living Dictionaries. Accessed October 2, 2018. https://en.oxforddictionaries.com/definition/initiation.

"Isis the Trickster Goddess." Isiopolis. Accessed June 10, 2019. https://isiopolis.com/2012/09/01/isis-the-trickster-goddess/.

"Isis." Center for Hellenic Studies, Harvard University. Accessed June 19, 2019. https://chs.harvard.edu/CHS/article/display/6542.6-isis.

Jastrow, Morris Jr. and Barton, George A. "Astarte Worship Among the Hebrews." *Jewish Encyclopedia*. Accessed June 20, 2019. http://jewishencyclopedia.com/articles/2048-astarte-worship-among-the-hebrews.

Johns, June. *King of the Witches: The World of Alex Sanders*. London and Edinburgh: Morrison and Gibb Limited, 1969.

Johnston,, Sarah Ilesed. *Religions of the Ancient World: A Guide*. Cambridge, MA: Belknap Press, 2004.

Jones, Leslie Ellen. *Druid, Shaman, Priest: Metaphors of Celtic Paganism*. Enfield Lock, England: Hisarlik, 1998.

Jones, Richard. "Part One: King Pausole and the Wican Rede." *Hermetic Library*. Accessed June 20, 2019. https://hermetic.com/jones/wican-ethics/part-one-king-pausole-and-the-wican-rede#note10.

Kerényi, Karl. *Dionysos: Archetypal Image of Indestructible Life*. Princeton, New Jersey: Princeton University Press, 1976.

Lada-Richards, Ismene. *Initiating Dionysus: Ritual and Theatre in Aristophanes' Frogs*. Oxford: Clarendon Press, 1999.

Lamond, Frederic. "Gerald Gardner." in *Fifty Years of Wicca*. Sutton Mallet: Green Magic, 2004.

Lancashire Folk-Lore. Ed. John Harland and T. T. Wilkinson. London, Frederick Warne and Co., 1867.

Leland, Charles Godfrey. *Aradia, or the Gospel of the Witches*. Edinburgh, London: Ballantyne, Hanson & Co., 1899.

Levi, Eliphas. *Dogme et rituel de la haute magie*. 2nd ed.. Paris : Germer Bailliere, 1861.

Lewis, James R. *Witchcraft Today: An Encyclopedia of Wiccan and Neopagan Traditions*. Santa Barbara: ABC-CLIO, 1999.

Müller, Ulrich. "The Grail Procession. the Legend, the Artifacts, and the Possible Sources of the Story." *Arthuriana* 16, no. 2. 2006.

MacKillop, James. *Myths and Legends of the Celts*. New York, NY: Penguin Books, 2005.

Magic and Witchcraft. Issues 1-10, ed. George Moir. London, Chapman and Hall, 1852.

"Magic Wands." Twilit Grotto: Archives of Western Esoterica. Accessed June 18, 2019. http://esotericarchives.com/wands/.

Majercik, Ruth. *The Chaldean Oracles*. Leiden: Prometheus Trust, 2013.

"Marioun Grant. 15/4/1597." Survey of Scottish Witchcraft Database. Accessed June 22, 2019. http://witches.shca.ed.ac.uk/index.cfm?fuseaction=home.caserecord&caseref=C%2FEGD%2F2141&search_type=searchpeople&search_string=lastname%3D%26firstname%3D%26residence%3D.

Mark, Joshua J. "Amun." *Ancient History Encyclopedia*. July 29, 2016. Accessed June 16, 2019. https://www.ancient.eu/amun/.

Mark, Joshua J. "Egyptian Gods – The Complete List." *Ancient History Encyclopedia*. April 14, 2016. Accessed June 20, 2019. https://www.ancient.eu/article/885/egyptian-gods---the-complete-list/.

McLean, Adam. *The Triple Goddess: An Exploration of the Archetypal Feminine*. Grand Rapids, MI: Phanes Press, 1989.

McManamon, John M. *Caligula's Barges and the Renaissance Origins of Nautical Archaeology under Water*. Ed Rachal Foundation Nautical Archaeology Series. College Station, TX: Texas A&M University Press, 2016.

Montgomery, James A. *Publications of the Babylonian Section Vol. III*. Philadelphia, Univ. of PA Museum, 1913.

Murray, Margaret A. *The God of the Witches*. London, Oxford, New York: Oxford University Press, 1970.

NearingHomer Jr. "The Legend of Julius Caesar's British Conquest." *PMLA Vol. 64, No. 4*. September, 1949. Accessed June 14, 2019. https://www.jstor.org/stable/459639.

O'Brien, Joan V. *The Transformation of Hera: A Study of Ritual, Hero, and the Goddess in the Iliad*. Lanham, MD: Rowman & Littlefield, 1993.

Ovid. *Metamorphoses*. trans. Henry T. Riley. London: George Bell and Sons, 1898.

"Paleolithic Art." The Columbia Encyclopedia, 6th ed.. Columbia University Press, 2018.

"Pan Cult." Theoi Greek Mythology. Accessed June 16, 2019. https://www.theoi.com/Cult/PanCult.html.

"Pan. mythology." New World Encyclopedia. Accessed June 17, 2019. https://www.newworldencyclopedia.org/entry/Pan_(mythology)#cite_note-Borgeaud-5.

Pfeiffer, Stefan. "The God Serapis, His Cult and the Beginnings of the Ruler Cult in Ptolemaic Egypt." in *Ptolemy II Philadelphus and His World*. ed. Paul McKechnie and Phillipe Guillaume. Leiden: Brill, 2008.

Phipps, Rollin. *A History of Alexandria*. Arlington, TX: The University of Texas at Arlington Press, 2004.

Pike, Albert. *Morals and Dogma of the Ancient and Accepted Scottish Rite of Freemasonry*. 2011 E-book edition. Richmond, VA: Jenkins, Inc., 1944.

Pitcairn, Robert. *Criminal Trials in Scotland Volume III.*. Edinburgh: William Tait, 1833.

Plutarch. *Moralia*. trans. Frank Cole Babbitt, Loeb Classical Library. 2003) ed., vol. Volume V. Cambridge, Massachusetts and London: Harvard University Press, 1936.

Pollack, Rachel. *Tarot Wisdom, Spiritual Teachings and Deeper Meanings*. Woodbury, MN: Llewelyn, 2015.

Pryke, Louise. "Ishtar." *Ancient History Encyclopedia*. May 10, 2019. Accessed June 17, 2019. https://www.ancient.eu/ishtar/.

Pryke, Louise. *Ishtar*. 2017 E-book edition. New York and London: Routledge, 2017.

Raddato, Carole. "Statue Group of Persephone-Isis and Pluto-Serapis with Cerberus." *Ancient History Encyclopedia*. May 18, 2019. Accessed June 25, 2019. https://www.ancient.eu/image/10673/statue-group-of-persephone-isis-and-pluto-serapis-/.

Ramaswamy, Sumathi. *The Goddess and the Nation, Mapping Mother India*. Durham and London: Duke University Press, 2010.

Rampton, Martha, ed. *European Magic and Witchcraft: A Reader*. Toronto: University of Toronto Press, 2018.

Regula, deTraci. *The Mysteries of Isis: Her Worship and Magick*. St. Paul, MN: Llewellyn Publications, 1995.

"Robert." Online Etymology Dictionary. Accessed June 22, 2019. https://www.etymonline.com/search?q=robert.

"Robin Goodfellow, His Mad Pranks and Merry Jests, 1639." British Library Collection. Accessed June 21, 2019. https://www.bl.uk/collection-items/robin-goodfellow-his-mad-pranks-and-merry-jests-1639.

"Robin." Online Etymology Dictionary. Accessed June 22, 2019. https://www.etymonline.com/word/robin.

Rolleston, T. W. *Celtic Myths and Legends*. 1990 ed.. New York, NY: Dover Publications, 1990.

Romanazzi, Andrea. *Guida Alle Streghe in Italia*. Rome: Venexia, 2009.

"Samhain at the Gates of Annwn." Eagles and Dragons Publishing. Accessed June 19, 2019. https://eaglesanddragonspublishing.com/.

Sanders, Maxine. "Dates", Email Correspondence with Brian Cain, June 23, 2019.

Sanders, Maxine. *Fire Child The Life and Magic of Maxine Sanders*. 2008 ed.. Oxford: Mandrake of Oxford, 2007.

Schiff, Stacy. *Cleopatra: A Life*. New York, NY: Hachette, 2010.

Scot, Reginald. *The Discoverie of Witchcraft*. New York: Dover Publications, 1972.

Spence, Lewis. *An Encyclopædia of Occultism*. New York, Dodd, Mead & Co., 1920.

Taylor-Perry, Rosemarie. *The God Who Comes: Dionysian Mysteries Reclaimed*. New York: Algora, 2003.

The Demotic Magical Papyrus of London and Leiden. ed. F.L. Griffith and H. Thompson. London, H. Grevel, 1904.

The Devils and Evil Spirits of Babylonia. trans. R. Campbell Thompson (London: Luzac and Co., 1904.

"The Gundestrup Cauldron: Largest and Most Exquisite Iron Age Silver Work in Europe." Ancient Origins. Accessed June 14, 2019. https://www.ancient-origins.net/artifacts-other-artifacts/gundestrup-cauldron-largest-and-most-exquisite-iron-age-silver-work-europe-020989.

The Hymns of the Atharva-Veda Vol. I. ed. Ralph T. H. Griffith. Benares, E.J. Lazarus, 1895.

"The Regius Poem." Pietre-Stone's Review of Freemasonry. Accessed June 4, 2019. http://www.freemasons-freemasonry.com/regius.html.

"The Thirteen Legendary Treasures of Britain." Ancient Origins. Accessed June 14, 2019. https://www.ancient-origins.net/artifacts-other-artifacts/thirteen-legendary-treasures-britain-002898.

"There was no cast of Roman priests." The Romans. Accessed June 4, 2019. http://www.the-romans.eu/society/Roman-priests.php.

Transactions of the Cumberland & Westmorland Antiquarian & Archaeological Society. vol. III, new series, ed. W.G. Collingwood. London: T. Wilson, 1903.

Valiente, Doreen. *An ABC of Witchcraft Past & Present.* New York, NY: St Martin's Press, 1973.

Valiente, Doreen. *The Rebirth of Witchcraft.* 2017 E-book edition. Wiltshire: Crowood Press, 1989.

Valiente, Doreen. *Witchcraft for Tomorrow.* Custer, WA: Phoenix Publishing, 1978.

Vasilatos, Nikos. *The Cretan Dagger.* Greece: Klassikes Ekdoseis, 1993.

"Venus of Willendorf." Great Discoveries in Archaeology. Accessed June 12, 2019. http://anthropology.msu.edu/anp264-ss13/2013/03/28/venus-of-willendorf/.

Ward, Terence P. "An Interview with Raymond Buckland, American Wicca Pioneer." The Wild Hunt, June 1, 2016. Accessed September 15, 2018. https://wildhunt.org/2016/06/an-interview-with-raymond-buckland-american-wicca-pioneer.html.

Wentz, W.Y. Evans. *The Fairy-Faith in Celtic Countries.* London, New York, Toronto and Melbourne: Oxford University Press, 1911.

Wilde, Lady Jane. *Ancient Legends, Mystic Charms, and Superstitions of Ireland.* London: Ward and Downey, 1888.

Wilde, Oscar. Complete Poetry, ed. Isobel B. Murray. Oxford, England: Oxford University Press, 1998.

Williams, Victoria. *Celebrating Life Customs around the World: From Baby Showers to Funerals, vol. 1.* Santa Barbara: ABC-CLIO, 2017.

Witt, R.E. *Isis in the Ancient World.* Johns Hopkins Paperback Edition, 1997 ed.. Baltimore and London: Johns Hopkins University Press, 1971.

Wood, Juliette. "Folklore Studies at the Celtic Dawn: The Role of Alfred Nutt as Publisher and Scholar." *Folklore.* 1999.

Wright, Brian. *Brigid: Goddess, Druidess and Saint.* 2011 E-book edition. Gloucestershire: The History Press, 2009.

Wright, Thomas. *Narratives of Sorcery and Magic, from the Most Authentic Sources.* New York, Redfield, 1852.

Yeates, Stephen J. *The Tribe of Witches: The Religion of the Dobunni and Hwicce.* Oxford: Oxbow Books, 2008.

Index

Alexander the Great   57, 86, 131-132, 134, 137, 152, 156-157, 169
Alexandria   86, 88, 90, 132-133, 135-136, 157-159, 163, 196, 203, 225-229, 234-238, 240, 242-244
 – Great Library   90, 133
Alexandrian Witchcraft   2, 6, 8, 18-19, 24, 29, 31, 35, 46, 48-49, 57, 61, 63-70, 103, 105-106, 179, 195, 198
 – DBG Line, the   65-66
 – Farrar Line, the   68
 – Kentish Line, the   67-68
Algard   66
Amun-Ra   152, 154, 156-157
Amun-Zeus   156
Anglesey   40, 45, 79
Anubis   133
Aphrodite   238
Apis   152, 156-158, 231, 242
Apollo   132, 155, 240
Aradia   4, 94, 97, 124, 145, 155, 164, 232
Ariadne   164, 166
Arianrhod   81
Artemis   121, 137, 143
Arts Magical   27, 34, 64, 101, 117, 202, 205, 209
Astarte   131, 143
Athame   183-185
Athena   87, 118, 132-133, 157, 197, 238, 241
Augustus   134-135
Bacchoi   165
Bacchus   3, 41, 84, 91, 150, 163, 172, 244
Beltane   284
Benevento   89

Black-Handled Knife, the   184-186
Blodeuwedd   81
Boline   291
Bone, Eleanor   5, 51, 57-58
Book of Shadows   48-49, 52, 58, 61-62, 69, 104, 182-183, 291
Bourne, Lois   5, 48
Bracelin, Jack   48
Brigid   122, 139-142, 237
Britain   38-45, 88, 98, 168
Brittany   263
Buckland, Raymond   1, 5, 20, 51-52, 54, 65, 186, 201
Cailleach   122
Caligula   135
Candles   201
Cardell, Charles   58
Cauldron   44, 82, 151, 169-170, 194-195
Celtic Trees and their Magical Correspondences   188
Celts, the   39-42, 44, 78-79, 82, 88, 122, 128, 139-140, 150-151, 167, 170-171, 195, 267
Censer   193
Ceridwen   82-83
Cernunnos   167, 169-171
Chalice   86, 232, 244
Charms   245
Cleopatra   133-135
Cochrane, Robert   191
Cole, Donna   56
Color Magic   270-271
Cords   198-199
Cornish Kinning Stones   257
Covens   7, 11, 15-19, 21-22, 25-35, 37, 47-48, 50, 56, 65, 70, 104-106, 118, 190, 292
 – Coven Rules   34
 – Fertility Covens   33
 – Healing Covens   33
 – Joining a Coven   18

– Specialized Covens   33-34
– Training Covens   32-34
– Worship Covens   32
Covenstead   30, 291
Crete   184
Crossroads   176, 266-267
Crowley, Aleister   216
Crowther, Patricia   5, 18, 50, 57-58, 60, 191
Cult of Diana   90, 92, 95-97, 144
Cult of Dionysus   41, 84-87, 160, 164-166
Cult of Isis   41, 86-90, 132, 134-135, 144, 158
Cult of Mithra   86
Curses   81
Dagger   179
Degrees of Initiation   11, 28-29, 69-70, 100, 102-106
Demeter   121, 133, 138
Devotional Altars   13
Diana   89-97, 124, 138, 143-145, 155, 196, 200, 240
Di Fiosa, Jimahl   59
Dionysus   84-86, 134, 160, 163-164, 166, 244
Divination   208, 262-265, 275
Druids   40, 78-80, 91, 128, 139-140
Egypt   40, 42-43, 86-88, 97, 100, 127, 131-134, 151-152, 156-157, 181, 187, 193, 203
Elemental Tools   179-180
Elements   11, 44, 83, 95, 194, 210-211
Eleusinian Mysteries   41, 85, 133, 138
Eleusis   85
Eostre   238
Ephesus   143
Etruscans   164
First Degree   36, 101-102, 104-106, 183
Freemasonry   100-101, 103
Full Moon   11, 14, 30, 119-120, 142, 200, 219, 241, 264, 272-276, 291
Full Moon Talisman   274
Gardner, Gerald   4-5, 18, 20, 28, 39, 43-44, 46-51, 58, 65, 69, 95, 101-106,

117, 145, 183, 198, 216, 291
Gardnerian Witchcraft   8, 18-20, 46, 48, 50-51, 55-56, 58, 61, 65-67, 104, 195
– Bone Line, the   51
– Kentucky Line, the   54
– Olwen Lines, the   51-57
– Sheffield Line, the   50
– Whitecroft Line, the   51, 54, 56
Ginzburg, Carlo   96
Goddess of Magic, the   89, 118, 123, 133, 136, 145
Goddess, the   81-82, 87, 89, 118-119, 122-124, 126-127, 130-134, 139, 142, 145, 157, 170, 226
Graves, Robert   120
Greece   134
Greeks   128, 132, 138, 157
Grimes, Edith Woodford   102
Grimoires   184, 187, 268
Gundestrup Cauldron   151
Gwion Bach   82-83
Gwydion   81
Habondia   243
Hadrian   135
Healing   23, 33, 123, 139, 225, 270
Hecate   121, 136-138, 145
Hermes   217
Herne   150, 168
Heselton, Philip   102
Holy Moon Water   276
Horned God, the   11, 147-154
Initiation   2, 9-10, 12, 19-21, 25-26, 59, 72-83, 85, 95, 97, 99, 101, 103-106, 218, 221
Invocation   234-235, 242, 244
Ishtar   129-131
Isis   43, 87-90, 92, 130-136, 143-145, 154, 157-159, 164, 196, 226-228, 232, 238, 241-243
Isis Oil or Incense   276

Julius Caesar   134
Jupiter   271
Kabbalah   268, 275
Kasprzynski, Pat   57, 59
Key of Solomon   184, 187, 269
Kybalion   217
Kyphi Incense   277
Lady Olwen (Monique Wilson)   51-52, 54, 60
Leland, Charles Godfrey   4-5, 17, 94-95, 145, 155, 164, 173
Lineage   22, 46-47, 49-50, 52, 56, 71
Lucifello   97, 155, 173
Lucifer   94, 155, 173
Magic   1, 3, 6, 13, 27, 33, 43, 62-63, 74-75, 89, 97-99, 101-102, 104, 119, 123-124, 127, 129, 133, 136-137, 149, 159, 179, 182-190, 192-193, 195, 197-198, 200-203, 205, 207, 209-213, 215, 224, 245, 266-272, 275, 292
Magical Systems   16, 64, 104, 266, 268
Magic Circle   211, 224, 278
– Casting a Circle   224
Magicians   210
Magic Mirror   200-201
Magic Words   291
Making Offerings   13
Manchester Coven   57, 63
Matres (Matronae)   122
Middle Pillar Ritual   223-224
Mighty Ones, the   78, 110, 211
Minoans, the   84
Mistletoe   91
Modona Horiente   96
Moon Goddess, the   11-13, 17, 30, 40, 94, 119-120, 123, 136-137, 140, 154, 159, 196-197, 273-274, 278
Morrigan (Morigu)   139
Murray, Margaret A.   95
Mystery Cults   84, 86, 101, 103
Mythology   123, 172
Nemi   90-91, 113, 135, 200

Nesnick, Mary   66
New Forest Coven   17, 28, 39, 47, 101-103, 106
New Moon   129, 138, 142, 247-248, 265, 272-274
New Moon Talisman   273
No-Socializing Rule   24, 26, 34-37
Occult   17, 43, 64, 101, 160, 162, 179-181, 204, 217, 221, 226, 228, 268, 292
Occultism   275
Olympians   163
Osiris   88, 131-132, 152, 154, 156-158, 227, 242
Osorapis   157
Pan   153, 159-162, 177, 196, 240
Pentacle of Alexandria, the   196, 228
Pentacles   195, 269
Pentacle, the   196, 228, 230
Persephone   121, 138
Pharaohs   87, 132
Philters   248
Planetary Magic   187, 269, 272
Priesthood   2, 9, 18, 21, 24, 34, 73, 77-78, 80
Protean Tradition   55
 – Protean Declaration   55
Psychic   204-206, 208-210, 225
Psychic Shield   224-225, 267
 – Psychic Shield Exercise   225
Ptolemies   163
Puck Fair   161
Quarter Lords   196
Recipes   276
Relaxation Ritual   222
Rex Nemorensis   91-92
Rites of Alexandria   226, 234-238, 240, 242-244
 – Eternal Rose Rite, the   230
 – Isis Invocation, the   232, 234-235
 – Rite of Serapis and Isis, the   231-232
 – Salutation of the Sun, the   228

- Serapis Invocation, the   231, 234, 242, 244
- Triad of Alexandria, the   226-229
- Witches' Mass, the   232, 238, 241-244

Ritual Baths   12

Robin Goodfellow   160, 175, 284

Romans, the   41-44, 78-79, 85, 90-91, 128, 134-137, 143-144, 155, 160, 267
- Roman Empire, the   41, 85-86, 89, 91-92, 128, 134-136, 144, 158
- Roman Republic, the   134

Sabbat Rites   194, 233
- Candlemas   30, 140, 233, 237
- Fall Equinox, the   30, 243-244
- Halloween   30, 189, 194, 233-235
- Lammas   30, 233, 242-243
- May Eve   30, 233, 239-240
- Spring Equinox, the   30, 238
- Summer Solstice, the   30, 156, 200, 241-242
- Winter Solstice, the   30, 155, 175, 177, 236

Sanders, Alex   6, 28, 39, 48, 57-62, 64-67, 103, 115, 179

Sanders, Maxine   6, 18, 35, 46, 49, 59, 62-64, 68, 105

Saxons   42

Scotland   60

Scourge   197-198

Second Degree   56, 101-102, 104-106

Selene   121, 134

Self-Dedication   73, 219
- Self-Dedication Rite   219

Self-Initiation   73

Serapis   43, 132-133, 157-159, 171, 196, 227, 231-232, 241-242

Serapis Incense   277

Seven Hermetic Principles   217

Sorcerers   3, 40, 123, 136, 138, 187, 258

Spells and Spellwork   138-139, 203, 245, 259, 266

Stang   191-192

Statues   135, 142, 157

Staves   187

Sumerians   78, 127, 269
Sun God, the   94, 132, 152, 154-155, 157, 236
Tables of Correspondences   287
– Occult Tarot Correspondences   290
– Table of Planetary Correspondences, the   288
– Table of Planetary Hours, the   289
– Table of Roman, Saxon, and Celtic Gods, a   287
Taliesin   82-83, 244
Tarot   180-181, 208, 275
Tatham, Sylvia   57, 59
Third Degree   28, 81, 102-103, 105-106
Threefold Law, the   213-214
Training   10, 12, 18, 20-22, 25, 28, 30, 32, 34, 56, 66-67, 70, 179, 205, 208
Triple-Fold Goddess   120
Underworld   79, 121, 130, 150, 166, 170-171, 233
Valiente, Doreen   5, 48, 58, 69, 102, 145, 191
Venus of Willendorf   126
Vervain   276
Vessels   192-194, 237-238
Visionary State, the   206-207
Wand   179, 187-189
White-Handled Knife, the   184, 186
– Secespita   185
Wicca   2, 38, 42, 292
Wild Hunt, the   150, 169
Witchcraft Tools   182
Witches' Rede, the   214-216
Witch's Pyramid, the   212
Working Partners   29

This page intentionally left blank.

About the Author

Brian Cain is a Witch and High Priest of the Alexandrian Tradition. He has been a devotee of Traditional Witchcraft since his early teens and was first initiated in 1994. Today he is the High Priest of the New Orleans Coven, the only practicing Alexandrian coven in Louisiana. He maintains strong ties to the magical roots of Witchcraft in the United Kingdom and follows the teachings of Alex and Maxine Sanders. His focus is on strong training in both priesthood and the Arts Magical.

With his husband, Christian Day, he co-hosts HexFest, a Weekend of Witchery held each August in New Orleans, as well as Festival of the Dead, a monthlong event series in Salem, Massachusetts that includes the Salem Psychic Fair and Witches' Market and the Official Salem Witches' Halloween Ball. Together they own Witchcraft shops Hex and Omen in Salem and Hex in New Orleans. They are also the founders and publishers of Warlock Press.

www.ingramcontent.com/pod-product-compliance
Lightning Source LLC
Chambersburg PA
CBHW030303080526
44584CB00012B/419